shared selves

Dear Vicki,

Thanks for being a part
of my ecosystem!

SMS

10/19

TRANSFORMATIONS: WOMANIST, FEMINIST,
AND INDIGENOUS STUDIES

Edited by AnaLouise Keating

A list of books in the series appears at the end of this book.

shared selves

LATINX MEMOIR
AND ETHICAL ALTERNATIVES
TO HUMANISM

SUZANNE BOST

**UNIVERSITY OF
ILLINOIS PRESS**
Urbana, Chicago, and Springfield

Publication of this book was supported by funding
from the Office of Research Services at Loyola
University Chicago.
© 2019 by the Board of Trustees
of the University of Illinois
All rights reserved
1 2 3 4 5 C P 5 4 3 2 1
♾ This book is printed on acid-free paper.

Library of Congress Control Number: 2019025036

Contents

Illustrations

Series Editor's Foreword

AnaLouise Keating

Humanism has played a key role in shaping our status-quo stories (unquestioned assumptions about reality), naturalizing a competitive individualism that defines selfhood narrowly, in oppositional terms: each human being is an autonomous person with impermeable boundaries, and self-definition occurs through exclusion. And, because I define myself by what I am not, I defend myself through separation and division: it's me against you, us against them. This status-quo story has not served us well, contributing to alienation, increased anxiety, and environmental degradation, as well as economic, racial, gender, sexual, and other growing disparities among us. In some of its most extreme manifestations hyper-individualism fosters neo-Nazism, fanatical nationalism, and other supremacist beliefs that thrive on hatred and division.

But individualism can take other forms as well, including a relational, networked selfhood in which each person thrives by recognizing interdependence with others. This relational individualism decenters the human and defines "person" broadly: *all* beings have personhood. As Gloria Anzaldúa beautifully suggests, even "[t]rees, rocks, [and] rivers . . . have consciousness" (*Light in the Dark* 24). Relational individualism replaces hyper-individualism's boundaried selfhood with what Suzanne Bost describes as "shared selves": a weblike approach to personhood and subjectivity in which "selves are intertwined with other humans and other-than-human environments."

Focusing on memoir, Bost explores the innovative ways Judith Ortiz Cofer, Irene Vilar, John Rechy, Aurora Levins Morales, and Anzaldúa redefine selfhood in "other-than-Humanist" terms. Whereas conventional memoirs that elevate the human and centralize the individual (boundaried) self might make memoir seem an unlikely choice, the memoirs Bost turns to have leaky boundaries that distribute agency widely. They defy conventional genre rules, turning individualism on its head and inside out, opening the isolated self up to other selves—sharing self with others, creating shared selves. Or, perhaps, they remind us that selfhood has *always* been shared, that each supposedly self-enclosed individual is radically interconnected with that which is "not-me." Bost herself illustrates this relational selfhood, loosening the boundaries between herself, these authors, and Latinx literature more generally—allowing herself to be changed by the complex conversations they enact. Through self-reflection and intellectual humility, she avoids adopting the oppositional scholarly voice Western academics have been trained to employ, an "authoritative academic voice" anchored in competitive individualism. She replaces pontification with conversation.

In short, Bost adopts a post-oppositional approach. Like other books in this series, *Shared Selves* investigates post-oppositional alternatives to the status-quo stories currently dominating our lives and impeding attempts to create more equitable worlds. I describe these alternatives as "post-oppositional" to underscore both their relationship to oppositional thought and their visionary promise. Post-oppositionality enacts relational approaches to knowledge production, identity formation, and social change that borrow from but don't become trapped within oppositional thought and action. "Post" functions as invitation, not as description. Post-oppositionality neither completely rejects nor entirely moves beyond oppositionality but instead enacts a complex dance with it, creating new perspectives as it does so. Although post-oppositionality takes many forms, these forms typically share several characteristics, including (1) the belief in our interconnectedness with all existence; (2) the acceptance of paradox and contradiction; (3) the desire to be radically inclusive—to seek and create complex commonalities and broad-based alliances for social change; and (4) the recognition that our knowledge is always partial, incomplete, and thus open to revision.[1]

Like the concept of shared selfhood, *Shared Selves* beautifully illustrates these and other post-oppositional traits, enacting useful interventions into Western academic scholarship. In dialogue with Anzaldúa, Levins Morales, and others, Bost offers an invitation to expand our self-definitions (and our understanding of [post]-Humanism), shift our focus beyond the boundaried human individual, and become curious about the many ways our lives intersect with and depend on others. As we do so, we discover, create, and enact "more inclusive and sensitive . . . ethics: feeling our intertwinement with the world."

Note

1. For more on post-oppositionality (and status-quo stories), see my *Transformation Now! Towards a Post-Oppositional Politics of Change.*

Acknowledgments

If I were to be true to the breadth of my other-than-Humanist aspirations in this book, my acknowledgements would be infinitely long. I will instead provide a sampling that gives a sense of the trans-species breadth of sources from which I draw knowledge. This is the first book I've written since giving birth (twice) and becoming a full professor. It might seem like an assertion of independence. But, if anything, the obligations of these two midlife events have led me away from independence. I am always tethered—to children, family, students, colleagues, and university administration, not to mention pets and a materially decomposing 100-year-old house. Ceilings have fallen down around me and been rebuilt; I have taken breaks from writing to paint new walls, bringing traces of latex, lead, and plaster dust into my work. One elderly cat declined very slowly—requiring daily cleaning of floors and the inescapable scent of urine—and a puppy was adopted—reorienting my relationship to my neighborhood based on frequent circular loops with a leashed dog as my first point of social encounter. Children needed to be dropped off and picked up at regular intervals; youth hockey games had to be watched; reading and writing often happened in the uncomfortable and chilly bleachers of ice rinks. Ideas were gathered in transit, in the shower, in overlong committee meetings. These "nonwriting" activities might seem like distractions, but each adds thoughts and things to this project.

Acknowledgments

I've been living and working in the same place for ten years now, staring at different views of Lake Michigan, getting lost and found in new encounters with crowded streets and Google maps. A secure position and collegial support at Loyola University Chicago have provided both quiet allies and (thankfully vocal) readers for this work; for this I am grateful to my dear friend, colleague, and writing partner, Badia Ahad-Legardy, in particular. I also want to thank my graduate students at Loyola, especially Victoria Bolf, for her writings about Latinx family and long discussions about feminism and yoga; Alex Christie, who has been an outstanding interlocutor and supplier of new ideas about posthumanism; Erica Chu, who helps to decenter my every thought about gender and sexuality; Katie Dyson, who helped me think through the tricky issues of suicide and abortion in chapter 1; and John Hawkins, who keeps me supplied with a lively collection of readings and films about dogs. Loyola has provided me with a leave of absence, a summer stipend, and a book subvention, along with a number of graduate assistants, to keep this project moving.

My ideas would not have become textual matter without Dawn Durante and the editorial staff at the University of Illinois Press, the (intellectual, professional, and personal) support of AnaLouise Keating and her "Transformations" series, and the various technologies that convert words on a screen to paper and ink. I appreciate my editors' willingness to accommodate my dialogic writing style and the many contractions, parentheses, epigraphs, and endnotes that come with it. I am also grateful that the possibility of digital editions might save some trees from being churned into pulp for *Shared Selves*.

A national network of scholars in Latinx studies, with whom I convene too infrequently but earnestly, has shaped my thinking to such an extent that I might call this book communal. To this end, I want to acknowledge those whose work directly influenced my own and those with whom I share conference drinks and meals: Lee Bebout, Norma Cantú, Laura Halperin, Tace Hedrick, Julie Avril Minich, Amelia Montes, Sandra Soto, David Vázquez, and Kelli Zaytoun among too many others to name. Aurora Levins Morales graciously welcomed me into her home in 2015 and visited Loyola in 2017, providing me with personal inspiration and intellectual fuel, especially around issues of disability justice, ecology, discourse, and appropriation. And long walks in the urban parks of Dallas with Stacy Alaimo and her dog, Carmel, more than ten years ago, still reverberate in my thinking about transcorporeal relations.

Acknowledgments

My intellectual work has also been nurtured by a non-academic community of neighborhood activists and friends, including my collaborators on a project we developed in our neighborhood school, Courageous Conversations on Race, and a pack of fellow moms who have talked ideas with me over wine, on the beach, and while watching our kids play. And though I am loath to construct hierarchies, the people I live with, my family—Stuart Wick, Samuel Bost Wick, and Elliot Bost Wick—have done the most to support and sustain me. They make everything I do possible.

shared selves

Introduction

Beyond the Self

> We need fresh terms and open-ended tags that
> portray us in all our complexities and potentialities.
> When I think of "moving" from a sexed, racialized
> body to a more expansive identity interconnected
> with its surroundings, I see in my mind's eye trees
> with interconnected roots (subterranean webs).
>
> —Gloria Anzaldúa, *Light in the Dark / Luz en lo
> oscuro* 66

I have always been attracted to memoir: the indulgence of reflecting upon one's own life, the voyeurism of gazing at another's presumably private experiences. It's a somewhat perverse pleasure. But, as I think increasingly about the various elements that come together in human experience, memoir has become interesting in another way: as a meditation on the permeability of human life. Gloria Anzaldúa, for instance, embraced "subterranean" roots and webs as part of her developing artistic, intellectual, and spiritual consciousness. Recently, many of the Latina writers whose publications in the 1980s brought me into intellectual adulthood—including Cherríe Moraga, Ana Castillo, Sandra Cisneros, Lucha Corpi, and Ruth Behar— have published memoirs as they enter their later years.[1] Reencountering these authors in memoir form highlights their histories of "changing consciousness" (to paraphrase the title of Moraga's 2011 *A Xicana Codex of Changing Consciousness*). Of course, these authors' novels, stories, essays, and poems have long hovered around a core of autobiography (following the personal-political connection), but these newer works emerge in a time when our understanding of human life and identity is different from the one promulgated during the heyday of identity politics (and critiques thereof) in the 1980s. These newer works have led me to think more deeply about the subject of Latinx autobiographical writing. The focus of my own work has shifted from the question of identity's realness (as a measurable property) to the parameters and perimeters of selfhood (as an embodied, relational, always emergent entity).

In my fields of Latinx, feminist, queer, and disability studies, simply writing about marginalized lives has the potential to shift norms. Gloria Anzaldúa, John Rechy, Aurora Levins Morales, and other Latinx writers have definite ethical motivations behind the stories they tell about themselves: highlighting the consequences of racism, ethnocentrism, misogyny, homophobia, and ableism; making visible experiences and bodies that are rarely at the center of the stories we see; and dramatizing a variety of human agencies and responsibilities. The writers I consider in this project have written extensively, almost obsessively, about their own lives—in a variety of media, scattered across a number of different texts. These repeated self-reflections ultimately move beyond the singular self of autobiography as their authors' personal histories intertwine with the histories of other people, animals, spirits, and the surrounding environment.

My epigraph, taken from Gloria Anzaldúa's never-defended doctoral dissertation, was published nine years after her death (and edited by AnaLouise Keating). Though that text is the product of writing and research conducted throughout the 1990s and early 2000s, it arrived in 2015 like a message from the grave with timely resonance for the present. Inspired by the onset of Type 1 diabetes and increasing fragmentation in our world following the September 11, 2001, terrorist attacks, Anzaldúa's later writings reflect an urgency to rebuild and connect, to embrace our linkages to "subterranean webs" that include humans, trees, and the earth itself. This interconnectedness among species resonates with recent intellectual and ethical developments in posthumanist theory as well as recalling a premodern (and pre-Humanist) indigenous worldview. These two frameworks help me to analyze what it means for Latinx writers, in particular, to conceive of their own lives as embedded with others. Rejecting the structures of Humanism, *Shared Selves* decenters the subject of memoir and highlights the webs of relation that mediate experience, agency, and life itself.

A brief meditation on the meaning of "Latinx" in current critical writing will help to clarify my stakes in this project. In terms of ethnicity, "Latino" means a great variety of things and carries a wide variety of political connotations—a refusal of the U.S. census term "Hispanic," an inclusive term for U.S. people of Spanish-speaking ancestry, or a depoliticizing move away from more particular and more nationalist terms like Chicano or Nuyorican. A number of recent books, including Marta Caminero-Santangelo's On Latinidad (2007), Cristina Beltrán's The Trouble with Unity (2013), and Ralph Rodriguez's Latinx Literature Unbound (2018), have provided nuanced accounts of the limitations of Latinidad as a pan-ethnic label.[2] I do not intend to thematize Latinidad itself as a central aspect of my argument. I initially employed the pan-ethnic framework in Shared Selves simply because I was writing about both Chicanx and Puerto Rican authors, and the umbrella term provided a handy way of linking them. But I began to realize that, as this project focuses on the complexity of selves, the difficulty of pinning down identity is also a central thematic. My argument that selves are intertwined with other humans and other-than-human environments makes it difficult to limit selfhood to any ethnic label. But the works I analyze are deeply embedded in particular encounters in which race and cultural frameworks (along with species and ecosystems) do matter very much. The fact that memoirs of Chicanx and Puerto Rican writers are particularly relevant for this study does not result solely from my own expertise in these literatures. The ecosystems that complicate selfhood in this project are constituted by experiences characteristically associated with Latinx cultures: colonialism, (im)migration, dispossession, cultural hybridity, environmental racism, insufficient healthcare, political oppositionality, and, sometimes, a nostalgic recovery of indigenous American cosmologies. By looking at these characteristics through a lens that goes beyond the human, I am also looking beyond sociopolitical labels that spring from Humanist aspirations (aspirations like competitive individualism, a search for objective truth, and the elevation of the human above the rest of life). Beltrán's definition of Latino as a verb and her embrace of the term "as a site of permanent political contest" whose "instability and incompleteness" enable "collective creation and fugitive enactments" (161) are particularly well suited to the way that I envision a self inhabiting an identity.

There is also the matter of gendering this framework. The suffix -x has been adopted to include people who don't identify with the binary gendering of "Latina/o." Yet some scholars and activists worry that universalizing "Latinx" diminishes the specificity of nonbinary identities (by applying the label to all). "Latinx" also potentially undermines the experience of binary-identified individuals who regard their gender as a hard-fought right or an essential, nonnegotiable quality. As of this writing, the usage and implica-

3

tions of terms like Latina/o, Latinx, and Latina/o/x are still in flux. I initially favored the bulky configuration "Latina/o/x," which I like precisely because it is bulky: it performs the impossibility of uniting heterogeneous people under one label. The Fall 2018 issue of the journal *Latino Studies* takes up this debate. I am particularly drawn to Nicole Trujillo-Pagán's argument that "a/o/x" is the only inclusive option, with the slash marks themselves enacting the multiple borders that Latina/o/x peoples cross. The "-a/o/x" also replicates the history of attempts to modify the mono-gendering of "Latino" by adding additional suffixes. While Trujillo-Pagán worries that -*x* alone displaces the feminist critique, Salvador Vidal Ortiz and Juliana Martinez, in the same issue of *Latino Studies*, point out that the -*x* carries a history of racial and ethnic difference that includes the term Xicana, which has been favored by many feminists and "canonized" by Ana Castillo's 1994 *Massacre of the Dreamers: Essays on Xicanisma* (taking the *x* from the indigenous term Mexica). I would add two additional historical references that the -*x* invokes: African Americans' rejection of white patronyms passed down from slavery (made most famous by Malcolm X) and my own memories of conducting research with the MLA International Bibliography in the 1990s, when "Latinx" would produce search results that included any term of more than five letters that begins with "Latin." So, for the purposes of this book, *x* marks a spot of contention, history, and efforts to include the shifting multiplicity and unwieldy selves that are my primary concern here.

My reason for writing about memoir has less to do with wanting to add to the already substantial critical field of memoir and autobiography studies and more to do with using life writing as a medium for thinking more broadly and deeply about what counts as human life. It might seem that memoir would be an irrelevant genre for studying other-than-Humanist selves. Isn't memoir simply a relic of Humanism's deflated myth of autonomous individuality? I argue instead that, for the writers I study, adopting the genre and breaking its boundaries is a political tactic that performatively challenges the myth of the individual and requires us to think more expansively about Latinx life. My first chapter responds to critical feminist and postmodernist studies of memoir's relationship to human subjectivity and analyzes the work of two Latina memoirists, Judith Ortiz Cofer and Irene Vilar, to lay the foundation for many of the assumptions I make in the chapters that follow about how selves get shared.

David Vázquez's *Triangulations: Narrative Strategies for Navigating Latino Identity* (2011) focuses on how Latino authors use life writing to embed their "I's" within collectivities and shared spaces:

> Reading Latina/o autobiographies as polyvocal and socially embedded reveals a rich continuum of narrative techniques that offer multilevel critiques of individual subjectivity, community formation, and national belonging. While the idea of socially embedded autobiographical writing is not new, I argue that the authors included in this study use their first-person personal narratives to imagine completely different spaces of belonging. (Vázquez 7)

I am indebted to Vázquez's emphasis on the communal, political subject in Latinx life writing, and I return to his work in my analysis of John Rechy. But while Vázquez focuses on how sociopolitical identity categories—"race, gender, sexuality, class, and national origin" (101)—"triangulate" literary subjects between and among identity-based communities, the communities I trace in *Shared Selves* move beyond the parameters of these sociopolitical identifications that are a feature of Western Humanist sociality. (I am including the constellation of anthropocentric ideas that emerged from Enlightenment Humanism—especially competitive individualism, which leads people to differentiate themselves from others, to assert their claim to objective truth, and to appropriate the nonhuman world for their own benefit—within this orbit.) Given the ways in which Latinx writers have invoked "pre-Humanist" indigenous cultures as intellectual and political influences, we are able to find selves in their works whose identifications remain tied to trans-species ecologies and mystical cosmologies. Yet calling these ideas "pre-Humanist" incorrectly assumes a temporal relation to Humanism that arrives in only some cultural and intellectual contexts. Ontologies developed outside of the Humanist orbit unsettle sociopolitical categories not by critiquing them from within but by appealing to forms of sociality where human identity categories do not bear the privileged meanings that segment our social spheres today.

Posthumanism has arrived on the academic front as a way to expand our thinking about ecologies, species, and relations, but this sort of thinking is new only from a perspective rooted in (liberal and neoliberal) Humanism. The Latinx writers I study draw from ontologies and epistemologies other than this one, and this other-than-Humanism provides a materially, culturally, and ethically grounded way of critically reading contemporary posthumanist theory. In an essay that critiques the intellectual Eurocentrism of posthumanist geography, Juanita Sundberg writes, "I am discomforted by the ways in which geographical engagements with posthumanism tend to reproduce colonial ways of knowing and being by enacting universalizing claims and, consequently, further subordinating other ontologies" (34). Zoe Todd likewise critiques posthumanism as a trendy "Euro-Western academic narrative" that essentially reinvents a wheel, developing ideas that resonate with existing indigenous cosmologies without invoking indigenous writers (7–9). What Todd asks for is self-reflexivity about our citation practices and the academic structures that perpetually center "Western" traditions and marginalize others (18). This self-reflexivity shapes my introduction and my methodology. Anzaldúa's other-than-Humanist epistemology is drawn from a feminist and queer reappropriation of precolonial (Aztec, in particular) goddess figures as well as a deep sense of connection between humans and the other-than-human environment. (This approach is political and somewhat romantic more than it is empirical, and it has been critiqued by scholars in the field.[3]) Levins Morales similarly takes her alternatives to Humanism from the Puerto Rican ecology that shaped her worldview, from the living presence of indigenous people on the island (and in the United States mainland), and from her own reliance on herbs and tinctures, as well as digital technologies, to maintain her health and mobility. Rechy's alternatives to Humanism, by contrast, emerge from a persistent queering of relationships, identities, and environments: defiance of monogamy and reproductive individualism, defiance of property ownership and heteronormative proprieties, and countercultural uses of space and time (such as lingering in parks all day rather than working a job).[4] I discuss all of these alternative epistemologies in greater depth in the chapters to follow.

In my 2009 book *Encarnación: Illness and Body Politics in Chicana Feminist Literature*, I argued that contemporary Chicana writers invoke pre-Columbian Mesoamerican traditions (like shape-shifting, shamanism, and corporeal sacrifice) in order to theorize forms of embodiment outside the circumscribed self of Enlightenment Humanism. This indigenous worldview focused not on a rational individual engaged in mastering the world but instead on a permeable collectivity in which health and identity were formed through the relations among human members of a community, animal counterparts (or nahuals), environmental fluctuations, and acts of the gods. Chicana (and, more broadly in *Shared Selves*, Latinx) literature thus provides a non-Eurocentric genealogy for many of the ideas associated with posthumanism today. While the early posthumanist theories associated with poststructuralism were primarily intellectual, challenging the universal "truths" and binary oppositions of Humanist reason, newer posthumanist writings, especially as developed by feminist ecocriticism, have sought concrete political outcomes from an understanding of transcorporeal interactions among humans and the more-than-human world. Though the affinities between Latinx Studies and posthumanism are rarely explored, recent explorations in posthumanist theory certainly resonate with the border-crossing epistemologies I associate with Latinx cultural productions.[5] (I choose the verb "resonate" to reflect the ways in which these two parallel traditions have similar reverberations yet distinct genealogies; resonance eschews the idea of cause and effect, or even direct relation, in its focus on the simultaneous.) Attending to this cross-cultural, trans-epistemological resonance enables me to build on the intellectual insights of posthumanism while retaining the historical and cultural grounding that informs Latinx politics, aesthetics, and thought. The metaphor of the web, which I develop in chapter 3, with its simultaneously organic and digital meanings, captures this simultaneity of the "premodern" and the post-, the sacred and the secular, the indigenous and the global.

I resist the conventional genealogy of the "post": both the assumption of linear temporality and progress that the term implies as well as the insular philosophical tradition from which most posthumanist theory derives. Latinx studies bears an ambivalent relationship to many of the -isms to which the prefix *post-* is attached, including Western intellectual developments like modernism and Humanism, drawing instead from a web of sources that implode the temporality of academic "posts." The term "other-than-Humanist" reflects this resistance and enacts the difficulty of pinning down the epistemologies in the texts I analyze to one shared term. (As I discuss above, the writers that are the subject of this book have distinct ways of and reasons for countering the individualism and anthropocentrism of Humanism.) Though "other-than-Humanist" still revolves linguistically around Humanism, this is part of my intention: to highlight the existence of other ways of relating to the world around us without Humanist individualism and anthropocentrism.

Yet, and perhaps counterintuitively, posthumanist theories help me to attend to the animist, the otherworldly, the irrational, and the ecological aspects of Latinx thought. Reading Latinx writing through the lenses of posthumanism reveals agencies and relations that are often overlooked: water, pesticides, and ideologies are among the other-than-human entities that are wrought up within Latinx becoming. Letting go of the frameworks of Humanism also allows us to read texts without looking for a privileged moral center, without expecting individuals to act as independent entities, and without looking for a linear narrative of development or discovery. Opening the net of what goes into a human life leads to messy, multidirectional stories.

I'm drawn to the chastening decentering of the human that follows from posthumanist critique and the different shades of agency that come from elements as varied as trees, dogs, air, and tables. Agency and power have been key terms in my political thinking as a feminist, but posthumanism has taught me to be wary of viewing either of these terms as stable qualities that an individual either possesses or does not. I've learned from posthumanists like Karen Barad that agency occurs in relations, or "intra-actions," among human and nonhuman, as well as among material and seemingly immaterial "relata" (her highly inclusive term for entities that meet in relation). The project of memoir itself leads many of the writers I study to focus their own permeability. In *Shared Selves*, I view these decenterings of the self as critiques of the Humanist hubris that keeps many people from recognizing the nonhuman (and even the human) others with whom we share our being.

Probably none of the Latinx authors I'm analyzing in this book would think of their work as posthuman or posthumanist.[6] Some prioritize indigenous epistemologies, and some explicitly reject the theoretical trajectory associated with today's posthumanism (through poststructuralism or predominantly white feminist ecocriticism/New Materialism). But the confluence of a surge in publications about posthumanism with a changing political landscape that has led to a resurgence of "inhumane" behavior (and a dismissal of the humanity of people of color, immigrants, women, and sexual minorities) suggests that we need new ways of thinking about the human today. In that quest, which is essentially an ethical one, I find many useful tools in posthumanist theory, especially for analyzing cross-species relations, expanding what we consider to be agency, and locating selfhood within relations among human and nonhuman beings with which our movements are intertwined.

Since posthumanism is still emergent and somewhat diffuse in its various manifestations, let me be clear about my theoretical sources. I particularly appreciate the feminist, queer, and ecocritical scholarship of Barad, Stacy Alaimo, Mel Chen, Jane Bennett, Claire Colebrook, and others who look beyond the human in their understandings of agency and world-making. In many works of these theorists, an emphasis on the human lingers to the extent that their frameworks are feminist, antiracist, anti-ableist, or oriented specifically against human hierarchies. Likewise, I'm not ready to move entirely past the human; instead, I want to understand how we can rethink the human through its relations with other-than-human agencies and ecologies. Unless we focus to some extent on the human, we cannot account for the disproportionate power that the human exercises in most of these relations (in the Anthropocene, by definition) and to alter this imbalance when it becomes destructive. Ecocriticism thus has an obvious shared investment with this approach, but so do feminist theory, queer theory, and disability studies in their search for ways of being and moving outside of universalized assumptions about the form and function of the human.

Though it precedes the advent of posthumanism, Donna Haraway's theory of the cyborg has certainly influenced its emergence. A product of biological studies (and science studies more generally), postmodernism, poststructuralism, postcolonialism, Marxism, and feminism, Haraway's work has been tremendously influential for my thinking about embodied more-than-human networks. From the cyborgs of her earlier work to the coevolving animal companions of her later work, Haraway offers an intellectual throughway from postmodernism to posthumanism that has never forgotten politics or material reality; indeed, women of color feminisms were central to her early thinking about networked identities.[7] Her 1980s cyborg deconstructed the binaries at the heart of our flesh (male/female, subject/object, nature/culture, human/machine) and inserted feminism and socialism right into the military-industrial complex.[8] Her work since then, relentlessly feminist and relentlessly material, has shown that feminist studies, queer studies, and animal studies are family. Haraway deconstructs the (implicitly Western, masculinist) subject of Enlightenment Humanism without instituting any other defended identities in its place. Instead, she focuses on permeabilities and shared agencies within the body politic. Understanding our world as a product of the conjoined relations of humans, animals, parasites, and databases is not just more realistic than a focus on the solitary thinking man; it also opens more potential avenues for transformation.

In terms of the latest wave of theorists of posthumanism, I take from Rosi Braidotti's *The Posthuman* (2013) a preference for posthumanisms with a critical edge and an urge to think experimentally about alternative forms of subjectivity. From Cary Wolfe's *What Is Posthumanism?* (2010), I take the idea that posthumanism, disability studies, and animal studies are allied in challenging assumptions about individualism, autonomy, human perfectibility, and human domination over nature. And from N. Katherine Hayles's *How We Became Posthuman* (1999) I take the imperative to restore a concern for the particular material contexts in which posthuman subjects emerge, deviating from the (implicit or explicit) disembodiment of both Humanism and poststructuralism.

Braidotti describes, in *The Posthuman*, a wave of "anti-humanist" critiques of the liberal subject that emerged with feminist, postcolonial, and antiracist thought in the later twentieth century, and the writers I study here are part of this "wave." (Indeed, it is Latinx literature that led me to my own critiques of Humanism.) Rechy's primary concern is depicting the queer variety within human life, which is shaped by space and environment as much as human community. Anzaldúa and Levins Morales both critique competitive individualism from a perspective that values monistic and indigenous traditions. Anzaldúa insisted that she "[knew] things older than Freud" and that her theories of identity construction emerged from her South Texas homeland and Aztec cosmology years before Judith Butler was deconstructing subjectivity (*Borderlands* 26; "Coming into Play" 12). Levins Morales likewise identifies as a "certified organic intellectual," rather than a postmodern one, and insists that the sources for her ideas are Puerto Rican ecology and a Taíno worldview ("Guanakán" 2; *Medicine Stories* 67). Experiences of alienation, distance from unitary identity categories, chronic illnesses, environmental politics, and resistance to global inequality led these writers to represent human subjectivity as embedded in webs of transcultural, transnational, transgendered, transcorporeal, and trans-species connection.

Jane Bennett's orientation toward posthumanism resonates well with these writers' work. At the end of an essay investigating the agency and vibrancy of nonhuman things, she concludes:

> [M]ine is not a *post*-human project. Quite to the contrary: it is my conviction that to really understand social practices it is necessary to acknowledge the non-human components that are always at work inside them. Ultimately, I am looking for a road that leads toward more sustainable consumption practices; things might have something to say about how to forge such a path. (Bennettt, "Powers of the Hoard" 269, original emphasis)

My project revolves around the ethical imperatives that emerge at the intersections among Latinx, feminist, queer, environmental, and disability studies; so, like Bennett, my orientation is primarily social. Yet sociality, as will become evident in the works I analyze in the chapters to come, includes the nonhuman to such a great extent that listening to what humans have to say also means listening to what things have to say. Unlike Bennett, I'm not sure it's useful to identify my project as for or against the posthuman. Concern for the future of humans must involve attention to our negotiations with the nonhuman world. Thinking of one without the other would be thinking with one eye closed. Call it prehuman or posthuman, call it globally responsible, or call it realism. It is all of these things. Our networks of webs are new and old. What is new, and what is post-, is a burgeoning variety of critical approaches for analyzing the ethics of being in cacophonous relations.

* * *

Memoir has been an important part of Chicanx and Latinx literary history, and memoirs have helped to shape what it means to come to consciousness as a Chicana, Chicano, Chicanx, Latina, Latino, Latinx subject. From Piri Thomas's recovery from drug addiction in Spanish Harlem (*Down These Mean Streets*, 1969) to Oscar "Zeta" Acosta's development from self-indulgent narcissism to Chicano leader (*Revolt of the Cockroach People*, 1973) to Cherríe Moraga's conversion from middle-class heteronormative assimilation to the "color of her mother" and the love of "dark women" (*Loving in the War Years*, 1983) to Esmeralda Santiago's journey from Puerto Rican *jíbara* to Nuyorican (*When I Was Puerto Rican*, 1993), much Latinx literature seems to present itself as a transparent story of identity formation, using the genres of life writing to create a heroic, racially and sexually conscious self. These works were important to the development of Latinx literature in part because of the successful narratives of selfhood that they present.

The texts I analyze in *Shared Selves* challenge the idea of a success story. Subject to racism, misogyny, homophobia, and chronic illnesses as well as legacies of colonialism and deterritorialization (as Puerto Ricans and Mexican Americans), the writers I analyze here highlight the continued compromises, contradictions, and collusions that shape their lives. Irene Vilar and Judith Ortiz Cofer experience selfhood as always intertwined with patriarchal control, corporeal and geographic upheaval, and the possibility of death. John Rechy drowns his own alienated narcissism and fears of rejection in underworld communities where selfhood is a staged performance. Aurora Levins Morales situates individual selfhood in a larger network of human and other-than-human entities that make survival for a Latina with chronic illnesses and disabilities both dangerous and possible. And Gloria Anzaldúa, in writing about her own experiences with illness, questions the primacy of life itself and imagines new forms of relation that do not rest on vitality or individuation. These writers' memoirs provide excellent sources for analyzing how selves are shared outside of the Humanist tradition.

My analysis of these texts builds from my work in feminist, queer, and disability theory—each of which has, in its own ways, critiqued Humanist conceptions of universal embodiment and the binaries that underwrite modern Western thought from simultaneously intellectual and political angles. Because of these roots (and routes), most of the Latinx writers I analyze here are women who have expanded the parameters of feminist thought. Levins Morales worked with Moraga and Anzaldúa on the first edition of *This Bridge Called My Back* (1981), a text that helped to develop a broad archive of sources for theoretical and political writing that foregrounds the experiences of women of color. John Rechy fits into this feminist/queer analysis not only because of the queer community and alternative kinship he represents but also because his work was influential to early Chicana feminists like Anzaldúa.[9] Memoir, especially telling about experiences that don't fit within literary conventions, has been at the heart of all of these writings.

I prefer the term memoir here, rather than autobiography or life writing, because the latter terms imply transparent representation of a self or a life, while memoir is muddier, including the imprecision and unreliability of memory as well as the aesthetic and intellectual manipulation of literary writing. My first chapter focuses on the processes of selection and fragmentation that Judith Ortiz Cofer and Irene Vilar highlight in their memoirs. In their defiance of coherence, these two Puerto Rican writers deterritorialize the genre of memoir in a way that reflects the disrupted foundation of the Commonwealth of Puerto Rico. They suture together conflicting accounts of a life to dramatize contests over knowledge between unequal powers. While disconnection is central to Ortiz Cofer and Vilar, Rechy and Levins Morales form imaginative connections, blending people and environments so that it becomes impossible to view the individual subject apart from the communities and ecologies with which they are intertwined. Unlike these more self-reflexive transhuman formations, Anzaldúa quietly assumes unconventional configurations of life in ways that keep readers and viewers on edge, questioning their previous assumptions about being in the world. Form (or genre) meets content in these writers' ethical challenge to the construction of lives; this intersection is my focus on *Shared Selves*.

The interdisciplinarity of my methodology has posed some problems for the organization of this book, which is informed by Latinx studies, posthumanist theory, feminist theory, queer theory, ecocriticism, and disability studies all together. Tracing each author relative to all of these approaches would make for very long chapters. So I have chosen to bring one theoretical approach to the foreground in each chapter: feminist theory in chapter 1, queer theory in chapter 2, ecocriticism in chapter 3, and disability in chapter 4. I hope that what will emerge is a sense of how feminist theory, queer theory, ecocriticism, and disability theory modify each other, in the context of Latinx culture in particular. I have already written, in *Encarnación*, about the resonances between disability studies and Latinx studies in their challenges to autonomy, individuation, and universal ideas of the human. In that book I focus on how identity and mobility are mediated by cultural and material contexts. Posthumanist theory has further helped to decenter the human individual; as in *Encarnación*, *Shared Selves* situates this decentered self in cultural and material contexts defined by race, gender, sexuality, and ability. Since *Encarnación* was published, feminist theory and queer theory have become increasingly diverse in their epistemologies, archives, and cultural contexts, yet disability studies, ecocriticism, and posthumanism remain dominated by Western intellectual sources and predominantly white theorists. (Notable exceptions include the important work of Mel Chen, Nirmala Erevelles, AnaLouise Keating, Julie Avril Minich, Jasbir Puar, and Priscilla Solis Ybarra as well as Levins Morales and Anzaldúa.) These fields still have much to learn from the cultural specificity and ethical rigor of Latinx studies.

Chapter 1, "Writing Latinx Memoir: Fragmented Lives, Precarious Boundaries," juxtaposes Judith Ortiz Cofer's mixed-genre *Silent Dancing: A Partial Remembrance of a Puerto Rican Childhood* (1990) with Irene Vilar's companion memoirs, *The Ladies Gallery* (1996) and *Impossible Motherhood: Testimony of an Abortion Addict* (2009), in order to examine the relationship between life writing and fragmented lives. Judith Butler's account of precarious life, Rosi Braidotti's critique of vitalism, and feminist autobiography studies inform my understanding of how these texts self-reflexively point to the contortions involved in the construction of memoir, especially the occlusion of violent or controversial events and the erasure of lives deemed unworthy of passing down. Ortiz Cofer and Vilar use different methods for highlighting fragmentation in the process of forming and narrating human lives. Ortiz Cofer compares the making of memoir to editing a film; she cuts and splices photographs, poems, and stories that overlap and conflict with each other in recounting her own Puerto Rican girlhood (which was punctuated with regular uprootings and movements between island and mainland). *The Ladies Gallery*, Vilar's first memoir, multiplies lives rather than fragmenting them, entwining (or sharing) her own story with the lives of her grandmother (the famous Puerto Rican nationalist Lolita Lebrón)

and her mother, tracing self-perpetuating histories of psychological instability and self-inflicted violence. *Impossible Motherhood* turns to the time
in which Vilar was writing *The Ladies Gallery* and points out the details of
the personal story that were suppressed in the earlier memoir, most notably
Vilar's addiction to conceiving and terminating life. This chapter lays the
groundwork for my subsequent analyses of memoirs that push against the
thresholds of human life and highlights the ethics of encountering otherness in these works.

Chapter 2, "Community: John Rechy, Depersonalization, and Queer
Selves," analyzes the emergence of Rechy's own life not only in his published memoir (*About My Life and the Kept Woman*) but also in his "fictional"
novels (especially *City of Night* and *Numbers*), his literary "documentary"
(*The Sexual Outlaw*), and an "interactive memoir" available on CD-ROM
(*Mysteries and Desire*). Rechy has been celebrated in gay and queer literary
circles for decades but receives comparatively less attention from scholars
in Chicanx studies (despite his Mexican parentage), in part because of what
is often regarded as his (seemingly apolitical) narcissistic individualism. I
think this charge is a misinterpretation. Beyond the apparent narcissism of
finding elements of Rechy's life (and dozens of photographs that show off
his muscular physique) over and over again in his works, something more
complicated occurs subtextually as bodies, identities, and places accumulate
and blur throughout Rechy's substantial *obra*. One of the primary qualities
of all of these works is excess. Not only does Rechy repeatedly return to
the same scenes, events, and characters across texts, but each book, within
itself, is excessive: long (300–400 pages), full of lavish lists describing people
and places in great detail. And with at least twelve books in circulation,
a vast web of connections links a Rechy-like character to an overwrought
network of people, streets, parks, bars, coffee shops, jails, hotels, animals,
deserts, mountains, dirt, and garbage. Landscape, buildings, and seemingly
marginal characters take the foreground at points and blend with the "life"
of Rechy or the semi-autobiographical male protagonists of his novels. (The
addition of "and the kept woman" in the title of his memoir is one obvious
instance of this.) The theoretical writings of Samuel Delany, Tim Deane,
and José Esteban Muñoz provide some of the scaffolding upon which I map
the shared agencies that depersonalize the self in Rechy's work and embed
it within queer communities and queer environments.

My third chapter moves to a writer whose authority is even more permeable. "Webs: Aurora Levins Morales's Animal, Vegetable, and Digital
Ecologies" begins with an analysis of the conjoined humans, plants, and

animals that people Levins Morales's autobiographical and semi-autobiographical writings, ranging from her first and best-known publication (the multigenre collection she coauthored with her mother in 1986, *Getting Home Alive*) to her recent work as a radical historian and activist in health and disability communities. I am particularly interested in the author's website, auroralevinsmorales.com, whose slogan, "it takes a village to keep the blogs coming," opens Levins Morales's authority to outside contributions and interventions. The site not only markets the author's work but also inserts the authority of the author into the unbounded ecosystem of the World Wide Web. Through the website she solicits financial donations to help cover medical care for her numerous illnesses and disabilities, she sells her services as a speaker and writing consultant, and she forms interactive communities based on webinars, blogging, and invitations to barter (exchanging writing services for massage or web management, for instance). This self-promotion embeds the author in a process of community building and shares the business of constructing the story (and the health) of the author with web browsers. The website models a new form of public archive and public memoir. I compare this digital network to the more "organic" ecologies Levins Morales writes about, some of which I was able to experience and embody in person when I traveled to her home in Cambridge, Massachusetts, to interview her in 2015. Ultimately, using the work of feminist ecocritics like Stacy Alaimo and Mel Chen, along with the posthumanist theories of Karen Barad, I develop a model of ethics based on accountability for the many participants in a web.

Chapter 4, "Life: The Gloria E. Anzaldúa Papers and Other-Than-Humanist Ontologies," examines little-known works by acclaimed Chicana writer Gloria Anzaldúa, who died from complications related to diabetes in 2004. In the enormous archive she left (consisting of more than two hundred file boxes of unpublished documents, notes, revisions, artwork, memorabilia, and other surprising ephemera), I found a complete memoir, written in the 1980s, titled "La serpiente que se come su cola" [The serpent that eats its own tail].[10] Analyzing this manuscript alongside some of the many doodles stored along with the written works in her archive highlights the degree to which Anzaldúa was focused on the matters of life and death. She believed that she died multiple times throughout her life; shape-shifting between species and identification with spirits were also part of her thought processes. In expanding life beyond the conventional bounds of the human, Anzaldúa also makes ethical demands: if our bodies are intertwined with plants and nonhuman animals, we must move through the world with greater care for and attention to our surroundings. Unlike posthumanist theorists who operate in the mode of negative critique, dismantling what we know of the human, Anzaldúa taps into precolonial indigenous iconography and her expansive imagination to depict bodies that defy the restrictions of empiricism and human life. Using the framework of disability theory, in particular Robert McRuer's critique of the neoliberal domestication of disability, leads me to foreground representations that challenge the meaning of life itself.

The book concludes with "Selflessness?"—a reflection on the significance of permeable subjects for the discipline of Latinx studies. The texts I'm analyzing elude mastery with their unwieldy interconnected subjects and intertextual webs. Rather than trying to pin any of them down to a single story, or identity, the best we can hope for is to engage them in conversation, to "speak nearby" them (to paraphrase Trinh Minh-ha) rather than objectifying them as stable objects. To engage these memoirs in conversation, I turn briefly to my own life—as a student, scholar, and teacher of Latinx studies—reflecting honestly on my own relationship to Humanism and the identity-based content of my field. As a white woman, I am an outsider, but as a published and tenured scholar-teacher, I am also most definitely within the network. From this liminal position, I hope to enact both empathy and humility, both cross-cultural identification and the incommensurability of different perspectives. Rather than offering any single lesson or conclusion, I see the most appropriate ending to this sort of work as an open door for future dialogue. I sketch out the possible dimensions of this open door as the book (un)closes.

CHAPTER 1

Writing Latinx Memoir

Fragmented Lives, Precarious Boundaries

> There the self is reshuffled by the voices of
> shadows, family, tradition, history, chance. . . .
> And just as those voices eventually become you as
> you write, you, in turn, to make your story meaning-
> ful, become part of those voices, a closing of the
> circle that is endurable only as you write.
>
> —Irene Vilar, *The Ladies Gallery* 19

How does memoir represent, or present, a self? What happens to a self in the process of being written? And what is the purpose of putting a self into narrative form? Irene Vilar suggests, in the epigraph to this chapter, that writing is a way of containing the multiplicity of voices that shuffle within and around a self. Writing the self gives it "meaning" to the extent that it creates a perimeter within which to interpret heterogeneous actions and experiences. As the circle of constructed meaning closes around the life, demarcating it and marking it, it also clearly excludes (or abjects) details that don't fit the narrative. The idea that there is something that is not "endurable" until it is translated into writing suggests that there is some-thing excessive or destructive that is being contained. Yet "endure" has two meanings (transitive and intransitive). To endure means "to bear or to suf-fer something," highlighting the experience of the self, as well as "to last," highlighting the permanence created by converting a self into text. The syntax of Vilar's sentence fails to clarify what is endurable (closing, circle, or becoming a part of the voices) and which definition of endure she means. These many dimensions to the endurance of a life are my subjects here.

Although I'm foregrounding memoir's role as an intellectual and ethical exercise, most writers of memoir come to the genre out of a belief that there is something interesting, something of value to tell about their lives. This is certainly the case for Vilar, who was encouraged by her first husband to write a dramatic intergenerational memoir. *The Ladies Gallery: A Memoir of Family Secrets*—which was originally published in 1996 with the same title as the mystical manifesto Vilar's grandmother Lolita Lebrón wrote from prison, *A Message from God in the Atomic Age: A Memoir*—shares the story of three generations of women whose lives revolved around psychological instability, including an impulse toward suicide.[1] Lebrón was a Puerto Rican nationalist who famously opened fire on the U.S. Congress in 1954 with the expectation (or hope) that she herself would be shot in the act and die a martyr.[2] Vilar's mother, Gladys Mirna Méndez Lebrón, was abandoned in infancy when Lolita left for the United States, married young to an unfaithful husband, and threw herself out of a moving car when Vilar was eight years old. *The Ladies Gallery* intertwines these historical biographies with Vilar's own suicide attempts and institutionalization, framing her own life as an echo of her foremothers' self-authored tragedies: "We inherit these secrets the way we inherit shame, guilt, desire. And we repeat" (*The Ladies Gallery* 4).[3] "We repeat" references the ways in which Vilar lives her life as a repetition as well as the ways in which her memoir repeats the family secrets. Whether repeating a secret means telling it or keeping it secret remains fruitfully unclear.

I am interested how these women push the boundaries of mental and physical coherence and how they question the preference for life over death. I am also interested in how the process of memoir-making puts these challenges to selfhood into representation. Thirteen years after publishing her first memoir, Vilar published another memoir, the controversial *Impossible Motherhood: Testimony of an Abortion Addict* (2009), which focuses on the period in which she wrote *The Ladies Gallery*. In this second memoir, she reveals events and circumstances that were left out of *The Ladies Gallery* and writes about the process of constructing her first memoir under conditions of mental instability and coercion. It is tempting, therefore, to read *Impossible Motherhood*—with its emphasis on the abortions and suicide attempts that were elided in *The Ladies Gallery*—as a more complete and truthful text. But it is also true that these details are emphasized in the later memoir as part of its ideological agenda; they probably receive disproportionate attention over other matters that might be elided in *Impossible Motherhood*. No single memoir will contain all of the details of a life. Most salient in the second memoir are the author/subject's submission to the man she calls her "master" and the fifteen abortions she had in fifteen years. This text, too, pushes at the boundaries of human agency, choice, and the line between life and death. The fact that Vilar wrote two memoirs that reveal two different sets of biographical details highlights both the contingency of life and the contingency of memoir.

I join my analysis of Vilar to a reading of an important work by another Puerto Rican writer, Judith Ortiz Cofer's 1990 mixed-genre *Silent Dancing: A Partial Remembrance of a Puerto Rican Childhood*, which focuses directly and self-reflexively on the process of constructing selves and constructing memoirs. *Silent Dancing* presumably narrates its author's coming of age story, but this story is fragmented from within by shifts between prose and verse as well as unexplained gaps and unresolved contradictions. As a result, the text muddies perceptions of its subject and undermines the process of translating a life into text. Ortiz Cofer ultimately highlights the artificiality of the lives that emerge in life writing. The ideal of memoir—to represent a coherent individual life—conflicts with the actual messiness of lives.

I am not the first to point out the ways in which women, queers, and other minoritized people conceive of selfhood apart from the (mythic) rational individual of Enlightenment Humanism. Indeed, in the 1980s, the heyday of deconstructive thinking about the subject, a number of critics turned to memoir and autobiography to highlight the social construction of subjectivity. (The emergence of the journal *a/b: Auto/Biography Studies* in 1985 is a testament to this correlated interest.) In her 1989 analysis of the role of Humanist selfhood in eighteenth-century autobiographical writing, Felicity Nussbaum points out that "we feel compelled as writers of ourselves and readers of autobiographies to construct a self, but that interest in a closed, fixed, rational, and volitional self is fostered within a historically bound ideology" (33). By highlighting the contingency of Humanism as an ideology, Nussbaum helps to pave the way for critiques of and alternatives to Humanism. Latina literary critic Frances Aparicio suggests that the link between the individual "volitional self" and autobiography nonetheless persists into contemporary U.S. writing:

> The autobiography has been a favorite genre in U.S. society because it reaffirms the ethos of individualism and of hard work, in other words, the American Dream. Thus, the Latino and Latina autobiographical narratives that reaffirm this myth, such as Richard Rodriguez's *Hunger of Memory* and Esmeralda Santiago's *When I Was Puerto Rican*, have been much

more successful in terms of sales and readership than those works which critique and challenge mainstream American ideology. (Aparicio 67–68)

Some of the Latinx works I analyze might *seem* to support this myth, but, according to my reading, ultimately undermine "the ethos of individualism" and the American Dream.

In "Women's Autobiographical Selves: Theory and Practice" (1988), feminist literary critic Susan Stanford Friedman examines the link between autobiography and Humanism. In response to George Gusdorf's argument (from his influential 1956 essay, "Conditions and Limits of Autobiography") that "autobiography is the literary consequence of the rise of individualism as an ideology," Friedman claims that this ideology excludes "women and minorities," whose culturally imposed group identities and conceptions of selfhood might be founded on relationality more than separate individuation (35). "The emphasis on individualism as a necessary precondition for autobiography," she writes, "is thus a reflection of privilege, one that excludes from the canons of autobiography those writers who have been denied by history the illusion of individualism" (39). I'm not sure if Friedman would include Judith Ortiz Cofer, Gloria Anzaldúa, or John Rechy in the "canon of autobiography," but these writers have certainly been successful in selling books and making their way onto course syllabi. Perhaps this is because they were published in a time when challenges to individualism were becoming more mainstream.

Many critiques of individualism from the 1980s are based on (sometimes essentialist, idealistic, or romantic) claims about ethnicity and gender (sociopolitical categories that fall within the framework of Humanism). In an essay in James Clifford and George Marcus's important 1986 collection *Writing Culture*, Michael Fischer focuses on the "proliferation" of autobiographical works in the 1980s "that take ethnicity as a focal puzzle" (195) and concludes that these works are ultimately oriented toward group traditions and cultural revolution: "What thus seem initially to be individualistic autobiographical searchings turn out to be revelations of traditions, re-collections of disseminated identities and of the divine sparks from the breaking of the vessels. These are a modern version of the Pythagorean arts of memory: retrospection to gain a vision for the future" (198). I am uneasy with the generalizations about minoritized cultures in this essay (beginning with Fischer's characterization of texts by minority writers as works that view ethnicity as a "puzzle"). He brings together autobiographers of "five ethnicities"—a decontextualized multiculturalism (fairly typical for the

1980s) that includes Armenian Americans, Chinese Americans, African Americans, Mexican Americans, and Native Americans—and offers romantic conclusions ("divine sparks"?) about the affirmative power of memory in these writers' works (201–02). But Fischer does draw attention to ways in which "ethnic" writers often challenge the individualism assumed to underlie autobiography.

Sidonie Smith has also written and edited a number of books about autobiography that critique, from a feminist and global perspective, the privileged understanding of subjectivity assumed to underlie the genre. In *Subjectivity, Identity, and the Body: Women's Autobiographical Practices in the Twentieth Century* (1993), Smith begins, like Friedman, from the premise that "Western autobiographical practices flourished because there seemed to be a self to represent, a unique and unified story to tell that bore common ground with the reader, a mimetic medium for self-representation that guaranteed the epistemological correspondence between narrative and lived life, a self-consciousness capable of discovering, uncovering, recapturing that hard core at the center" (Smith, *Subjectivity, Identity, and the Body* 17–18). These conventions of autobiography "served to power and define centers, margins, boundaries, and grounds of action in the West" (18). The "rational, free, and autonomous" self circulated as the standard subject, agent, and citizen, the one with a coherent life to narrate. When people excluded from this narrative enter into autobiographical discourse, for Smith, they do so with cacophony, with "mess and clutter" that dislodge the "hegemonic discourses of the universal subject" (22–23). Smith considers, in an essentialist fashion that is also characteristic of the period, that the female body constitutionally participates in this dislodging:

> The female body opens up to foreign influences, foreign infiltration, foreign insemination, to foreign meaning and control. It is the breached boundary that destabilizes inner and outer, that invites further penetration by the dominant order, the very source of oppression. It is the opening through which leaks out the (endogamous) life of the people. . . . In the body politic, female sexuality saps the male of his privileges, as it threatens to erase his original identity. (144)

As with Fischer's account of ethnic autobiographies, here there is something at the root of female sexuality that defies the bounded self of Humanist autobiography.

I quote these earlier studies at length because I've benefitted from their accounts of the link between autobiography and Humanist selfhood and I value their arguments that self-writing by minoritized peoples challenges this bounded subject. I also spend time on these approaches in order to clarify what I am *not* saying in this book: I am not saying that there is something about "women and minorities" that makes them inherently more permeable or radical to Humanism. Rather, political strategies developed by Latinx writers deliberately disrupt conventional understandings of selfhood since these understandings are the grounds of racism, misogyny, and homophobia. If the writers I analyze "sap" the dominant subject of its privileges (to paraphrase Smith), it is not because of a biological leakiness but because of a strategic effort (feminist, queer, and decolonial) to think a different sort of subject. Though it is true that historical circumstances lead to distinct conditions of identity emergence, I do not want to make any general claims about "group identities," as Friedman, Fischer, and Smith seem to do.[4] No text is a transparent reflection of the life it narrates (though literature written by "minority authors" is often read as autobiographical or sociological data).[5] As I explain in the introduction, this is the reason why I favor the term memoir over autobiography: a memoir is not an empirical study of the self but, rather, an aesthetic engagement with what one remembers about the past and what one cares to share in the present.

In addition to not fitting neatly into linear stories, neither of the writers' lives I analyze in this chapter fits into familiar identity molds; they experience a sort of "excess" in their movements between nations and cultures. Ortiz Cofer links the fragmentations of her memoir to childhood and adolescent experiences shuttling between Puerto Rico and New Jersey, Spanish and English, hot and cold, Puerto Rican and "American" gender norms, which developed into "cultural schizophrenia" as well as a sense of being a "cultural chameleon" (*Silent Dancing* 17, 124). (The contradiction between these two terms is palpable: how can one be both chameleon—for whom changing colors is an inborn condition that does not affect the integrity of its body—and schizophrenic—a pathology Ortiz Cofer describes as an "undoing" [124]?) These constant uprootings lead to lapses in memory, unresolved contradictions, withheld secrets, and opaque mysteries. Quinceañera, for her, was a "crossroads," where she felt herself pulled in the "many directions a woman's life can take" (148). This internal conflict was not just about coming of age; for Ortiz Cofer it was about discovering that the rules of courtship in New Jersey didn't apply to the rules of courtship in Puerto Rico and that she didn't know how to succeed in either place. In the poem that comes between the chapters about courtship in Paterson and courtship on the island, she describes herself and her brother as "red balloons set adrift" who "lost their will to connect," traveling like nomads with their homes on their backs (138). The most significant lines in this poem, from my perspective, claim that "In time we grew rich in dispossession / and fat with experience" (138). I picture the siblings' varied and contradictory experiences pushing against their flesh from inside, excessive; dispossession forms its own sort of wealth, a possession made of discomfort and loss.

Like Ortiz Cofer, Vilar's girlhood and adolescence were spent shuttling between households and schools in Puerto Rico, New Hampshire, Spain, and upstate New York. In each place she is marked by cultural alienation: not "American" enough in Spain because she'd never been to New York City, and not "Latina" enough in Syracuse because she wasn't like the Nuyoricans (Vilar, *The Ladies Gallery* 43, 217). Ultimately, she rejects all of the ethnic models presented to her: "just as being a gringa didn't tempt me, neither did being Albizu's transcendental woman. . . . Ivan saw me as a Latin American, but I felt myself to be just another woman among so many on campus: blondes, brunettes, black, dark-skinned" (48).[6] Unlike her mythic grandmother, who did model herself after Pedro Albizu Campos's nationalist ideal, Irene identifies instead with an anonymous list of women defined by their different colors.

One might say that there is something particularly Puerto Rican about this kind of dispossession: being a product of an island that is tethered to the United States while still floating in the Caribbean, denied independent national status, pulled between competing visions of gender, race, and success. "Status is judged by unique standards," Ortiz Cofer writes, "in a culture where, by definition, everyone is a second-class citizen" (*Silent Dancing* 56). She describes the ridiculousness—under the program of enforced English-language immersion during the "Operation Bootstrap" era—of being told that roosters say "cock-a-doodle-doo" rather than "cocorocó" when the reality of children on the island told them otherwise.[7] The frames of intelligibility that Puerto Ricans were offered by U.S. colonialism conflicted with the realities of their experiences. Colonialism also plays an important role in Vilar's challenge to conventional representations of life: "My nightmare is part of the awful secret, and the real story is shrouded in shame, colonialism, self-mutilation, and a family history that features a heroic grandmother, a suicidal mother, and two heroin-addicted brothers" (*Impossible Motherhood* 5). Part of what made motherhood, or even life itself, "impossible" for her was the inheritance of loss, her grandmother's self-sacrifice in the defense of Puerto Rican nationalism, poverty on the island after profits shifted to U.S.

corporations and undermined the agricultural economy that had sustained families like Vilar's, and the history of U.S. interference in the Puerto Rican birthrate by experimenting on Puerto Rican women with new birth control technologies and performing unnecessary sterilizations. (Vilar's mother was one of the many women on the island who had a hysterectomy performed for unclear reasons [*The Ladies Gallery* 150].) These conditions undermine not just the integrity and coherence of an identity but the ability of a self to thrive.

In their introduction to *Puerto Rican Jam* (1997), Frances Negrón-Muntaner, Ramón Grosfoguel, and Chloé Georas call Puerto Rico's condition one of "illusory autonomy," in which "discourses of autonomy have obscured how (subordinately) integrated Puerto Ricans are to the United States' economic and political structures" (12). For Negrón-Muntaner, Grosfoguel, and Georas, this integration "has not resulted in a loss of cultural identity . . . but in an overt hybridization and multiplication of Puerto Rican identities played out by different subjects" (14). Puerto-Ricanness is often coded through the tropes that link island and mainland, like a bridge or an airbus, in defiance of the bounded self or the bounded nation. I do not, however, want to overstate the role of nationality in shaping the kinds of lives I analyze in this chapter; other contexts—families, illness, ecosystems, globalization—also fragment lives from within and without. There are (intellectual and ethical) benefits to rupturing the Humanist (and nationalist) self. Vilar's and Ortiz Cofer's memoirs reimagine life and build powerful feminist critiques from conditions of precarity. In *Precarious Life*, Judith Butler invokes Emmanuel Levinas's insistence that encountering an other (in particular, the face of an other) makes ethical demands. In Butler's interpretation, the face that initiates this ethical encounter—since it is *other*—reflects the precarity of life and thresholds of difference that cannot be captured by the human form. Since normative schemas limit what a livable life is supposed to look like, Butler calls us to highlight the ways in which precarious lives exceed the conventional frames of representation:

> For Levinas, then, the human is not *represented by* the face. Rather, the human is indirectly affirmed in that very disjunction that makes representation impossible, and this disjunction is conveyed in the impossible representation. For representation to convey the human, the representation must not only fail, but it must *show* its failure. There is something unrepresentable that we nevertheless seek to represent, and that paradox must be retained in the representation we give. (*Precarious Life* 144, original emphasis)

For Butler, "schemas of intelligibility" perpetuated, for instance, by mainstream media decide "what will and will not be publicly recognizable as reality" (147). In order to represent those who are unrepresentable in the shared conventions of the dominant culture, one must first point out the violence committed by those normative conventions. The writers I analyze in this chapter break the rules of memoir to dramatize their friction with racial, sexual, national, physical, and mental norms—with excess, diffraction, or exclusion—and put readers in a position of ethical encounter with an other.

What do we do when we are presented with fragmented lives? Smith worries that "any autobiographical practice that promotes endless fragmentation . . . might be counterproductive," and though "the resistant autobiographer lingers in the space of negativity where she refuses attempts to universalize any 'us,' 'we,' or 'I,' . . . she may be caught in an endless self-qualification that takes her further away from any community of interest and political action" (Smith, *Subjectivity, Identity, and the Body* 156). Ultimately, I wish to expand this idea of "community of interest and political action" to include both fragmentation and excess, dispossessed lives and intertwined lives. Building from Butler's Levinasian ethics described above, I will demonstrate how Ortiz Cofer and Vilar use fragmentation not just as a form of critique but also as a form of solicitation: soliciting reader involvement, broader frameworks for representing lives, and generosity toward those who stand outside autonomous subjectivity. Though she does not embrace fragmentation, literary critic Lourdes Torres similarly emphasizes how Latina writers (Gloria Anzaldúa, Cherríe Moraga, Rosario Morales, and Aurora Levins Morales, in her analysis) "realize that a noncontradictory, unified self is impossible within the discourses they traverse" leading them to reject the "stifling subject positions" offered by conventional discourses and to "forge new possibilities" through their radical autobiographies (Torres 282). For Torres, the reader of these works "is prevented from fixing the authors in any stable position and must begin to question her desire to do so" (284). The texts thereby engage readers in a process of letting go of their conventional ideas about human life.

My next section analyzes the processes of accounting for dispossessed lives as demonstrated in Ortiz Cofer's *Silent Dancing*. Then I turn to Vilar's paired memoirs to highlight the ways in which they represent diffuse or incoherent selfhood, undermining the singularity of life itself. These texts create friction more than seamless narratives, and I conclude with an analysis of how readers are involved in an ethical process as they work through this friction.

25

Memoir in Practice

What is the purpose of calling this collection
non-fiction or a memoir?

—Judith Ortiz Cofer, *Silent Dancing* 13

What is at stake in calling a text memoir? By posing her genre choice as a question, Ortiz Cofer characterizes the relationship between text and life as a problem. While she tethers *Silent Dancing* to life, she also emphasizes that there is no one-to-one correspondence. She ultimately uses the term "*ensayo*" (which means both essay and rehearsal/practice, according to her preface [12]) rather than memoir or autobiography. This dancing around questions of genre emphasizes fluidity, a rehearsal rather than a fixed work. The text's subtitle calls it a "partial remembrance," indicating the limitations of memory as well as the limitations of the text in containing a life. In an essay about writing *Silent Dancing*, Ortiz Cofer further distances her work from memoir by suggesting that "I realized that memoir was not the right label for what I wanted to accomplish in these narratives, as it has come to be attached to celebrity or notoriety, neither of which I possess in enough quantity to justify a book about my exploits" ("¿La Verdad?" 26). This claim diminishes the value of the life being captured, while "partial remembrance" diminishes the ability to capture a life. Ironically, the subtitle of the essay in which Ortiz Cofer so adamantly rejects the term memoir describes *Silent Dancing* as "A Memoir in Prose and Poetry"; it is and is not a memoir.[8]

Silent Dancing is also a sort of anti-bildungsroman that takes apart its subject at the same time that it builds it. Ortiz Cofer highlights the artistic process that goes into representation by splicing prose and verse versions of the same events in alternating (and sometimes conflicting) chapters that demonstrate how the genres work differently. (Ortiz Cofer describes the relationship between the poetry and the prose as one of "refraction" rather than reflection ["¿La Verdad?" 27].) In one of many references to photography and filmmaking, the preface begins by pointing out: "As one gets older, childhood years are often conveniently consolidated into one perfect summer afternoon. The events can be projected on a light blue screen; the hurtful parts can be edited out, and the moments of joy brought in sharp focus to the foreground. It is our show. But with all that on the cutting room floor, what remains to tell?" (*Silent Dancing* 11). The matters edited out of the film, presumably the "hurtful parts," lie on the cutting room floor, but Ortiz Cofer includes them as part of her subject. This metaphor enables us to see not the content but the existence of the excess that did not survive the process of selecting images for the "show." Ortiz Cofer makes us aware of loss and the unendurable parts that we can't see. In a later passage she turns from film to weaving as her metaphoric art form: "I wanted to try to connect myself to the threads of lives that have touched mine and at some point converged into the tapestry that is my memory of childhood" (13). "Threads of lives" suggests a web of connections; rather than giving this web a perimeter, she focuses on the points of convergence within the web and locates these points not in her actual childhood but in her memory of it.[9] So telling the story of *a* Puerto Rican childhood tears one thread out of the context in which it is embedded, erasing the pattern, and we are left with a jumble of threads and snippets on the floor. Indeed, in the sometimes abrupt shifts between the alternating fragments of prose and poetry in *Silent Dancing*, the text is full of palpable holes.[10] Ortiz Cofer emphasizes, in an interview with Stephanie Gordon, that her *ensayos* in *Silent Dancing* feature herself not as a central character but "as a witness" to her own life as well as those others with which she is embedded ("Ensayos: Essays of a Life" 13). This is a text with no single center and no clear boundary: Ortiz Cofer is "not interested in 'canning' memories" (*Silent Dancing* 13) but in unfurling problems.

One "hole" in the text is violence, which rarely takes the foreground but, instead, gets projected onto otherwise nonviolent images. (Ortiz Cofer's early reminder in the preface that "hurtful parts" can be edited out of a memoir is important to bear in mind.[11]) For instance, the poem "Christmas, 1961," which describes a photograph of the narrator dressed as an angel for a Christmas play, uses language that, in other contexts, would indicate some sort of violation: "In the exposed print, / the flowers will bleed at the edges / of my ghostly shape" (59). The language describing the actual moment when her mother took the photograph implies danger: Ortiz Cofer writes that "I am nearly blinded by" the radiance of the mother, who "had swallowed the sun," and she sees, in the "eye of the lens," "a tiny world burning" (60). Since the world burning is in the lens of the camera, it is equated with the daughter being photographed. Ortiz Cofer indicates that this picture was sent to her father who was, at that time, at sea with the U.S. Navy, and there is a reminder in the poem that soon he will be "lost to us for months" during the Cuban Missile Crisis, but there is no obvious reason for the image of the little girl to be bloody, ghostly, or burning. An indented and italicized stanza follows this one and intrudes upon the otherwise chronological description of the picture-taking:

Who knows how fear can change the face
of everything? The colors
of a picture left in an empty house
will fade to yellow. The paper
will cocoon around a moment
in a reversed metamorphosis. (59)

It is possible that the "fear" here refers to anxiety about the father's deployment during the missile crisis, but why would this fear "change the face" of the daughter in the picture taken months before, and in what supposed empty house is this picture later decaying? Since she was wearing "tissue paper wings" in the photograph, the "reversed metamorphosis" suggests some sort of regression of the child from beautiful butterfly to cocoon, but this is an odd metaphor. Indeed, there is no explanation for this reference to empty houses and cocoons; maybe it was left on the cutting room floor. All we are left with is faded memories and incomplete stories of loss.

There are also several stories that are told differently from different perspectives, usually differentiating the narrator's interpretation of events from her mother's or grandmother's.[12] *Silent Dancing* ends with an unresolved dispute between mother and daughter. There was a mysterious incident during a party when the daughter was two years old and her father had just returned from being stationed in Panama. The daughter remembers being left alone in a crib, crawling out, and falling into a fire. But the mother won't even let the daughter finish telling her version of the story, reminding her that she was only a baby and, implicitly, couldn't remember correctly. The mother becomes angry, leafs through a photo album to find evidence to defend her own version, and points at a picture of the daughter in a fancy dress asking, "Does that look like a child who was neglected for one moment?" (164). But what the daughter notices is that she is not smiling in the picture and that the eyes in the two-year-old's face "tell me that she is not a part of" the celebration going on around her (164). The mother insists that her version "*es la pura verdad* [is the pure truth]," but the narrator ends the chapter with a remark addressed to readers: "that is not how *I* remember it" (165, original emphasis). Following this account, *Silent Dancing* ends with a poem that references this picture:

There is a picture of me
taken soon after: my hair clipped close to my head,
my eyes enormous—about to overflow with fear.
I look like a miniature of those women

in Paris after World War II, hair shorn,
being paraded down the streets in shame,
for having loved the enemy.

It seems like a big reach to compare a two-year-old in a party dress to women who were publicly shamed for loving "the enemy" (presumably Nazis) during World War II, but it is a reach that Ortiz Cofer creates with this juxtaposition. Moreover, the photograph referred to in this debate is on the cover of the book (or, at least, the photo on the cover of the book looks like the one described in this poem), encouraging readers to return to the image of the solemn girl in a lace dress holding a baby rattle and to compare her to a "fallen" woman. This is like the yellowed picture in "Christmas, 1961": Ortiz Cofer presents us with fragments—story, poem, picture—and leaves the gaps between them to guesswork. Regardless of what readers might conclude about this comparison, it is made evident that any interpretation would be disputed.

Archival records—photographs, home movies, poems, and remembered versions of oral stories—accumulate throughout *Silent Dancing*, but these are always incomplete and cryptic. Readers are like detectives sorting through evidence, but this archive works against conventional notions of research: it undermines conclusions and asks questions rather than supporting any story with data. Although a memoir might be supposed to smooth out controversies and ambiguities, this one does not. This text is, after all, literary, not the work of a historian, and we do well to bear in mind that the function of the literary is not to preserve facts (recalling the "canning" metaphor in the preface) but to create ethical and aesthetic encounters.[13] Memoir is a hybrid genre: it is literary but expected to refer in some way to reality. Ortiz Cofer points out the impossible contradiction within this hybridity by undermining empiricism at every turn. She also thwarts the idea that memoir is supposed to foreground *a* life since most chapters in *Silent Dancing* focus on other characters she encountered; some names emerge for just a few lines (Lorenzo, Vida, Salvatore, plus countless unnamed cousins, aunts, and uncles), forming the larger tapestry referred to in the preface. There is a kind of humility about this approach to memoir: rather than foregrounding the exploits of an individual, the life of the individual blends with others in a less hierarchical fashion. The story Ortiz Cofer shares is, itself, a shared one. What emerges from *Silent Dancing* is not a life but a collaborative process of negotiation and reinterpretation. In her account of the text, Carmen Haydée Rivera claims that "the reader is left with a barrage of information hovering between the biographical account of [Ortiz Cofer's] life and her artistic creativity"; ultimately, the reader is "unable to separate fact from fiction" (100). We know that we don't know the truth with any certainty, but does it matter? The memoirs I am most interested in favor situated knowledges, imaginative exploration, and ethical engagement.

Fragmented Lives

> "(When you decide you are going to die, something in you splits. You live two lives, half of you cries in a chapel, the other half writes an index card.)"
> —Irene Vilar, *The Ladies Gallery* 35

In this puzzling sentence (and in paradoxical parentheses that defy the magnitude of her claim), Vilar links thoughts of suicide to crying and writing. Index cards are a recurring motif in both of Vilar's memoirs, and they seem to perform conflicting functions: one as a constructive method of assembling fragmented ideas for a book (a memoir) and the other as the pathological gesture of a mentally unstable woman obsessively trying to grasp an elusive reality. The half of herself that is writing index cards is not necessarily any more in control of herself than the half that is crying in the chapel. Indeed, she seems to lose control over the content of the cards she writes upon.

> Things hadn't been going well for me lately, and the refuge I needed was somewhere else. Perhaps in my index cards. I had been shuttling between the library and my room armed with index cards that were becoming increasingly oppressive, but Mama's overpowering voice went on; hundreds of voices sprang from hers, talked among themselves, spoke to me, about me, on my behalf, voices from my index cards—the illusion of a busy life—notes for a diary I would one day turn into a critical book about Three Sirens. . . . But what I imagined was a clever project was fast becoming a chaos of three-by-five cards I couldn't bother to read because they brimmed with pride, wanton self-assertiveness, self-conscious family epigrams, too glorious to be taken seriously now, now that I could barely stand on my own feet. (*The Ladies Gallery* 13)

These fragmented and rambling sentences reflect the disorder in the narrator's mind as well as the overwhelming amount of input that she's trying to sort out. She also apparently fears the self-assertion of planning to write a memoir. The cards themselves become oppressive, taking on agency and voices of their own. They embody excessive vitality and self-assertion right at the moment that the narrator is literally losing footing as a person. This long passage comes from the beginning of *The Ladies Gallery*, but once one has read more of the text, one realizes that the moment this passage refers to is the day before Vilar's first suicide attempt. This chronology makes memoir writing itself seem like a destructive process, one that undoes the mental and physical stability of the author/subject.[14] (More information about the actual assembly of the index cards into the shape of *The Ladies Gallery* appears in Vilar's second memoir, *Impossible Motherhood* [98].) Piecing together information placed throughout these conflicting and nonchronological memoirs makes it seem like the texts themselves are full of three-by-five cards that readers must (but can't) put in order to create a fuller picture, to establish cause and effect, chronology, and coherence.

Like Ortiz Cofer's, Vilar's work revolves around lives that are fragile, malleable, and at times unrecognizable. In trying to give shape to these precarious lives, Vilar's two-book memoir disrupts chronology and life-building with repeated reminders of death, loss, and mental instability. *The Ladies Gallery* begins and ends in a mental hospital (days before the miscarriage that serves as the final moment of the text's chronology). The three parallel stories this book tells—of Lolita's growing nationalist fervor and subsequent mystical visions in prison; of her daughter Myrna's depression and eventual suicide; and of the granddaughter Irene's journey from Puerto Rico to Spain to Mexico and, eventually, to a psychiatric hospital in Syracuse, New York—are all punctuated with italicized first-person accounts of Irene's time in the hospital. (The stories of nonhuman beings, like coffee and the Puerto Rican sugar economy, provide additional context for this multifaceted memoir.[15]) Irene recounts the diagnosis of one of her doctors: "According to the doctor, part of my problem is that I'm very open, I don't establish boundaries. When I leave the hospital I'll know how to say no. For her [the doctor] that's being somebody" (208).[16] In the next paragraph, Vilar allows another patient at the hospital to literally "make up" her face, "reanimating . . . with a touch of crimson" the self she felt had been lost. When she opens her eyes and sees herself in the mirror, she wants to cry "not so much over what I saw, . . . but over what I was discovering (or not discovering) about myself" (208–09). For "Dr. O.," "being somebody" means having clear boundaries, and boundaries are kept by saying "no" to outside forces. But immediately after this prescription Irene has clearly not said "no" to an outside influence trying to "reanimate" her face with artificial colors. Irene seems to regard herself as a fluid construction, and she allows this construction to be permeated by the influence of others (including both the psychiatrist and the makeup artist in this scene; later she will be permeated by many others). It's not clear what she was "discovering (or not discovering)" about herself, but the fact that she's not sure if it is or isn't a discovery, is or isn't "myself," suggests fundamental ambiguity.

This uncertainty of boundaries is characteristic of the portrayal of mental illness throughout the text. For instance, one of the more visible signs of Irene's mother's mental instability (beyond the more readily explicable acts of attacking her husband's clothes with scissors or threatening his lover with a machete [138, 140]) is her preference for wigs and false eyelashes toward the end of her life, rendering her often unrecognizable to her family. The patients in the mental hospital are similarly tenuous in their existence, "broken form[s]" (238). One patient, an anorectic, is literally invisible, her body "looking more and more like the folds of her bedcovers" so that people think she is not in the room (113). The narrator's miscarriage at the end of *The Ladies Gallery* is also about losing the boundaries of her self: "Down below, between my legs, I thought I felt cold pinches and everything began to turn into a dialogue between the needles and my body, and the operating table might just as easily have been a dissection table. . . . I no longer felt myself rooted to anything on earth. My only links were to the metal railings on the gurney . . . time, the hands on the clock flowed on, the memory of something that had ceased to exist" (318). The only boundaries to this body are, as Laura Halperin notes in her astute analysis of Vilar, "medicalized" (the gurney, the needles, the operating table). The self is defined by this dialogue with professionals who might just dissect her. But what "ceased to exist"? Time? Memory? The self? Halperin reads this passage optimistically, suggesting that "her arguable depiction of herself as the 'something that had ceased to exist'" relegates the medicalized self to the past (51), presumably liberating an actual self from the grip of the clinic. I read this passage, however, more as a sign that the body/self is defined by its tendency to slip away.

From the perspective of disability studies, Laura Kanost embraces the fact that Vilar "represents mental illness as one pivotal life experience among many," resisting the demands of "autopathography" (Thomas Couser's term) that illness be regarded as a separate, exceptional form of experience (Kanost 108). I would suggest, by contrast, that all of the events in Vilar's life are narrated through a lens of pathology (lives that are difficult to endure). Illness is not separate or exceptional because it is the norm. But this norm is a specific effect of cultural and historical circumstances that Vilar critiques through the mechanism of life writing (economic imperialism, the violation of women's reproductive rights, infidelity, misogyny). By pointing to lives that are somehow imperiled, she highlights conditions that lead to imperilment and, implicitly, challenges us either to change those conditions or to accept that our living, itself, is a situation of peril, a precarious state of vulnerability. This vulnerability is similar to the dispossession expressed in Ortiz Cofer's work, but violence is less suppressed in Vilar, and actual injuries take the foreground.

While *The Ladies Gallery* thematizes mental illness and suicide, *Impossible Motherhood* adds pregnancy and abortion to those experiences. This juxtaposition intertwines mental health with physical health as well as self-destruction with reproduction. In *Impossible Motherhood*, Vilar writes: "I basked in the thought of killing myself, in the same way I would make love without birth control: without thinking about the consequences" (53). Though this description poses suicide and conception as allied forms of irresponsibility, I would suggest that this framing eclipses the sense in which both acts are also about taking control over the production and termination of life. This tension between controlling and relinquishing control over life is central to the text. As a salient example, the miscarriage I analyze above is actually the result of taking "an overdose of a cathartic" (*The Ladies Gallery* 318) after cancelling and rescheduling an appointment to see a doctor about an abortion.

This theme of relinquishing and seizing control is mirrored by the process of memoir production, which is foregrounded throughout *Impossible Motherhood* with numerous self-reflexive meditations on the writing of both memoirs. Vilar's relationship with her first husband, a former professor who was much older than she, is entirely absent from the first memoir: "The transference horror script I lived out with the man I loved and became pregnant by multiple times, as I wrote my life down during those years, is absent in that memoir, tucked away under the noble rug of family history" (*Impossible Motherhood* 34). Like Ortiz Cofer, Vilar edited the "horror script" out of the first memoir: the psychologically abusive relationship with the man she called her "master" as well as the fifteen abortions that punctuated their marriage. She references what she "should have written"— that she wanted to carry a pregnancy to term, for instance—as well as how she conceded to end *The Ladies Gallery* the way her husband thought she should (100–101). "I quiet the shame of my half-truths," she writes, "by reminding myself that all the provisional selves that seem to be my true makeup don't have to be reason for despair" (101). Whether these provisional selves are those she has lived or those she has written into her memoir is unclear, but what stands out most to me is the idea that selves are provisional. She discovers that her personal history "alters constantly as more is 'remembered' or released into my consciousness, recasting in this way my sense of self and the lives I've lived" (35). Readers are keenly aware that Vilar has written one incomplete, potentially dishonest memoir and would do well to be skeptical of the illusion that the second memoir is a more reliable corrective with truer insight into which actual self Vilar is or was.

The Ladies Gallery establishes a direct parallel between writing and pregnancy: "the only thing I had to offer was a family history and my body" (The Ladies Gallery 321).

> And so I began to write, bits and pieces and self-figurations, as if by writing "I"—the much despised "I" of Virginia Woolf—a personal history would become a valid, legitimate source of progress and direction. But the bits and pieces of this pronoun became the life stories of my grandmother and my mother, all kinds of stories set free to roam like a medieval incubus, impregnating everything it touched in its cruel transmigrations. (322)[17]

I find it interesting the Vilar compares the written "I" to progress, as if the writing constitutes the self. This interpretation is furthered by the incubus image: the stories run amok and impregnate everything they touch. The pronoun (I, itself) is fragmented into bits and pieces that become the life stories of others, growing new generations back into the past rather than into the future (somewhat like Ortiz Cofer's tapestry). This description of memoir writing as "cruel transmigration" seems like a perverse form of (re)production. In correlation to this, an earlier sentence suggests, within parentheses, that "(. . . I can be her, she can be me, one can always edit oneself, one can always abort)" (The Ladies Gallery 321). This interchanging of self and other is described in terms of editing and abortion, as if the generation of lives within a memoir also involves the termination of other lives or possibilities.

The second memoir foregrounds not just the secrets withheld in The Ladies Gallery but also the manipulative editorial power of the "master" who initially suggested that she write the book to keep her occupied, while he was writing his own, during their extended stays on his yacht. She writes that she began to enjoy the project after reading Simone de Beauvoir's Memoirs of a Dutiful Daughter.

> As I became more involved with my book, he began to fight hard to keep my identity in check. Each time I wrote a memory down, he reminded me

of Paul de Man and the death of autobiography. "I" would always remain an ideological construct, and so a fiction of sorts. I was never to believe in the importance of what I was doing beyond the practicality of writing a book that organized our common schedule and could potentially bring us money. As for me, I was to embark on a writing life to create a cohesive whole I could live with, ignorant that what I amplified and allowed to recede through the quiet sleight of hand that were his edits of my work, would become a life I could not live with. (*Impossible Motherhood* 98–99)

Recalling the link between editing and abortion in my previous paragraph, the master's "edits" seem like a form of murder. (Invoking de Man and the "death of autobiography" furthers this parallel.) Vilar's husband fights against her "I" by using the excuse of deconstruction and also by diminishing her memoir to a matter of convenience rather than a story worth writing. It's not clear if Vilar agrees that "the 'I' would always remain an ideological construct" or if she repeats this point in order to critique it.

Another passage in the midst of this discussion about the self written into *The Ladies Gallery* establishes tension between the individual and her surrounding context:

Only the suicide attempts are given in detail, but even these are lacking an identifiable referent that inspired them. It's as if the movement toward self-annihilation was happening in a vacuum, the vacuum of a history attractive enough in its tragic sense to be understood as the reason for it all. My misery at the center of the book is historically romanticized, and the personal, domestic truths of a self's struggles are for the most part missing. (99)

The idea of self-annihilation happening in a vacuum suggests that the first memoir evacuated the context (presumably her marriage and her abortions) in which Vilar attempted suicide. There is an opposition between the "historically romanticized" first person in the first half of the last sentence (the decontextualized self) and the "personal, domestic" self at the end of the sentence. But the idea of a "personal, domestic" self sounds as mythic to me as the historically romanticized heroine of Puerto Rican nationalism. The fact that the "personal" self is described in the third person further distances even the supposed "truths" of the self from the self.

In her analysis of the theme of abortion in *Impossible Motherhood*, Mary Thompson suggests that Vilar's text forces us to recognize that "we are and are not the rational actors upon which pro-choice rhetoric and legislation is predicated" (133). Thompson questions the degree of accountability the subject of Vilar's memoir bears, given her entrapment within intersecting systems of oppression (135). This relates to my point above: how personal can a self or her choices be given her embeddedness in cultural, historical, and material conditions? Halperin importantly situates this framework of constrained choice within the context of the mass sterilization of Puerto Rican women as a part of U.S. population control policies from the 1930s to the 1970s. Many thousands of women, particularly those living in poverty, were encouraged—and sometimes misled—to consent to sterilization. Halperin points to a "paradoxical and incompatible juxtaposition of choice and coercion" that emerges from this history and "undermines neoliberal ideas of individual agency" (27, 49). I want to highlight this point and add to it: the colonial situation of Puerto Rico, in general, leads to dependency and exploitation, undermining the individual integrity of the island and its citizens. Vilar emphasizes this precarious condition and emphasizes precarity and lack of autonomy in her self-representations. Halperin ultimately describes Irene's repeated suicide attempts and repeated abortions as a form of self-sacrifice that "can be likened to, and ostensibly follows from, Lolita's self-sacrifice in the name of Puerto Rican independence, with both Irene's and Lolita's sacrifices plausibly serving as forms of protest over the unbearable conditions in which they live" (52). Abortion and suicide seem to converge here as parallel acts in which a body turns upon itself (especially if we view the fetus as part of the pregnant woman). Yet we would do well here to think more deeply about the kind of self that is subject to sacrifice in Vilar's memoirs. Mental instability undermines coherence, choice, and agency. Pregnancy, abortion, and suicide are all conditions that make the self both subject and object, dividing it against itself. Fetus and woman are both separable and inseparable, invariably defined in relation to each other even as they remain distinct. There is no "personal, domestic" self in pregnancy or abortion since these are states of relation.[18] The choice to focus on these conditions affects Vilar's overall attitude toward selfhood and memoir, rendering both matters of complexity greater than the proprietary dynamic "self-sacrifice" implies.

Vilar's representations of pregnancy are often paired with reflections on her precarious self. For instance, in *Impossible Motherhood*, pregnancy is described as making the self "less sub-human": "Sexuality spun a casing of shame around me, slowly concealing my origins and ties to my past. But pregnant, my life felt less sub-human. In this unique state I felt hope" (51). Yet this optimism is undermined by her husband's refusal to raise a child with her: "Every pregnancy was a house of mirrors I entered and lost myself in, numb to the realities of a fetus, my partner's wishes, and the impossible motherhood I was fashioning" (202). The house of mirrors reflects conflicting images that overtake Vilar's integrity: she "lost [her]self" in the competing realities of fetus, partner, and motherhood. Reproduction presents unforeseen futures and possibilities, represented as an increase in selfhood: "Feelings of inadequacy, helplessness, and disorder faded in the face of the possibilities of my reproductive body" (202). But this increase is never about the individual alone: pregnancy involves dialogue with others: "It was a violent, intensely emotional drama that kept me from feeling alone" (203). Loneliness disappears with the introduction of relationship, drama, and potential violence.

Many writings about pregnancy and abortion focus on the linked but often opposed rights and agencies of mother (or potential mother) versus fetus. I appreciate Karen Barad's deviation from this trend: from the perspective of her posthumanist "agential realism" (developed in her 2007 book *Meeting the Universe Halfway*), mother, fetus, and a host of other material and discursive apparatuses (including ultrasound imaging machines and political rhetoric) produce each other intra-actively in pregnancy: "The fetus is a complex material-discursive phenomenon that includes the pregnant woman in particular, in intra-action with other apparatuses" (Barad 218).[19] This insight moves us away from the duality of mother/fetus; both are produced through technologies and ideologies that shape and exceed their human (and protohuman) boundaries. This insight also highlights the injustice of "the recently intensified discourse of hypermaternal responsibility" that places "the full burden of accountability" onto the "mother" (a term that defines the woman only as a function of the fetus):

> The real questions of accountability include accountability for the consequences of the construction of fetal subjectivity, which emerges out of particular material-discursive practices; accountability for the consequences of inadequate health care and nutrition apparatuses in their differential effects on particular pregnant women; accountability for the consequences of global neocolonialism, including the uneven distribution of wealth and poverty; and many other factors. (Barad 218)

A posthumanist approach like Barad's views pregnancy as an ecological system much wider than the conjoined bodies of woman and fetus and moves us beyond the liberal Humanist discourse of individual rights and responsibilities. Moreover, while the Humanist narrative frames suicide and abortion as endpoints (the terminus of a life), the posthumanist perspective regards these events as temporal nodes where intersecting phenomena meet and produce other phenomena as effects (a temporal version of Ortiz Cofer's tapestry, perhaps).

Barad's view no doubt derives to some extent from the work of Donna Haraway, who argued in her 1997 book *Modest_Witness@Second_Millennium. FemaleMan©_Meets_OncoMouse*™ that the fetus, like the whole earth, owes its existence as a "public object" to "visualizing technologies" (174). Technology mediates (or creates?) our apprehension of these entities that would not be otherwise visible to us. The range of technologies available and the kinds of images they make public are not ideologically neutral developments. (The poster-sized images of late-term abortions wielded against defenders of women's reproductive rights are a case in point.) Reproductive "freedom," fetus, and mother are constructed through technical, political, and cultural vocabularies. Haraway suggests: "Under these conditions, looking for a feminist doctrine on reproductive technology, in particular, or on technoscience, in general, would be ludicrous. But understanding feminist technoscience scholarship as a contentious search for what accountability to freedom projects for women might mean, and how such meanings are crafted and sustained in a polyglot world of men and women, is not ludicrous" (191). Since both suicide and abortion involve some form of destruction as well as an affirmation of agency, we could view these acts as literal, and potentially liberating, reconstructions of the subject. But given the role of economically powerful institutions (like the medical-industrial complex or the media whose truths are filtered by corporate advertisers) in defining what life, health, and family look like, we must not view Vilar's actions in isolation as individual self-assertions. What freedom (or health or happiness) means is a complicated issue that involves a larger web of relations. We should consider Vilar's multiple abortions—along with her suicide attempts and mental instability—as social-political-institutional events that involve multiple agents. From this multipoint approach, the repetition of abortion and suicide in Vilar's memoirs is neither excessive nor perverse; it merely indicates a repeating convergence of particular material and discursive agents. If these repetitions are viewed as "wrong," changing the pattern would require changing the social, material, and ideological context, including, perhaps, the frameworks for gauging wrongness versus rightness.

Vilar's choice to focus on these controversial subjects forces us to confront the meaning of health, freedom, and individuality. In the prologue to *Impossible Motherhood*, she writes, "In opening up the conversation on abortion to the existential experience that it can represent to many, for the sake of greater honesty and a richer language of choice, we run risks" (2). It is difficult to think about abortion or suicide apart from politics and ethics, and Vilar is clearly aware of how her abortion "addiction" could be mobilized in support of both pro- and anti-choice rhetorics. But the larger histories and stories in which these life events are embedded in her memoirs ask us to regard them not in isolation but as part of a larger web of relations (including colonialism, patriarchal marriage, and the commodification of women's bodies). Though Mary Thompson worries that Vilar's use of the word "addiction" "irresponsibly" implies that women are "personally 'accountable'" (135), the meaning of "personal" is really what is at stake here. As Vilar writes, "the human fetus is so unlike anything or anyone else" (*Impossible Motherhood* 1). Neither "thing" nor "one," the fetus is a fragment, one component of a complicated relationship. Focusing on the story of the fetus should remind us that every subject is a fragment of larger relationships. We might say that Vilar's memoirs focus on a variety of fragments in a variety of human/nonhuman states, a catalogue of fetuses embedded in ideologically inf(l)ected material-discursive wombs.

Be/holding the Fragment

> The song of the Sirens is the great paradox that suicides and madmen know. It is the paradox, too, of every book on suicide written by suicides; they make their nests from the skeletons of dead authors. It's contagious—beware.
>
> —Irene Vilar, *The Ladies Gallery* 323

> It is only when writing is liberated from life, when one no longer grounds systems of inscription on the supposedly self-maintaining organism, that one disrupts the normalizing figure of bodily life.
>
> —Claire Colebrook, *Death of the Posthuman* 216

"Suicides and madmen" share the pleasure of having heard the song of the Sirens. They have crossed some sort of threshold that enables them to hear that which more contained selves do not. The pronouns are ambiguous in the first epigraph above. Who or what is the "they" that makes nests out of skeletons, and what is contagious? This ambiguity makes "beware" a doubly ominous warning because we're not sure what to watch out for, but there seems to be a threat to life in the books of suicides. Contagion suggests that readers are literally brought into the story against their will and to their potential peril, taking in the paradox of a suicide's life. I conclude this chapter with some thoughts about the ethics of engaging with these memoirs of precarious lives.

In *Death of the Posthuman*, Claire Colebrook aims to rethink vitalism in such a way as to disrupt the reproduction of the human as parasitical life form. One way to do this is to loosen the distinction between life and death: "Every living being borders on death; or perhaps it might be more accurate to say that every being has one side turned towards the non-living. Without that border between life and non-life, without the living being closing itself off to some extent from the fullness of life, there would be a pure influx, intensity, or becoming without any resistance or stasis" (Colebrook, *Death of the Posthuman* 208). I see this approach not as a counter-vitalism but as a step away from the binary of life/death in which life is constantly defending itself against its opposite. Rosi Braidotti likewise asks that, rather than pathologizing "self-destructive practices" (she includes abortion, addiction, and suicide in her list), we "think alongside them and with them": "This amounts to a radical redefinition of the boundaries of the human and the terms of his or her embodiment. It also generates new and more complex forms of compassion or deeply shared affinity in others" (*Transpositions* 233). This is not a matter of embracing death but of allowing some death into life. If we take the subject of Vilar's memoirs as a model—a self whose life includes mental illness, suicide, pregnancy, abortion, and motherhood—we can see what it might look like to loosen the perimeters around "life." Vilar is a suicide who survives, whose survival is defined by a history with death. And, by the end of *Impossible Motherhood*, Vilar is an "impossible mother": she is mother to a daughter whose life is defined in relation to abortion. By not titling her second memoir "Possible Motherhood," Vilar keeps motherhood from being the apotheosis or the endpoint. Even after she has given birth, she still participates in a motherhood that is impossible because she still lives in a world where motherhood is not a "free" or individual choice and where mothering (or, rather, parenting or family-ing in general) is often denied the financial and emotional support that it needs. Mothering for Puerto Rican women, given the history of enforced sterilization on the island, exists in tension with the demonization and annihilation of Puerto Rican motherhood. Thinking with this history of "destruction" inhibits simplistic celebrations of life and enables sympathetic engagements with death. (In this way, I disagree with Thompson's reading that *Impossible Motherhood* creates a progress narrative that embraces middle-class motherhood as the ultimate resolution [Thompson 153–54].)

Vilar's work, and Ortiz Cofer's, present life as always precarious, always involved with destruction. I would argue that this ambivalence is part of these writers' ethical critiques. Returning to Colebrook, rethinking life enables us to imagine a different future: "The promise of concepts—or the difference of concepts from any already given life—yields a politics of futurity" (*Death of the Posthuman* 217). It's impossible to say that this is a future in which there will no longer be genocide or femicide or that this will be a future in which human life is decoupled from environmental destruction. Such progress narratives are built on wish fulfillment defined by the deficiencies of our present moment. If we change how we do life in the present, our problems will simply be otherwise. The possibility I take from these writers is the suggestion that human life could be done differently. Vilar and Ortiz Cofer adamantly disrupt the norms of bodily life (to paraphrase my second epigraph above) by coupling life with its supposed opposite, by highlighting the violence that underwrites human life, and by echoing the violent exclusion of marginalized bodies from the dominant narrative.

These writers disorient readers in their approach to memoir. For all of the reasons I discuss in the preceding sections (foregrounding omissions from the narrative, pointing out the violence and instability that haunt life, emphasizing the impossibility of telling a coherent life story), their memoirs put readers off balance. We are denied the Humanist triumph narrative expected of memoirs. And we are denied the image of a remarkable individual whose life we might learn from. Instead, the pedagogical value of these texts lies in their disorientation.

If we accept death as a part of life, must our ethics refuse to choose between life and death? Should we not feel impelled to save the life of another? I think these questions are beside the point. There is no other whose life and death are not also in some way involved in our own. Braidotti explores "a system of ethical values that, far from requiring a steady and unified vision of the subject, rests on a non-unitary, nomadic, or rhizomatic view" and takes "sustainability" as her "central point of reference" (*Transpositions* 4–5). The "nomadic subject" of Braidotti's work is "nonetheless functional, coherent, and accountable, mostly because it is embedded and embodied" (4). Yet I'm not sure that the subjects I analyze here are coherent, and we would have to think long and hard about what "functional" means in the context of this work.

One way in which these memoirs educate readers is by presenting them with depictions of lives they might deem unlivable (of suicides, madmen, victims of untold violence). These "impossible" lives complicate straight-forward identification with the subject of the text. Confrontation with such subjects elicits a variety of ethical possibilities: trying to identify with an undesirable subject position, trying to dis-identify with the abject other, try-ing to understand what the other is made of, projecting a familiar story onto the other, or merely appreciating the other in its difference from oneself. I would emphasize the benefits of the last approach as a way of recognizing our connections with an other while also honoring their otherness. Lately I've been thinking about empathy, which is other-oriented and relational, as an alternative to identification.[20] Empathy is an action and a choice that involves looking into another from outside and taking into oneself some of that other's feelings; it thereby rests on permeability and elicits reciprocal transformation. I particularly like Carolyn Pedwell's sense of empathy as "surrendering oneself to *being affected by* that which is experienced as 'for-eign'" (Pedwell 38, original emphasis). The idea of sharing life with unlike elements in an ecological web is a theme that recurs throughout my study of memoir in *Shared Selves*.

The tension between connection and difference brings me back to the subject of pregnancy. Pregnancy is a form of contagion to the extent that one body takes in another, along with its physiological needs, digestive expul-sions, potentially conflicting blood type, and distinct genetic material. The shared vitality of pregnancy undermines the distance upon which objectiv-ity is assumed to rest. As in Barad's theory of intra-action, the distinction between intra-acting elements is difficult to perceive (or conceive). Barad solves this problem with her idea of the "agential cut"—an in-situ differ-entiation between apparatuses in intra-action—but this concept is, to me, the most difficult one in her work. She writes that "ontological separability" is "agentially enacted . . . within phenomenon" (175): "The crucial point is that the apparatus enacts an agential cut—a resolution of the ontologi-cal indeterminacy—within the phenomenon, and *agential separability—the agentially enacted material condition of exteriority-within-phenomena—provides the condition for the possibility of objectivity*" (175, original emphasis). This separability is the basis for Barad's view of ethics: "different agential cuts produce different phenomena," so the process of establishing this objec-tivity-within-phenomena has ethical implications. "[W]hat we need," she concludes, "is something like an *ethico-onto-epistemology*—an appreciation for the intertwining of ethics, knowing, and being—since each intra-action matters, since the possibilities for what the world may become call out in the pause that precedes each breath before a moment comes into being and the world is remade again" (185, original emphasis). Of course, in this framework, no apparatus has individual agency to determine what "comes into being," but, presumably, within the complex matters of intra-action, there is a "pause that precedes each breath" in which future worlds are shaped.

Ethical action is not determined by what "one" does in that pause. For Barad, subjectivity itself "is not a matter of individuality but a relation of responsibility to the other." The "ethical subject" is not individually embodied but embedded in relations (391). Separability is impermanent, an idea of differentiation among relata that are constantly shifting and sharing their being. "Ethics is therefore not about right response to a radically exterior/ized other, but about responsibility and accountability for the lively relationalities of becoming of which we are a part" (393). It is difficult to imagine responsibility and accountability without individuality, but this is precisely the problem that pregnancy, abortion, mental instability, and other contagions of selfhood pose. No *one* is responsible. Recalling Colebrook, this is a different way of doing life, one that leads not to competition between discrete entities but to shifting and sharing, permeating and differentiating, recognizing and not recognizing the others that are within and without. Ethics, in this life, must be negotiated with others.

If a life is neither a stable object nor a solitary one, the meaning of suicide shifts. Suicide is not the action of one individual in isolation; nor is there one sole victim. (These claims are obviously supported in Vilar's memoirs since she claims suicide as an intergenerational act and feels herself to be a product—as well as an agent—of suicide.) Moreover, suicide exists on a slippery scale of life and death rather than at one end of a binary, as evidenced by the fact that some suicides write books. For Vilar, sharing her life with her first husband (along with her choices about reproduction and the construction of her first memoir) was also a form of suicide: lost control over the boundaries of her own body as well as lost control over her memoir. Pregnancy is another form of suicide: loss of an original sense of selfhood, denial of individual sustainability, and the ultimate surrender of the fetus in birth, loss, or termination. We might even view reading and writing as forms of suicide: opening our conceptions of the world to the community of engagement established in a text. Perhaps any engagement in relation—which is to say, any living in the world—is suicide in that the self is partially constituted by the others with which one is in relation. This is not to diminish the power (or the horror) of suicide as a unique act but, rather, to point out that our view of it conventionally assumes individual autonomy and separability. Viewing lives and selves in relation highlights the variety of births and deaths—as well as acts of love and acts of violence, large and small—in which we are all involved.

Suicide, abortion, and mental illness are not the source of the decentered lives shared in the chapters to follow, but they provide a visceral framework for unsettling the boundaries of the self and the parameters of memoir. These subjects also establish an ethical imperative for the recognition of the others each life is intertwined with. This intertwinement takes distinct forms in my readings of John Rechy, Aurora Levins Morales, and Gloria Anzaldúa—queer communities, material or digital webs, and imagined kinships beyond the human—each with distinct ways of engaging readers in ethical action. Michael Fischer's 1986 essay "Ethnicity and the Post-Modern Arts of Memory," which I critique early in this chapter for its generalizations about "ethnic autobiographies," foresees some of these conclusions about the ethics of reading others: "Contemporary ethnic autobiographies partake of the mood of meta-discourse, of drawing attention to their own linguistic and fictive nature, of using the narrator as an inscribed figure within the text whose manipulation calls attention to authority structures, of encouraging the reader to self-consciously participate in the production of meaning" (Fischer 232). Fischer concludes that this characteristic "is not merely descriptive of how ethnicity is experienced, but more importantly is an ethical device attempting to activate in the reader a desire for *comunitas* with others, while preserving rather than effacing differences" (232–33). Community assumes different meanings even among Latinx writers, but each of the texts I analyze elicits readers' participation in making meaning as well as making community. And each models the disorienting and self-estranging process of being a self in a community of others. Ethical action is no simple matter in comunitas, since we share choice and agency with known and unknown others, but ethical action is also all the more imperative because of this sharing.

CHAPTER 2

Community

John Rechy, Depersonalization, and Queer Selves

New York had become a symbol of my liberated
self, and I knew that it was in a kind of turbulence
that that self must attempt to find itself.
—John Rechy, *City of Night* 20

There was still, too, the narcissistic obsession with
myself . . . the desperate, strange craving to be a
world within myself.
—Rechy, *City of Night* 120

It would not be unreasonable to regard John Rechy as a narcissist. In fact, he repeatedly points out the narcissism in himself and his characters throughout his work. And to the extent that memoir is conventionally associated with narcissism and exhibitionism, Rechy's generic choices support these associations. He has written one memoir, *About My Life and the Kept Woman* (2008), and an autobiographical "prose documentary," *The Sexual Outlaw* (1977), and several of his twelve novels are semi-autobiographical, especially *City of Night* (1963), *Numbers* (1967), and *This Day's Death* (1969). His newest novel, *After the Blue Hour* (2017), details the experiences of the author John Rechy sharing life stories with a cruel narcissist during a summer stay on a private island. Indeed, one of the more salient aspects of Rechy's body of work, in tension with its insistent claiming of gay publics, is its autobiographic content.[1] There is also a biography of John Rechy,

Charles Casillo's *Outlaw: The Lives and Careers of John Rechy* (2002), and an "interactive memoir" on CD-ROM, *Mysteries and Desire: Searching the Worlds of John Rechy* (2003), which blends fact with fiction by juxtaposing quotes from Rechy's novels with photographs, audio interviews, and news clippings about the real John Rechy. Many of his publications contain photographs of the author, not just on the back covers but sometimes in lengthy photo inserts of Rechy posed in front of the architecture and landscape of El Paso, his original hometown, and Los Angeles, his adopted home. When I visited the John Rechy archive at Boston University, alongside the numerous clippings documenting his accomplishments were nearly a hundred photographs of the author, many of them in provocative poses with unbuttoned shirts, low-slung pants, or bikini briefs. (Some of these photographs were taken for physique magazines.) Rechy's seems to be a self-referenced corpus.[2]

Toward the end of *City of Night* (Rechy's first, most acclaimed, and most autobiographical novel), Rechy describes narcissism as "defensive," a "self-love that implies a completeness within yourself—and yet implies a huge incompleteness—your devouring need of others to sustain each battered return to the Mirror" (*City of Night* 356). The narcissistic self is needy, oriented toward the others whose witnessing gaze confirms its existence. Yet the recurring image throughout *City of Night* is of the semi-autobiographical "youngman" gazing not into a mirror but out a window, from the beginning of the novel when, as a child, he watches a sandstorm blow outside his El Paso home to the end of the novel when he watches the Mardi Gras parade from the window of a hotel room in New Orleans. In one emblematic scene when the youngman actually looks into a mirror, his own reflection is not even revealed. While sitting in a hustler bar, silently listening to the gossip of the men around him, the youngman dismisses his own image in a panel of mirrors hung over the bar: "Looking up, I see my own reflection now in the panel of mirrors; and reflected behind me, that life that has fascinated me greets me victoriously: All along this long closed-in bar, the composite face of this submerged world stares defiantly at me" (153). The youngman shifts his gaze from himself, the reflection readers never see though the narrator reportedly does, to the "composite face" of the men "reflected behind" him, so that it is as if he is again looking out a window at a diffuse world passing by rather than in a mirror.

Though one might be tempted to describe *City of Night* as a bildungsroman, like *Silent Dancing* and Irene Vilar's memoirs, the novel details the unmaking of its narrator as much as his making. Throughout Rechy's work, the seemingly narcissistic individual is always on the verge of losing himself in an anonymous and "turbulent" world (the window rather than the mirror). The worlds that define him are both human and other-than-human: communities of male hustlers, scores, and queens as well as the (often tenuous) underground/queer ecosystems carved out by these communities in parks, bars, and bathhouses. The first epigraph in this chapter comes from the beginning of *City of Night*, when the unnamed "youngman" is breaking away from a racially divided El Paso to create himself apart from his all-absorbing Mexican family and his judgmental community. He already knows, though, that he is going to find this "liberated self" not alone but within a turbulent world. At the same time, his narcissism leads him to believe that this turbulent world will be found within himself. The confusion between outside and inside in these paired epigraphs marks the perimeter of the self as a space of encounter, where the world within meets the world without. In many ways, the youngman is transparent as he moves through the novel. He adopts the postures of the streets he walks and fades into the background as the novel shifts focus from his youth to the stories of the characters he meets on his travels across the United States and Europe. Each of these encounters presumably shapes him, but the "him" is barely perceptible as he sits quietly listening in the bars or on the street corners while the narrative focalizes on other characters. He will point out the surface of his body—especially the skin tone, eye color, and physique that make him attractive to others—but then study the context in which his handsome surface assumes meaning. Toward the beginning of Rechy's memoir, he reports that a neighbor once called him "a ghost boy": "'You don't talk to anyone. You seem to be studying others around you, judging others. You act as if you're not where we are'" (*About My Life* 38). Being a silent observer, in this account, dematerializes his presence. If he is perceived as a "ghost," he must lack the apparent qualities of a living person; perhaps this is because his constant orientation toward others troubles human individualism.

Even the "memoir," *About My Life and the Kept Woman*, fails to focalize on the author individually. Both the title and the plot of *About My Life* join the author's story to another, to two different "kept" women, in fact: a cousin who was the mistress of a prominent Mexican politician and a former classmate who rejects her Mexican heritage, claims royal Spanish ancestry, and, passing as such, marries a wealthy man who knows nothing of her background.[3] What makes these women remarkable (to the narrator and to the communities who gossip about them) is that they sacrificed their original identities in order to achieve wealth and glamour; their success in doing so forever removes them from their families and ties them to the men who support their created identities. These women assume nearly mythological status in the eyes of the character John Rechy, who envies their ability to adopt the postures and costumes of the social elite with convincing grace.[4] Their performances are the context in which Rechy makes sense of his own life. Two constant threads are woven throughout the narrative: the author/narrator recalling the time he watched Marisa Guzman (the first "kept woman") smoke a cigarette alone, on the margins of a family gathering, and his regular visits to his sister to catch up on the gossip about Alicia Gonzales (the second "kept woman"). Rechy is like these women in key ways, leaving his hetero-patriarchal family behind to achieve fame and success by passing within and writing about queer underworlds that his family would never understand. Checking in with the two kept women, recalling their beauty and reflecting on their exile, is paradoxically what tethers the author/narrator to his own life's trajectory, confirming Rechy's claim that narcissism is oriented toward others.

Rechy's embeddedness in communities of exiles keeps his work from being self-referenced in any conventional way. Rather than focusing on a singular self, this corpus covers a communal way of life. And rather than documenting these shared lives in any coherent fashion, the cacophony and friction between the many iterations of "Rechy's" story defy expectations for life writing. One of the qualities of Rechy's work that is most palpable is multiplicity, excess even. Most of his novels are longer than 300 pages (stacked on my floor they reach well above my knees), and the prose within them is lush: long detailed descriptions, lists, repetitions. Characters, events, and references reverberate between the separate works and create an intricate intertextual web. One never forgets that one has entered a literary labyrinth. The messiness of this corpus appropriately mirrors what I take to be the messiness of its content: the communality of selves and the proliferation of outlaw spaces that form a diffuse underground network. In talking about this lush body of work, and the lush body of criticism that has emerged around it over the past fifty years, it is difficult to pin down any singular point. (In sifting through the multiplicity within Rechy's corpus, my own sentences end up overcrowded with words, and this chapter itself has accumulated endnotes and parenthetical layers like mold.)

Casillo opens his biography of Rechy with the claim:

John Rechy likes to talk about the three ranks in the hierarchy of literary liars. At the top of this list he places the autobiographer, for daring to say, "This is exactly how it happened." Rechy argues that events are censored and transformed by time and can never be re-created from memory exactly as they occurred. Second in his rank of liars is (dare I say it) the biographer. Rechy takes issue with a writer claiming, "I am capable of knowing another's life," feeling instead that one can only hope to capture a "shadow of a life. A shade of it. A reflection." (Casillo 1)

An emphasis on the unreliability of memory and the distortion of representation characterizes much of Rechy's work. Characters are always mediated, reflected in mirrors or in the gazes of others; in this way, they are products of another, projections of the witness's or author's desires. Rechy's writing style is overtly artistic, opaque rather than transparent, and he manipulates narrative form and genre in ways that challenge conventions of life writing.[5] Characters are often imprecise or elusive, and actions are blurred by dark, smoky, or drug-induced distortion. They don't resolve into individuals.

In *About My Life and the Kept Woman*, Rechy wonders whether literature—in imposing order and meaning upon chaos—hides, blurs, or preserves the lives it tells about (307).[6] Not only do the repeated references to masks and role-playing—conventionally queer forms of representation—undermine any possibility of "preserving" a "real" life, but also the many references to literature throughout Rechy's work remind readers of the layers of artistry that go into any story.[7] Rechy writes frequently about his own writing, telling and retelling the stories of the evening his mother, brother, and he walked around and around a table collating three copies of the 500+ page *City of Night* and also of writing *Numbers* on a notepad held by his mother while driving on the highway from Los Angeles to Texas. Both of these stories highlight the labors of creation (and manipulation) that come between lives and texts. In his more recent critical analysis of Rechy's work, Juan Bruce-Novoa distinguishes between two layers of narration in *City of Night*: the nearly silent first-person narrator (the Rechy character) who presents a "camera-eye style of journalistic narration" and the author himself whose "play of authorial orchestration of formal elements and motifs produces [a] literary identity" ("Rechy and Rodriguez" 18, 22). This interpretation of a "dual Rechy"—the mute hustler soaking up life on the streets versus the highly literate author—makes it impossible for Rechy's works to be autobiographical in any strict sense; indeed, the hustler at the center of the narrative speaks a different language (mostly jive slang like "oh man, dig" [*City of Night* 346]) from the author telling his story. Rechy comments about these two aspects of his life being in tension throughout his work, with men who pick him up disbelieving that he could write a novel and critics of the novel disbelieving its veracity. To be a successful hustler, he has to suppress his intellectual and creative abilities, and as a writer he relishes his ability to manipulate the devices of canonical literature.

I focus in this chapter on three of Rechy's works that play with the genre of memoir and the conventions of human individualism in distinct ways. *City of Night* is a novel that revolves around details from Rechy's own life, in chronological fashion, but focalizes, serially, on other characters that the narrator encounters. Drag queens, hustlers, eccentric "johns," and other lonely seekers who inhabit the queer underworlds receive more detailed life histories and characterizations than the "youngman" (modeled after Rechy himself) who studies these characters. The voices and stories of these seemingly minor figures decenter any one life story. Every other chapter tells the story of one character (Mr. King, The Professor, Miss Destiny, Skipper: A Very Beautiful Boy, etc.), and these alternate with chapters that focus on environments rather than individuals. (These impersonal chapters all share the title "City of Night.")

The Sexual Outlaw also alternates between chapters oriented toward characters and those oriented toward context. While *City of Night* is multifocal in its account of heterogeneous characters, *The Sexual Outlaw* is diffracted by different disciplinary angles. Rechy calls *The Sexual Outlaw* a "prose documentary."[8] Most of the narrative focalizes on the semi-autobiographical "Jim" with a minutely detailed account of three days spent "sex-hunting" in Los Angeles: seeking paid sex in the "hustling" zones, cruising for lovers in underground locations, and accumulating large "numbers" of anonymous sexual encounters. This three-day chronology (marked by date, time, and location) is interrupted with alternating chapters that present supporting "evidence" in the form of mixed media news clippings, interviews with John Rechy, and political essays/lectures that explain the author's views about the politics of sexuality.[9] The disjointed, collage-like nature of this text makes Jim's "life" seem emblematic of larger structures rather than being meaningful in itself. *About My Life and the Kept Woman* also follows details from Rechy's life in a chronological fashion, but this life is tethered to two others and a fascination with "camouflage" (*About My Life* 347), blurring any examination of "John Rechy" himself.

Most of the criticism of Rechy's work revolves around its relation to queer and Chicanx traditions. Questions of identity and autobiography have been central to this line of discussion. In this chapter, after establishing Rechy's relation to queer of color selfhood, by way of a dialogue with Gloria Anzaldúa, I turn my attention to the depersonalization of identity in Rechy's work, the ways in which any self is formed in a communal, environmental nexus that defies singular identification (including racial and sexual identification) and defies coherent autobiography. The self whose story Rechy tells is oriented away from itself and toward the "seething world" (*City of Night* 21) that makes it possible. The following section focuses on the queer environments and queer contagions. The third section turns to two works of homage dedicated to John Rechy—the CD-ROM *Mysteries and Desires* and the performance art of Tim Youd—to examine the ways in which audiences are invited to participate in the life and world of John Rechy, and the chapter concludes with an examination of how these qualities align with theories of the posthuman.

Outlaw Sexuality and Queer Depersonalization

> *That* was the spooky part; that's what the Park
> was all about . . . and the numbers. Losing
> control and losing identity.
>
> —John Rechy, *Numbers* 235, original emphasis

Rechy's body of work exceeds any singular framework one might apply to it. His publications span the time period from the early emergence of the Chicano and gay rights movements to the contemporary evolution of broader and more fluid terminologies, like "Chicanx" and queer.[10] In his 1978 essay "Common Bonds and Battles," Rechy rejected the label "gay" because of its history as a pejorative term, and in a 1995 interview with Debra Castillo he rejected "queer" for the same reasons (its association with hatred and violence). Indeed, in speaking with Castillo, Rechy rejects all identity labels as being too restrictive: "Labeled by the sexual persuasion, ethnicity, or the gender of the writer, such literature is guaranteed a restricted audience of like persuasion" ("Interview" 113). While many of us might disagree with this claim about restricted audience, the point about limitation remains. Gloria Anzaldúa makes a similar point about identity in her 1991 essay "To(o) Queer the Writer":

> Identity is not a bunch of little cubbyholes stuffed respectively with intellect, race, sex, class, vocation, gender. Identity flows between, over, aspects of a person. Identity is a river—a process. Contained within the

river is its identity, and it needs to flow, to change to stay a river—if it stopped it would be a contained body of water such as a lake or a pond. The changes in the river are external (changes in environment—river bed, weather, animal life) and internal (within the waters). (Anzaldúa, "To(o) Queer the Writer" 166)

Identity, in this depiction, is contextual but not fixed. Cubbyholes would stifle the river/self, which must remain fluid, taking up elements from its ecosystem and sending parts of itself out into the surrounding elements.

As a gay Chicano and a lesbian Chicana, both Rechy and Anzaldúa were uncomfortable with the available (white) terminology for referring to sexuality. The term that Rechy does embrace in the interview with Castillo is "outlaw": "'Outlaw' suggest defiance, an acceptance of being 'outside the law.' It carries an implication that the law itself may be wrong, therefore to be questioned, overturned" ("Interview" 113). Like rivers, outlaws defy authority and resist confinement. It is noteworthy that "outlaw" is also a choice, an active stance against laws deemed unjust, resembling the wide-ranging travels and the (officially illegal) hustles that define the lives of Rechy's (first- and third-person) characters. In this sense, "outlaw" resonates with early uses of the term "queer" as an act of resistance to false binaries and normative identity categories.

Yet, as Jasbir Puar and others have demonstrated, queerness also came to be a neoliberal, biopolitical, domesticating project, one that works "in collusion with" whiteness:

The paradigm of gay liberation and emancipation has produced all sorts of troubling narratives: about the greater homophobia of immigrant communities and communities of color, about the stricter family values and mores in these communities, about a certain prerequisite migration from home, about coming-out teleologies. We have less understanding of queerness as a biopolitical project, one that parallels but intersects with that of multiculturalism, the ascendancy of whiteness, but may collude with or collapse into liberationist paradigms. (Puar, *Terrorist Assemblages* 22)

Anzaldúa, too, worried about the whitewashing that occurred with the term *queer*: "In the '60s and '70s it meant that one was from a working-class background, that one was not from genteel society," but "these working-class words (. . .) have been taken over by white middle-class lesbian theorists in the academy. Queer is used as a false unifying umbrella. . . . When we seek shelter under it we must not forget that it homogenizes, erases our differences" (Anzaldúa, "To(o) Queer the Writer" 164, 166). The implicitly white supremacist narratives of "gay liberation" resonate with the narrative of Rechy's sexuality (as well as Anzaldúa's, as it is depicted in *Borderlands / La Frontera*): closeted and rendered perverse in his smothering Mexican home and only discovered simultaneous to "liberation" from his family, culture, and homeland. Rechy's resentment at not being considered a real "Chicano writer" (Rechy, "Interview" 113) could stem from this narrative of cultural alienation, from the assumption that he felt he had to choose between Chicano and queer.[11] His bicultural identity (his father was a Scottish immigrant to Mexico, his mother native Mexican) is another aspect of his misalignment with singular racial, cultural, or sexual categories.

In one of her interview questions, Castillo tries to steer Rechy toward queer theory's "possibilities for exposing the contingency of heterosexuality and whiteness as normalizing functions," but he tells her that he doubts he'll ever use the word "queer" in reference to himself ("Interview" 114). For my own argument here, however, I find queer theory to be the best framework for analyzing the variety of queens, hustlers, sadomasochists, and heterogeneous men, women, and trans people who populate Rechy's sexual underworld. Anzaldúa, too, ultimately concludes that "there is still more flexibility in the 'queer' mold, more room to maneuver" (Anzaldúa, "To(o) Queer the Writer" 166). Returning to the end of my quote from Puar above, despite its collusion with neoliberal domesticating projects, "queer" also colludes with liberation.

What makes Rechy and his work "queer" in my analysis is not just about sex and gender, though the young Rechy's obsession with designing clothes for women and his refusal to participate in masculine sports with his brothers would have made him a candidate for this sort of "queering" long before he started having sex with men. One of Eve Kosofsky Sedgwick's broader definitions of queer hinges on "experimental self-perception and filiation" (*Tendencies* 9). Judith/Jack Halberstam similarly links queer life to "subcultural practices, alternative methods of alliance, forms of transgender embodiment, and those forms of representation dedicated to capturing these willfully eccentric modes of being" (*In a Queer Time and Place* 1). Throughout his work, Rechy (and his autobiographical characters) definitely experiment with different modes self-perception and filiation; as an "outlaw," he moves willfully outside of normative routes, and as a hustler, he is deliberate about his adoption of particular presentations of masculinity. Like Anzaldúa's metaphor of the river, this wandering identity is defined by place: in heteronormative El Paso, in proximity to his family, the Rechy character keeps to himself; in Times Square, Pershing Square, Griffith Park, or New Orleans during Mardi Gras, he loses himself and his body in queer masses. This traveling selfhood is consistent with Halberstam's idea of queer geography, in which "the notion of a body-centered identity gives way to a model that locates sexual subjectivities within and between embodiment, place and practice" (*In a Queer Time and Place* 5). One of the qualities that makes the self in Rechy's work queer, in my argument, is its orientation away from the individual human body toward more permeable relations among bodies and environments. Sexual queerness, itself, as becomes evident in the next section of this chapter, leads to "eccentric" or experimental ways of inhabiting space and of making space amenable to queer sexual practices.

My epigraph that opens this section, from Rechy's novel *Numbers*, describes cruising in Griffith Park as being about "losing control and losing identity." In this light, seeking sex with multiple anonymous partners is antithetical to personal coherence. Calling this process "spooky" suggests ghostliness and dis-ease. Right before this passage from *Numbers*, the character Johnny resolves to cease his pursuit of finding (and counting) multiple sexual contacts in the park: "It'll be only with people with identity—men *or* women—not just 'numbers'" (235, original emphasis). Having sex with a number eclipses identity. Despite this resolution, however, Johnny nonetheless continues to collect numbers of anonymous sexual encounters. This is not a singular orientation, as indicated by the fact that it could be with "men *or* women," and anonymity is part of the (guilty?) pleasure. Rechy's autobiographical characters are sustained by these encounters, obsessively losing themselves in the confusion of bodies. In *The Sexual Outlaw*, as well:

> Clustered throughout under the crumbling boards in the water-decayed cavern, other outlaw torsos shine darkly in the mottled light. The sound of sucking, of sliding flesh. Sighs. Sounds of orgasm float through the darkness. Two more outlines have materialized about Jim—he feels more mouths. His mind explodes with outlaw images: men and men and men, forbidden contacts, free, time crushed, intimate forbidden strangers. (*The Sexual Outlaw* 26–27)

In this passage, it is not clear whose flesh is where, who is sighing, or who is orgasming. In this queer confusion, the "forbidden" and the "stranger" become intimate and immanent: a kind of haunting in which the individual gets lost. Jim's mind explodes as if it, too, were experiencing orgasm. The lack of control is both physical and intellectual. The image *is* spooky—"outlines" "materialize" seemingly out of nowhere—but it's the kind of haunting that one might welcome with open arms.

What is the identity that is lost in these encounters? Recalling Puar's critique of the whitewashing of queerness, one might interpret these impersonal encounters as enacting a loss of cultural identity, distancing Johnny from his Mexican family. But reducing sexual partners to anonymous "numbers" also takes away their humanity. In his analysis of *Numbers*, David Johnson describes cruising as an "ahuman" relation: "not people, not human beings: just organs and apertures, holes, openings; community as a certain spacing of the inhuman" (Johnson 464, 461). (This conversion of human to orifice becomes overt in the Mardi Gras section of *City of Night*, when the faces around the youngman begin to blur and "swirl in one enormous, composite, gobbling mouth" [318].) Though Johnson doesn't make much of the distinction between "ahuman" and "inhuman," I think it really matters here. "Inhuman" sounds cruel, an inversion of human values, while ahuman moves outside those values, is perhaps agnostic toward them. Johnson suggests that the ahuman relation is not just queer; it is an economy of masses rather than individuals: "unlike identitarian communities of the same, the community of bodies-in-common does not inscribe violence as the very condition of existence, as an effect of the value of identity" (464). Identity, for Johnson, is problematically tied up with self-possession and thus with the possibility of appropriation (and violence or violation). This view is, in my interpretation, consistent with posthumanism's refusal to abide by the limits of Humanist selfhood and Humanist plotlines. But Johnson's choice of prefixes distances his reading from the temporality and critical genealogy of posthumanism: inhuman and ahuman are both alternatives to human values (whatever we regard those to be) that bear no necessary relation to postmodernism, New Materialism, or other schools of thought associated with posthumanism.

I would argue that the idea of the human, and the Humanist narratives associated with this idea, are too narrow for the queer peoples and worlds of Rechy's work. Individual coherence, domestic accumulation, reproductive inheritance, and the settings conventionally associated with these are not capacious enough to account for the marriages of transgender "queens," the male hustlers who self-identify as heterosexual even while soliciting sex with men, the numbers of anonymous sexual encounters in parks and under bridges, the intense and defining love the "youngman" in *City of Night* has for his dog,[12] or the mixed crowds of evangelicals, drug addicts, and hustlers that gather in Los Angeles's Pershing Square. When faced with what passes as "human" in the conventional world (like racism, physical abuse, and extreme economic inequality, especially as embodied in Rechy's depictions of the violent and dilapidated domestic sphere of his childhood), it is no wonder that Rechy's characters would want to define themselves outside of this framework. I like the term "ahuman" since it reflects an opposition to the human, something more political and immediate than that which gets theorized as posthuman. Ahuman refuses the terms of the human altogether.

This ahuman orientation also resonates with the defiance of laws and identity "cubbies" associated with an undomesticated queerness. Rechy describes the promiscuity of cruising and hustling in the era before AIDS as a "revolutionary" lifestyle, an affirmation of existence and an emphatic embrace of a criminalized sexuality. (One might say that, in the era after AIDS, this gesture is even more revolutionary.[13]) In *The Sexual Outlaw*, he writes:

> The promiscuous homosexual is a sexual revolutionary. Each moment of his outlaw existence he confronts repressive laws, repressive "morality." Parks, alleys, subway tunnels, garages, streets—these are the battlefields.
>
> To the sexhunt he brings a sense of choreography, ritual, and mystery—sex-cruising with an electrified instinct that sends and receives messages of orgy at any moment, any place.
>
> Who are these outlaws?
>
> Single men, married men; youngmen, older ones; black, white; your brothers, your fathers; students, teachers, bodybuilders, doctors, construction workers, coaches, writers, cowboys, truck drivers, motorcyclists, dancers, weight-lifters, actors, painters, athletes, politicians, businessmen, lawyers, cops. (*The Sexual Outlaw* 28)

This passage doesn't tell a story of individuals; it describes a political rite that involves many men in a plural unit. And these men are described as generic types, crushed together in one list whose seriality depersonalizes the experience but also facilitates communal identification.[14] The emphasis on roles, choreography, and mystery suggests artifice rather than core identity. And what is produced in this "orgy" is a community joined by shared rites and shared risks rather than particularity. Though Rechy repeatedly identifies himself and his autobiographical characters as bystanders—"I watched other lives, only through a window" (*City of Night* 18)—and nonjoiners—"I don't really like 'joining' anything" (*The Sexual Outlaw* 178)—the communities he depicts are corporate entities with indistinct boundaries.

Rechy's autobiographical identity, too, is indistinct, especially when considered as the product of the different representations across his publications, as a composite of the "youngman" from *City of Night*, "Jim" from *The Sexual*

Outlaw,[15] and "John Rechy" from *About My Life* (as well as "Johnny Rio" from *Numbers*, Endore from *Rushes*, Jim from *This Day's Death*, and John from *After the Blue Hour*). In both *City of Night* and *About My Life*, the central character is the son of a beloved Mexican mother and an embittered Scottish father with an illustrious past as a musician in Mexico. In *The Sexual Outlaw*, Jim is more generally "a mixture of Anglo and Latin bloods" (23), and Johnny from *Numbers* is half Irish and half Mexican, from Laredo rather than El Paso. In both *City of Night* and *About My Life*, the central character is a loner who suffers through the dust storms of El Paso as a child, studies literature and hikes to the top of Cristo Rey mountain, has a brief stint in the army after college, joins the male hustling scene in New York, and then moves between major U.S. cities on a journey that involves not self-discovery as much as "sex-hunting" with others. In his adult journey (the focus of Rechy's other autobiographical novels), his identity as writer exists in tension with his anonymous cruising, even when his own sexual exploits are the subject of his writing, because hustlers and sex-hunters are supposed to lack the intelligence and the interiority of authors. (Across these works, the characters' writing life is routinely disbelieved or, at best, regarded as a fascinating contradiction. While promiscuous sex defies consistent or particular identity, the author of a published work is expected to be a singular individual.)

Rechy also describes his autobiographical characters' identities as being discontinuous: in the memoir, John is unable to reproduce in El Paso "the person [he] had become in Times Square" (*About My Life* 230), he is surprised and disturbed when "Johnny Rio" is recognized on the streets as John Rechy (287), and "imposters" start claiming the identity of "John Rechy" since the "real" Rechy was trying to live his life anonymously rather than coming forward in his particularity ("by keeping my identity private, I was making it possible for others to claim it") (308). The stability of identity is further undermined in the Mardi Gras celebration that appears toward the end of both *City of Night* and *About My Life*, when masquerade and carnival liberate individuals from their expected selves and identity is reconstituted by a series of masks. At the end of *City of Night*, the youngman's mask begins "to crumble," he tells a stranger on the street that "Im not at all the way you think I am" (*City of Night* 341),[16] and a very specific character named Jeremy, attracted by this vulnerability, pulls Johnny from the swarms of the streets to the seclusion of a hotel room. Yet, after an extensive discussion in which Jeremy and the youngman talk about the potential distinction between appearance and reality and the possibility of long-term romance,

Johnny flees from this self-reflection and returns to the streets, "mythless to face the world of the masked pageant" (369). The possibility of a stable self that would preserve an individual history is invoked and rejected.[17]

Similarly, the final scene in *About My Life* depicts John trying, figuratively, to unmask a woman from his childhood: to reveal that the wealthy San Francisco socialite Isabel Franklin-Schwartz, who has been passing for "Spanish" royalty, is "really" Alicia Gonzales, a poor Mexican girl from El Paso. Yet, in the end, Johnny protects the woman's false identity and tells her husband, when the latter threatens to divorce the wife who "doesn't know who she is," that he had merely confused Mrs. Schwartz with a photograph of another woman (*About My Life* 354). The final paragraphs turn to the figure of the "kept woman" from the memoir's title, a shadowy figure who was idolized by both Johnny and Alicia when they were children, and concludes with a previously forgotten memory of the kept woman claiming her name: "'I am . . . Marisa Guzman. You probably know me as the kept woman of Augusto de Leon. No I am not ashamed of who I am'" (356). These final words are presented as an "implied judgment on Alicia Gonzales—and on me—for all our subterfuges and masquerades"; the implication of this textual construction is that the other characters have not similarly owned their own names or disowned the socially imposed shame associated with their transgressive sexual behavior. The John Rechy character is not as clearly individuated as Marisa Guzman, the kept woman (whose status as being "kept" nonetheless ties her to Augusto de Leon).

This oscillation between self and others characterizes much of Rechy's work, and the loss of self is overtly thematized in *The Sexual Outlaw*, where he emphasizes the link between the "profligate sharing" of "gay liberation" and a lack of "interior awareness" that "reduces" men to "shadows, shadows" and "mouths in alleys and parks" (243, 286). *The Sexual Outlaw* opens with an account of "Jim's" extensive muscle-building workout, described as a "mysterious rite of destruction and construction" in which "the body is rushing fresh blood to pulsing muscles, making them stronger and bigger." The detailed attention to each muscle (pectorals, lats, abdomen), each weight, each repetition performs this destruction and construction for the reader, who witnesses the body literally being formed by pulsing blood and stretching, crunching muscles. (This denaturalization of the body is later augmented when Rechy argues that the sculpted body should be exhibited just like the books or paintings that artists "spend hours, days, months, and years on" and which are "acceptably exhibited, put out for display" [*The*

Sexual Outlaw 67–68].)[18] The muscle-building scene ends with Jim standing before the mirror watching his own "cock strain[ing] against the sweat-bleached cut-offs" (22). This image of self-adoration goes with him to the beach, where he poses naked on the sand imagining "how his body looks to others" (23), but once others arrive to adore him, he loses himself in a jumble: "male and male and male, hard limbs, hard cocks, hard muscles, strong bodies, male and male" (27).

One of the final sections of *The Sexual Outlaw* is titled "Contradictions, Ambivalences, and Considerations"; here, Rechy worries that the "fragile connections" between "one and many" might "cancel identities": "Always the possibility of a soulless reduction of bodies to limbs and orifices—all limbs, any orifice" (287). These are the peripheries of bodies, the extremities and the points of access, the places of contact with others and the world outside, the skins where we meet. Rechy worries that this reduction might lead to a "loveless sacrifice of all human contact. The ultimate in non-feeling and alienation" (287), but aren't limbs and orifices where we reach out to each other, where we most often feel sensation? On a material level, there is no contradiction between the "profligate sharing" of these parts and the vulnerability and "humanity" that Rechy seems to worry about losing. Interiority is accessed through orifices. Selfhood is marked at the boundaries where bodies meet. The human is defined in communion with others.

In his analysis of *The Sexual Outlaw*, David Vázquez argues that "because the novel represents Jim's struggle as a product of the tension between existentialist individualism and a desire for communal affiliation, it can never fully embrace a communal identity" (114).[19] Rechy's protagonists do seem to long for community as an antidote to individual isolation:

> As a child, I was often overwhelmed by a feeling of devastating sorrow for everyone, for everything. At those times, I would stand on the ragged porch of our house on Wyoming Street in El Paso and I would pray into the black sky: "Please help everyone." Years later, after long sex-hunting on the streets, that feeling of isolated horror, infinite sadness, would recur. Black, black depression would pull me down, lower and lower, until I felt that I was drowning in darkness. (*About My Life* 275)

I wouldn't, however, interpret passages like this as "existentialist individualism." Community seems to be the source of selfhood, with individual isolation represented as the source of "black, black depression." One of the reasons Rechy's characters participate in hustling and counting "numbers" is as an evasion of individual existence. Rather than defining an individual self and a particular romance (the Humanist plotline), the sex-hunting character participates in something more like communal existentialism, forming a community and defining his meaning and purpose in relationships with others. It is only in community that "parks, alleys, subway tunnels, garages, streets" become "battlefields," and it is only in community that "choreography, ritual, and mystery" assume any meaning (*The Sexual Outlaw* 28). One can't assign new meaning to places or gestures without others consenting to this same meaning (or this same "consensual reality," to paraphrase Gloria Anzaldúa).[20]

This shift from the idea of an individual self (with its individual repressions, projections, and masks) to a consensual multiplicity resonates with a passage in *A Thousand Plateaus*, in which Gilles Deleuze and Félix Guattari elaborate their critique of the Freudian model of selfhood through an analysis of Freud's infamous "Wolf-Man." Rather than pinning down this interspecies sensibility to a singular entity that abides by the laws of human consciousness, Deleuze and Guattari point to wolves' "generic multiplicity" (27). Unlike the Freudian human—whose symptoms can be explained by his individual trajectory, his individual ego, and his particular repressions— wolves exist not as one but as part of a community (or, less humanistically, a pack) where the practice of precise counting does not apply, where there are "nine, six or seven" wolves.[21] "In becoming-wolf, the important thing is the position of the mass, and above all the position of the subject itself in relation to the pack or wolf-multiplicity; how the subject joins or does not join the pack, how far away it stays, how it does or does not hold to the multiplicity" (29). Yet, as he sought to diagnose the "Wolf-Man" in isolation, Freud kept imposing singular interpretations, such as "animals could serve only to represent coitus between parents," and reduces the composite to a singularity: "when the thing splinters and loses its identity," Freud would find a word to "restore the identity or invent a new one" (28). What I take from Freud's mistake (and Deleuze and Guattari's diagnosis of this mistake) is the idea of "crowd phenomena," teeming bodies that are irreducible to conventional logics and identities (30). This is an important framework for understanding how "outlaws" and "underworlds" work: these oppositional consciousnesses rely on communal consensus about the laws, agreement to a shared choreography or shared way of repurposing space. An individual act of defiance is enough to get the individual in trouble; it's not enough to start a revolution. A multiplicity is more likely to shift some ground.

Queer Environments

It is thus not lack of cleanliness or health that
causes abjection but what disturbs identity,
system, order. What does not respect borders,
positions, rules. The in-between, the ambiguous,
the composite.

—Julia Kristeva, *Powers of Horror* 4

From the dust of El Paso, to the steamy YMCA in Manhattan, to the dilapidated hustler bars of Los Angeles, Rechy focuses on cluttered environments that are filmed with dirt, grease, and smoke. Sticky-floored movie theaters, bathrooms crowded with men having sex, parks where the outcasts loiter: these are the places that house the queer communities whose lives he presents. These are generally dark, and in many ways reproducible across any city in the world, apparent as Rechy's characters move between Paris, Dallas, New Orleans, and Chicago and find the hustler bars, bathhouses, and cruising parks in each.[22] Rechy was often asked by writers and publishers from his professional world to give them a tour of the underground he describes in his novels.[23] The "ultra-chic" writer-agent Wendy Elliot Hyland is one such person who asked to see "the city behind the city" (Casillo 241–42). She told Charles Casillo about Rechy showing her the dark tunnels and alleyways where drug deals were made and hustlers picked up scores: "He showed me back doors in restaurants that led to an entirely different world. . . . It was like picking up a rock and seeing the colony of ants that exists underneath" (Hyland qtd. in Casillo 242). The image of the colony of ants is perfect: they are indistinct and overlooked but, once noticed, discovered to be thriving in their own system of labors and their alternative ways of using the same space that the "mainstream" world moves through.

Importantly, this is not an "entirely different world," as Hyland claims, but an orientation that conflicts with dominant uses of our shared world: a queer public. Samuel Delany's *Times Square Red, Times Square Blue* (1999) focuses on the inclusive forms of relation enabled by this repurposing. He describes the "asystematic" contacts (public sex, loitering, even just talking) that used to occur among gay men in Times Square, in public yet "outside the knowledge of much of the straight world" (Delany 194, 199). Delany argues that these contacts (which often cross race and class lines) are essential to establishing a sense of sociality, cosmopolitanism, and human exchange, as opposed to the supposed safety and isolation of more restricted groups and networks. Just as masking and performance protect an individual self from judgment, these "masked" spaces (back doors and hidden alleys) serve as protection; they are queer spaces that don't attract outside invasion because they are recognizable only to those who choose to see them. In his analysis of *The Sexual Outlaw*, Rafael Pérez-Torres suggests that the "deserted urban terrain [Rechy] claims as his own geography serve[s] to reinscribe the marginalization of the sexual outlaw" (205). I see it a bit differently: rather than being deserted, this terrain is alternatively inhabited, used against the grain. Claiming garages or tunnels, conventionally unused by night, for male-male sex gives these spaces new meanings as a time/place for "outlaws." While Pérez-Torres sees Rechy's term "gay world" as ultimately ironic, with the "gay" spaces defined (restrictively) by constitutive opposition to heterosexuality, I think there really is a queer kind of worlding. The repurposed places where broken boards become shields and dirt and fallen leaves become beds reconfigure the relationship between bodies and things defined by the dominant culture. In these places where dirt is cleansing (Jim washes his hands in it in *Sexual Outlaw* [75]), the conventional standards of pollution, the conventional ranking of in versus out, is disavowed. Unlike the Hollywood portrayed in the movies, the alleys and garages and tunnels near Hollywood Boulevard are a double city, occupied in the dark by a community of outlaws that is shaped and sustained by its alternative occupation of a shared ecosystem. The title of Rechy's first novel makes it clear that the night enables and defines this community.

As conceived most famously by anthropologist Mary Douglas, dirt is matter "out of place." According to Douglas, dirt is a fundamental part of the formation and maintenance of cultures: a "byproduct of the creation of order," the "rejected bits and pieces," whose role is "to threaten the distinctions made" by any system (Douglas 161–62). Things are marked as dirt when they are perceived as "a threat to good order, and so are regarded as objectionable and vigorously brushed away" (161). Dirt is thus "a relative idea" (36), but it's one we need in order to maintain classification systems. The dirt I remove from my vacuum cleaner includes hair, food crumbs, and soil blown in through the doors and windows. What makes these things "dirt" to vacuum up is not their matter but their mislocation (on the floor instead of on my head, plate, or garden). They threaten the order we establish when determining how to make a house, and their elimination is the stuff of housekeeping.[24] Things become dirt, and bodies become outlaws, through processes of abjection. Since dirt is a taboo configuration of the matter of normative bodies and things, it is by definition a threat to the norm. It has emotional and political heft. In the context of mainstream health and domestic sciences, which focus on the means of its elimination, dirt is contrary, perverse, and unreasonable. But from the queer perspective of John Rechy's worlds, dirt shows us how to undermine the foundations of stigma and to create more fluid selves. Dirt protects the queer underworlds in Rechy's corpus, signaling a way of belonging outside of dominant conventions.

In *Powers of Horror*, Julia Kristeva extends Douglas's anthropological argument to the level of the symbolic structures that shape human existence. "Defilement," for Kristeva, "is what is jettisoned from the 'symbolic system.' It is what escapes that social rationality, that logical order on which a social aggregate is based" (65, original emphasis). Read in this light, Rechy's embrace of abjection reconfigures what we think of as the "logical order" of sociality. In the same way that the hustler's manner of interfacing with large numbers of anonymous lovers could be seen as ahuman, the sociality of Rechy's underworld is arational, operating outside of received logic.

> There looms, within abjection, one of those violent, dark revolts of being, directed against a threat that seems to emanate from an exorbitant outside or inside, ejected beyond the scope of the possible, the tolerable, the thinkable. It lies there, quite close, but it cannot be assimilated. It beseeches, worries, and fascinates desire, which, nevertheless, does not let itself be seduced. . . . Unflaggingly, like an inescapable boomerang, a vortex of summons and repulsion places the one haunted by it literally beside himself. (Kristeva 1)

The revolution happens at the level of ontology ("dark revolts of being") and epistemology ("beyond the scope of the possible, the tolerable, the thinkable"). These spaces are so queer that they cannot be reabsorbed by society; they resist that sort of order. And those who abide within the abject ("haunted," "literally beside himself") will likewise never be conventionally human.

In *City of Night*, during Mardi Gras, throngs of "young faces . . . dot white-winter highways" and head in the direction of "Away, New Orleans" (*City of Night* 283): "Like flotsam from the world's seas, the vagrants of America's blackcities are washed into New Orleans" (309). These descriptions make New Orleans an elsewhere, a receptacle whose status as "Away" puts it off the map. The fluidity that "washes" the rejected bits of other cities into New Orleans is perversely cleansing: that is, it cleanses according to an unclean logic. In a bar called "The Rocking Times," a queen sitting by the door criticizes newcomers for letting air into the "wombgrayness" of the bar and "purifies" the air with puffs of gray smoke from a cigarette (326). The youngman finds a place to stay, predictably, at the YMCA, where "hot-water steam mushroomed about [him], protecting" (319). The showers of the YMCA—from the first place the youngman stays in New York, where the constant sound of showers masks the sounds of sex, to the eerie image of the shower as a protecting mushroom of steam in New Orleans—similarly create an anti-abjection: they absorb, dull, and blur rather than sort and purify. (Rechy's depiction of the YMCA as an underground haven for gay male sex was taken up by the Village People's famous 1978 song by that name.)

The haziness of queer spaces blurs not just sexual activities but also human identity itself. Among the crowds in the "public head in Cindy's bar," with "scribble-blackened wall[s]," "malebodies were clamped to each other, kissing, sexhuddling. Standing at the crowded urinal next to me, a man reaches for me mutely, automatically: the unconcerned, mechanical gesture of someone picking up something from the sidewalk. *I could be anyone!*" (336, original emphasis). Not only does the youngman become anonymous here, but sex itself becomes indistinct, as unremarkable as picking up trash from the sidewalk. The anonymity of the sexual underground is magnified during Carnival, when everyone is masked, out of place, and only marginally human: werewolves, Medusas, bats, vampires, clowns, and "a creature draped in weeping seaweed, dead seahorses glued to the legs" (336–37). After days in New Orleans, the youngman begins to feel "sad for the whole rotten spectacle of the world wearing cold, cold masks," yet he does ultimately return to this rotten spectacle on the "grinding streets" after rejecting the possibility of sincere, monogamous love (the logic of the Humanist narrative) (341, 368). Rather than leaving New Orleans with Jeremy (the first lover with whom youngman shares his name, though we ourselves don't see that name),[25] he returns to the grinding public that dulls specificity. Later, at an all-night "moviehouse," with "excessively hot" air and "derelicts" sleeping on the floor, the youngman falls asleep and then wakens to three cockroaches crawling on his arm and "a man squatting before me on the floor, his hungry hot hands on my thighs, his moist lips glued to the opening of my pants" (377–78). The movie theater, where no one seems to be watching the movie, is repurposed as a safe space for sleeping and oral sex. The fact that this theater is home to both derelicts and cockroaches cements its association with the refuse of the dominant culture, refuse that crosses species boundaries.

I would argue that Rechy's characters' relation to refuse is not pathetic: it is a reconfiguration of the trajectories of abjection.[26] It is an outlaw spatial orientation, a chosen rerouting of the structures that support possession and cultural convention. The ways in which outlaws inhabit space are more radical than the occupation of a park or a building during a legally sanc-tioned public protest since they operate tangentially to both the law and the official place designations. In his analysis of art critic Douglas Crimp, José Esteban Muñoz argues for the "transformative potential of queer sex and public manifestations of such sexuality" as a "respite from the abjection of homosexuality and a reformatting of that very abjection"; reclaiming "spaces and acts" that have been rendered abject within heteronormativity pushes us toward a queer futurity (Muñoz 34). This interpretation applies to Rechy, as well. Claiming spaces with exuberant public sex between men does not simply offer a remapping against heteronormative designations: it is an act of world-making.

Yet, as surely as the sex these men are having will be revealed by the advent of AIDS to be potentially deadly, this way of inhabiting space is not always safe. As Frederick Luis Aldama says of *The Sexual Outlaw*, in spite of the "utopic" and transgressive impulses of the sex-hunters' move-ments through Los Angeles, they are "forced to move in the shadows of a city that is itself in decay," "a city that constantly threatens to swallow [them] with its natural disasters that lead to impenetrable orange skies and mudslides" (Aldama 63). The threat of violence and intrusion from outside queer communities (including police arrests and homophobic attacks in addition to the natural disasters Aldama invokes) is mirrored by the threat of violence inside (such as the sadomasochistic practices Rechy criticizes, especially in *The Sexual Outlaw*). AIDS emerged in the 1980s to resignify the source and matter of these threats.

Audience Participation and Communal Memoirs

> I've been flashed. I've been mooned.
>
> —Tim Youd speaking about his performance
> retyping John Rechy's work (Miranda, "I've
> Been Flashed" n.p.)

As Linda Singer described it in her final book, *Erotic Welfare* (1993), the culture of fear that followed the advent of the AIDS epidemic was governed by a "logic of contagion": "Communication has become communicability; access is now figured as an occasion for transmission and contagion" (28). The panic surrounding epidemics drives humans to seal off their bodies from other humans as well as from potential nonhuman transmitters (mosquitoes, bacteria, etc.), but the outlaw logic of Rechy's queer underworlds defies these self-defensive measures. Joining the outlaw community is a stance against the policing of boundaries (homophobic, xenophobic, germophobic). Promiscuity generates community and defies the proprietary boundaries that govern sanctioned heterosexual couplings (couplings that potentially lead to reproduction and the inheritance of properties). Deleuze and Guattari link contagion to the operations of packs and herds: "We oppose epidemic to filiation, contagion to heredity, peopling by contagion to sexual reproduction, production. Bands, human or animal, proliferate by contagion, epidemics, battlefields, and catastrophes" (Deleuze and Guattari 241). While it is certainly risky to play around with epidemics and catastrophes as generative events, it is true that they create community, unlike the individuation of family. These communities are made of lateral relations rather than heredity and open-ended multiplicity rather than family units: "contagion, epidemic, involve terms that are entirely heterogeneous: for example, a human being, an animal, and a bacterium. . . . These combinations are neither genetic nor structural; they are interkingdoms, unnatural participations" (Deleuze and Guattari 242). Again, Deleuze and Guattari might be too glib in their embrace of the "unnatural" couplings of contagion, but it is precisely this kind of inversion of heteronormative order that Rechy invokes, the propagating "interkingdoms" that defy the cultural logic of purification that Douglas writes about.

Embracing promiscuous sex is even more revolutionary after AIDS than it was when Rechy wrote about promiscuity as a political gesture in *City of Night* or *The Sexual Outlaw*. Tim Dean's *Unlimited Intimacy* (2009) highlights the radical resignification of sex and illness under AIDS. Dean is perhaps best known for analyzing the affirmative ethics of "barebacking" (anal sex without a condom); his larger argument about contagion among gay communities is most relevant here: "The AIDS epidemic has given gay men new opportunities for kinship, because sharing viruses has come to be understood as a mechanism of alliance, a way of forming consanguinity with strangers and friends. Through HIV, gay men have discovered that they can 'breed' without women" (Dean 6). The intimacy, consanguinity, and lifelong commitment of sharing of sero-status (positive or negative) undermine the fear of contagion. Rather than associating gay sex with death, barebackers reconfigure the potential transmission of unprotected sex as generative, life-giving. This counterintuitive association is, according to Dean, related to a larger critique of state-mandated health policies. To the extent that conventional medicine institutes universalizing norms of health and views gay sex through primarily proscriptive lenses, "outlaws" may engage in barebacking in an effort to resist "health" as an instrument of "normalizing" power (Dean 66). In this light, sickness (HIV infection, in particular) is an act of defiance and builds solidarity among outlaws.

Readers and fans have sought entry into Rechy's underworlds, choosing community and pleasure rather than fear. This is consistent with Dean's argument about breaking down barriers and forming new networks of intimacy. Rechy's depictions of cruising and anonymous sex have earned him a certain cult status, and new outlets for Rechyan outlaw expression have emerged, including some possibilities for communal memoir. *Mysteries and Desires: Searching the Worlds of John Rechy*, the 2003 interactive CD-ROM created by the Labyrinth Project, enables readers to participate in the "mysteries and desires" of Rechy's underground worlds using what was (in 2003) a new digital platform. There are three different "realms" in this so-called "interactive memoir": "Memories," "Cruising," and "Bodies."

"Memories" is a virtual archive; when viewers enter, they are presented with one of three quotations about memory and character by Søren Kierkegaard, Sigmund Freud, or Marcel Proust. Following this entry is a collage-like array of images (photographs of the author and his family, pictures of his books and awards) through which viewers navigate using their computer mouse; clicking on certain items enables one to listen to audio recordings of interviews or to read media clippings that immerse one in the life of John Rechy. In this process, viewers are selecting the materials that go into their experience of the memoir, constructing a narrative by making choices about what to click on, or what not to, and in what order. Actual photographs from Rechy's past are sometimes pasted onto cartoon-like backdrops, blurring the real, hyperreal, and surreal.

In "Cruising," after hearing the command that one must get one's body "ready for the hunt" (extracted from the opening of *The Sexual Outlaw*), viewers become participants in the "sex-hunt" as they navigate through a virtual Griffith Park, listening to the birds and crickets in the background, and choose which men to click on. In this realm, Rechy reads aloud from his work with music aurally superimposed, making it like a participatory, multisensory version of his books. If you move to a certain alcove in the park, one man, posed with his leather jacket off his shoulder and his hand on his crotch, is approached by another, and they engage in a choreographed sex-dance that takes them from the park to a bar. Viewers even have some agency over the choreography they witness by making different selections on a virtual record player to the side of the screen. (The record player was already a relic of old technology in 2003, making this process an overt reference to archives from the past and distant technologies.)

The "Bodies" realm is designed like a game. The "home" image is of Rechy posed in front of a two-dimensional photograph of a church with a car waiting in the street to take viewers to the "Cruising" realm. In the background, one hears Rechy read the phrase "I become that panting breathing," invoking bodies in a sensory way. In order to experience the "Salvation," "Confession," or "Passion" that the CD's "map" promises for this realm, viewers must figure out how to enter the church and then determine which images from a stained-glass panel are links to other rooms. Some lead viewers into images of the bodies of saints. One leads to a confessional, where the priest asks for details of the unseen penitent's sexual exploits. Alternatively, one might find oneself listening to a lecture on "persona" and viewing a list of different character exercises that Rechy uses in his creative writing classes. One image leads to a history of bodybuilding that consists of cartoons, physique drawings, and an interactive "pump iron" icon. Back on the street, if one discovers the possibility of scrolling to the right of the church, there is a hidden entrance to Selma Avenue, one of Los Angeles's hustling alleys that appear throughout Rechy's work.

As their eyes track the scenes across their computer screens and their hands manipulate their trajectory through these realms, viewers are sutured into the process of composing a story. It is possible, with a computer mouse, to (virtually) "pump iron" or get picked up by a "score" and become like a Rechy character. In this way, viewers can play at being Rechy the author and play at being his autobiographical characters at the same time, experiencing the queer blurring that characterizes so much of Rechy's work. The idea of creating an "interactive memoir" in the first place is fascinating, defying the conventions of authority associated with memoir and rendering the process both communal and variable. The life is different with each viewer and each entry into the realms of Rechy's past. It is not the property of the author.

More recently, performance artist Tim Youd has taken on the persona of John Rechy, the author, by publicly rewriting Rechy's books on an Underwood Model S typewriter that is a near duplicate of the one upon which Rechy wrote *City of Night*.[27] Youd began typing *City of Night* in 2016 at LACE gallery on Hollywood Boulevard (where he used a microphone to amplify the sound of the typewriter and to inject it into the regular noise of the boulevard); in July 2016, he moved his performance to the entrance of Griffith Park to type *Numbers*. In both performances, Youd welcomed audiences to enter the exact locations Rechy and his characters/communities repurposed as queer underworlds, and, while playing at being Rechy characters, audiences were also watching a simulation of the literary documentation of this world (Youd typing the novels). The performances thus offered an experience of both the content and the production of Rechy's work. Youd claims that he's been flashed and "mooned" by passersby during his performance: "While it can have a carnivalesque atmosphere, there has also been a good deal of real engagement in terms of people stopping to try to understand what I'm doing" (Miranda, "I've Been Flashed," n.p.). Youd likely chose the term "carnivalesque" with *City of Night* in mind, implying that the performance of Rechyan writing involves the same kind of disorienting masking and estrangement that one finds in a community of Mardi Gras revelers.

The idea that another could write the novels of John Rechy undermines the uniqueness of authorship. This performance, however, doesn't exactly suggest that Rechy's work is reproducible; nor does it entirely depersonalize Rechy. Youd communicates a real reverence for the original author: he sought out Rechy's "blessing" before beginning the performance and even made a pilgrimage to Rechy's own typewriter (which is wrapped up for safekeeping). Youd describes his performance as "devotional," compares it to meditation, and claims to experience a form of "out of body" ecstasy at times (Miranda, "Artist Tim Youd Retypes" n.p.). Youd's process of typing Rechy's novels is thus supplementary to Rechy's own history of writing those novels. In fact, Youd types the entirety of "his" novels onto one page (actually, two pages layered together), typing letters on top of letters in thick layers of unreadable ink; this process ultimately punctures and tears the paper, converting the paper, itself, into a material artifact (as opposed to a transparent medium for immaterial ideas). Youd later frames the papers as devotional diptychs, records of his own labor rather than replicas of the original novels.

While typing, Youd also notices aspects of Rechy's writing style that "probably would have gotten beaten out of him if he had gone to writing school. . . . Like not using punctuation, using a lot of ellipses, changing the tone of the narrator, flashing forward and backward within a paragraph, changing tense within a paragraph" (Miranda, "I've Been Flashed" n.p.). From being in the experience of writing these kinds of sentences—with tension between time periods and unfamiliar markers of organization—Youd claims to have been able to "understand this state of anxiety and doubt" that Rechy's narrator is engaged in (Miranda, "I've Been Flashed" n.p.). He says that Rechy dropped by the Hollywood Boulevard gallery space to watch him type at one point and writes of the experience of watching Rechy watch him type Rechy's words. This kind of mirroring recalls my discussion of narcissism at the beginning of this chapter. Rechy watching Youd act like Rechy shows the author an image of himself as imagined by another. This retyping process also creates a unique form of intimacy between the men, not in terms of orifices but in terms of entering into the mind of another, reproducing the hand movements of another, tethering one's artistic practice to another's. Youd enters into the creative moment of writing John Rechy's work neither as an independent creator nor as a re-creator but as a devotee, an echo, an excess. The fact that passersby are incorporated into the performance makes them a part of a Rechyan community at the same time that these passersby create community for the artist.

This performance seems emphatically "safe" when compared to the content of Rechy's books and the intimacy that Rechy seeks through cruising. After all, the matter exchanged is writing, not semen. But I would argue that what Youd does to writing is a very Rechyan move: his redundant efforts and displayed performativity highlight the embodiment of writing and the physical labor of the writer (something Rechy gestures at in his descriptions of the processes of collating and editing *City of Night* and writing *Numbers* on the console of his 1965 Mustang while driving across the Arizona desert). And Youd's choice to put all of the ink onto one double-sheet of paper emphasizes the materiality of the book, giving the book a kind of body with thickness, accumulated layers, and scars. (This materiality is also emphasized in the physical thickness of Rechy's own lengthy books.) Youd renders the process of authoring promiscuous, with too many men involved in the writing, and he gives the book a kind of excessive corporeality. The fact that viewers are welcomed into the production process makes the writing even more promiscuous: it's a public event involving anonymous masses. And the fact that the typed-upon papers are, upon completion, framed as a diptych elevates them as sacred icons—artifactual records of a historical embodied practice. Genuflecting before them involves more of the body than reading typically does.

As of this writing, Rechy is still alive (at eighty-eight years old), and fans and devotees come together in multiplicity to continue the propagation of this life, which has, by far, exceeded the boundaries of one individual body. His most recent publication, *After the Blue Hour*, presents another ode to the idea of commingling lives. This text is based on an event from

Rechy's own life in which a fan invited the author to spend a summer with him on a private island.[28] In the novel, the primary activity consists of Paul, John Rechy's narcissistic host, narrating his own life story—episodically, repetitiously, lavishly—with a particular focus on his unconventional sexual experiences. When John asks Paul "'Why have you been telling me all this?'" the answer is "'So that you will tell me as much about your own life'" (Rechy, *After the Blue Hour* 60). And John Rechy proceeds: "I was born in El Paso Texas. . . . My mother was Mexican; my father was Scottish" (60), as he has written in so many of his other publications. But Paul, a listener who wants to control the narrative, is impatient and asks for more details about John's sexual experiences. Probably many readers are able to identify with Paul's desires at this point. Paul, again echoing the imagined desires of many Rechy readers, also asks John to explain the logic of his writing style: his shifting verb tenses, his irregular use of capitalization, his belief that autobiography is a lie (25–26, 86–87). Ultimately, John realizes that Paul wants to blend life stories with him, wanting John to write Paul's life alongside his own, "believing that through kindred knowledge, as he saw it, I would set down the facts of his sordid life, connected to my own, juxtaposed—'two of a kind'" (138). Paul seeks community. Ultimately, in what might be Rechy's final publication, life stories overlap even more completely than they did in *About My Life and the Kept Woman*. John and Paul, lying side-by-side in swimming trunks, "two of a kind," "kindred," "connected," and "juxtaposed," create at the level of narrative the kind of entanglement that ultimately occurs when John finally joins Paul and his lover in a particularly violent sexual act. Bodies blend just as their narrated lives do, and John Rechy's final words are direct quotes from Paul: "Island . . . island" (212). This novel presents blending lives as both risky and inevitable, somewhat terrifying but also desirable.

Other-Orientation

> What seems salutary about cruising is how it can involve intimate contact with strangers without necessarily domesticating the other's otherness.
>
> —Tim Dean, *Unlimited Intimacy* 180

Tim Dean argues that the cultures of cruising and anonymous sex enact an affirmative ethics that "involves not just hunting for sex but opening oneself to the world" (Dean 210). This "unlimited intimacy" with a stranger "entails a discipline of challenging to the point of dissolution an individual's boundaries, in order to achieve boundlessness" (46). Dean continues,

> In such a practice, contact or intimacy is desired not only with other persons but also with something more impersonal: The impersonality of anonymous group sex facilitates access to an impersonal intimacy that barebackers often characterize as sacred, rather than profane. In light of this understanding, I would suggest that impersonal intimacy disentangles intimacy from personhood. (46)

Rather than regarding as negatively dehumanizing practices like having sex through "glory holes" (where all that is seen of a potential partner is his penis), Dean interprets this anonymity as a refusal to "domesticate" the stranger, embracing uncertainty and vulnerability. In this light, we have much to learn from queer sexual subcultures: making ourselves open to others, welcoming strangers as strangers rather than insisting that they form themselves into the image of the same. Rechy challenges Humanist conventions by involving such "undomesticated" others with his individual story, "disentangl[ing] intimacy from personhood." In his work, individuals are replaced by revolutionary actants sustaining an ecosystem that counters the ontologies and epistemologies of "mainstream" society.[29] The ways of relating among these characters are oriented around transgressions of boundaries, including the limits of the human body, incorporating others within other-than-human environments.

About My Life opens with a scene in which the narrator worries about being engulfed in a giant tumbleweed: in the blowing dust of El Paso, he sees a tumbleweed approaching him, growing larger as it "raged along the blocks collecting splinters loosed from other dry weeds." He tries to dodge it, but it crashes against him:

> Trying to break away from it, I flailed at it, but it pushed against me, finally capturing me within its cage of dried twigs, shredding my skin bloody. Trapped inside the tangle of dead weeds, I pushed and pushed, until I had disemboweled it. In nests of seared weeds, it spun away, tumbling across the horizon, gathering its shed parts, racing across the city, and, finally, back into the hellish desert. (Rechy, *About My Life* 39)

In the ecosystem of El Paso, dust overcomes everyone and everything, coats surfaces inside and out, swamps all barriers, despite the narrator's attempt to assert himself as an exceptional individual (a star student, a writer, an artist). Rechy interprets this encounter with the tumbleweed as emblematic of his fears of being trapped in all that El Paso represented to him as a child, especially the poverty of his family and the surrounding Mexican American community and the patriarchal violence that made his home an unsafe place. The tumbleweed in this passage is an ambivalent, inchoate form of home or community, a "nest" of dead weeds. Though Rechy disembowels it, it later "gather[s] its shed parts." The fact that so many of the photographs of himself that Rechy publishes in his books depict the author with his family or in the deserts of El Paso suggests that his identity remains embedded in this tumbleweed.

Many of the settings of Rechy's publications coincide with the "greater Mexico" within the United States, and Rechy's characters' outlaw occupation of Texas and California resonates with Chicanx reclamations of the homeland, Aztlán.[30] Yet Rechy's work is often excluded from the Chicanx literary canon because it is insufficiently oriented around the racial, cultural, and nationalist concerns at the heart of other Chicano novels of the 1960s and '70s. Rechy's emphasis on sex might seem to be individualistic or agnostic about culture and nationality, but, as we have seen, Rechy's writing is insistently communal, environmental, countercultural, and political in its orientation. His queer world-making reappropriates the lands that were Aztlán along with those that were French (like New Orleans) or Dutch (like New York). This noncontiguous region layers queer occupation on top of the layers of U.S. colonialism: an outlaw orientation that puts Rechy at the forefront of queering identity-based canons and could also put his work at the forefront of posthumanist ethics.

In *Giving an Account of Oneself*, Judith Butler argues that "there is no 'I' that can fully stand apart from the social conditions of its emergence," which means that there is no "purely personal" self and that "the very terms by which we give an account, by which we make ourselves intelligible to ourselves and others . . . are social in character" (7, 21). This account resonates with Rechy's work. The ways in which he "giv[es] an account" show acute awareness of the community wrought up with himself and the ethics of narration. A life story is not the sole property of an individual but a tumbleweed sent out into space to gather unknown others. I believe Rechy is careful not to "domesticate" the others in his shared story but, rather, continually reminds us of the haunting, the alienation, and the impersonal sociality that shape his queer ecosystem.

Webs

Aurora Levins Morales's Animal, Vegetable, and Digital Ecologies

> Lightning blazing behind it, a wolf appears in the doorway. . . . This is my true self. . . . [I]t changes shapes, becomes buffalo, becomes anteater, always flickering back to its true shape of wolf. . . . I try to tell them, "My totem is the wolf," but they don't know what a wolf is. . . . They think I mean a dog. I say, "But you can't imagine the utter wildness and beauty of a wolf." They don't understand me and I know it is urgently, desperately important. For their survival and mine and the world's.
>
> —Aurora Levins Morales, *Getting Home Alive* 16

Aurora Levins Morales's relationship to both identity and genre has been radical from the start: oriented toward political activism and dismantling Eurocentric conventions. This passage from a brief prose piece titled "Wolf" opens the 1986 mixed-genre collection *Getting Home Alive* (1986), which she coauthored with her mother, Rosario Morales. *Getting Home Alive* is a collective memoir, commingling the life stories of its authors and their foremothers. It follows in the tradition of other feminist of color self-narratives of the 1970s and '80s (like Maxine Hong Kingston's *The Woman Warrior*, Audre Lorde's *Zami*, and Cherríe Moraga's *Loving in the War Years*), enacting the beliefs that the personal is political and that the underrepresented life stories of women of color need to be told. But *Getting Home Alive* is unique, not just because it is dual-authored but because of the "wildness" of its content. Why does Levins Morales begin a collection that is ostensibly about human cultures and generations in the body of a shape-changing wolf?[1] What is most significant for me here is that the other people in "Wolf" are unable to see the wildness of the animal. They understand dogs, animals domesticated within human terms, but this wolf that is also anteater, buffalo, and woman is beyond their language and their comprehension. The story *Getting Home Alive* sets out to tell, for the sake of the world's survival, is bigger than the women of color who author it; its wide ecology teaches us how to see the animals, plants, and even the rain with which we make the world.

When publications by and about Latinas and U.S. women of color feminists surged in the 1980s and '90s, Aurora Levins Morales was a central figure, known for her contribution to Cherríe Moraga and Gloria Anzaldúa's ground-breaking collection, *This Bridge Called My Back: Writings by Radical Women of Color* (1981), as well as *Getting Home Alive*. These works share three qualities that are central for my argument in *Shared Selves*: they present individual authority as part of a collective effort, they take personal experience as a foundation for broader political reflection, and they move between and beyond genres in order to approach their subjects from unconventional angles. Many of the authors associated with *Bridge* have fallen out of the spotlight and moved on to other kinds of work, and this is also somewhat true of Levins Morales. Though she has remained a writer and an activist, the onset of chronic illness and the revelation of past sexual trauma oriented her writing in a different direction, focused on creating therapeutic histories, healing communities, and Internet connections. Thus far, scholars have not had much to say about her newer work, work I find to be both revolutionary and timely.

Her poetry and prose, from the 1980s to her newest digital incarnations, hover around the idea of memoir. Like John Rechy, Levins Morales circles back again and again to many of the same personal and collective histories not redundantly but productively, unfolding the self and her contexts from multiple angles and mobilizing these stories for a variety of ethical projects. *Getting Home Alive* tells about the author's girlhood in Puerto Rico, her coming to feminism in the United States, the influence of her indigenous and Jewish ancestries, her identification with the ecology of Puerto Rico, and broader structures of deterritorialization, colonial violence, and sexual trauma that underlie all of these. Most of the published criticism about Levins Morales, including my own earliest scholarship, reflects on the interweaving of cultures, voices, and genres in *Getting Home Alive*.[2] There

75

is also a coauthored "sequel," *Cosecha and Other Stories* (2014), which was published shortly after Rosario Morales's death, based on a collection of writings they had been gathering.

Levins Morales's singly authored works return to many of the same stories and places but with a distinct critical angle and a sharper ethical imperative. *Remedios* (1998), *Medicine Stories* (1998), and *Kindling* (2013) offer what she describes as "medicinal history" (*Medicine Stories* 5): healing self and community by reimagining the oppressive stories in which we are embedded. These works reflect on not just the author's personal *mestizaje* but also on the wider outcomes of global commerce and imperialism, from the first populations in Africa through the European conquest of the Americas. For *Remedios*, Levins Morales conducted extensive historical and botanical research, contextualizing her story within a larger ecology of violence and adaptive response. In this broad history, the perseverance of humans, animals, and plants offers lessons for survival in conditions of abuse. Critics have seemed more hesitant to embrace the imaginative, interdisciplinary reach of Levins Morales's historical work than her earlier personal narratives.[3]

Kindling focuses more tightly on the author's own health and analyzes more deeply how stories can function as therapy. For instance, when doctors and insurers refused to recognize her illnesses (epilepsy and multiple chemical sensitivity, in particular), Levins Morales turned to Re-Evaluation Counseling, a group therapy based on the performance of personal stories and collaborative efforts to imagine alternative endings with healing narrative pathways: "new stories that open up different possibilities of self" (*Kindling* 42). Her website extends these healing processes to networks real and virtual, sharing stories, selling books, and offering her services as speaker or writing coach in trade for massage, air filters, or nontoxic flooring. Monthly payments can earn sponsors certificates of contribution to the author's works. As the website proclaims, "It takes a village to keep the blogs coming" (www.auroralevinsmorales.com).

A somber indictment of the status quo emerges in these stories about toxic environments, transcorporeal suffering, and the shallow minds and shallow pockets of U.S. medical insurers, all of which drove Levins Morales to plead for donations online. This outright solicitation makes many readers uncomfortable, but, I argue, it takes Levins Morales's newest work beyond the critique of past violence toward a creative process for future transformation. Communal authorship, narrative therapy, and digital exchange expand the boundaries of literary genres for twenty-first-century cultural expression. These emerging genres also offer new kinds of relationship. Levins Morales's website deploys stories as material objects with the power to heal, either through the broad dissemination of their therapeutic content or as commercial objects exchanged for products that sustain the author's life and health. These stories disrupt conventional economies and circulate between and among bodies, challenging conventional understandings of the human self.

Ecocriticism is central to understanding the ways in which bodies are intertwined with trans-species ecologies in Levins Morales's work. I turn to ecocritics Stacy Alaimo and Mel Chen in the final section of this chapter to unravel the other-than-Humanist dynamics of Levins Morales's environmental illness. But there is an epistemological disconnect between Levins Morales's environmental writing and the discourse of academic ecocriticism, which still tends to revolve around the ideas and concerns of the dominant culture. Priscilla Solis Ybarra's original book, *Writing the Goodlife: Mexican American Literature and the Environment* (2016), has helped me to think about this disconnect. According to Ybarra, most Mexican Americans and Chicanxs "never became environmentalists" because they were never separated from nature; their culturally particular way of valuing nature was based not on human domination and exploitation but on connection (what she calls "the goodlife"):

> While the American project of environmentalism denotes an explicit quest to find alternatives to exploitative approaches to nature, goodlife writing shows how the Mexican American and Chicana/o culture enacts values and practices that include nature all along. Goodlife values can be found in Mexican American writings published as early as the late nineteenth century, at the same time that these writings maintain a connection to pre-Columbian practices and epistemologies. (Ybarra 7)

This alternative genealogy is consistent with Levins Morales's orientation to Puerto Rican and Taíno culture and practices. Ybarra explicitly opposes the hybridized indigenous/Mexican relation to the land to "the Enlightenment/modern concept of human intellect and transcendence" (14), and the same could be said for Levins Morales's hybridized indigenous/Puerto Rican relation. Ybarra even wonders if the term "environment" applies to the ways in which the subjects she analyzes perceive the natural world around them (25). This fundamental difference derives from a worldview outside of Humanist anthropocentrism as well as from the experience of being dispossessed by settler colonialism.

[T]he culturally marginalized never wholly bought into the modern world-view that centers on nature/culture dichotomies. As such, they do not embrace environmentalism as moderns and even postmoderns understand it, given that the postmodern is positioned dialectically in relation to the modern. . . . As a result, they did not have to develop an environmental critique to solve the nature/culture divide: their approach is at once nonmodern and decolonial, but it still offers environmentalism an alternative set of traditions and insights with which to approach today's challenges. (Ybarra 16)

It was the dominant culture, after all, that created the Anthropocene and its attendant ecological destruction; perhaps the answers to this problem should come from outside of anthropocentric epistemology.

In this chapter I begin with Levins Morales's coauthored works and an analysis of the communal and trans-species subjectivities that emerge there. Then, I move on to her work as a radical historian who gathers global histories not in the name of empiricism but for the sake of their healing powers.[4] Levins Morales's histories do not just decenter the most documented figures; they also move beyond the centrality of humans in conventional accounts of history. Weaving the stories of plants and animals into her historical practice emerges from a premodern sense of the interconnectedness within nature and, I argue, is further allied with contemporary posthuman networks. The final section considers what life and memoir look like in these (prehuman and posthuman) webs, ultimately turning to Levins Morales's website as a model for other-than-Humanist ethics. The chapter's trajectory thus moves from human collectivities toward wider networks, opening beyond the author and her life and into the global ecology of which we are all a part.

Coauthorship and Collective Subjectivity

> For this kind of broth, there can't be too
> many cooks.
>
> —Aurora Levins Morales, *Cosecha* 10

Like a verbal incarnation of the patchwork quilt pictured on its cover, *Getting Home Alive* consists of dozens of essays, stories, and poems that alternate between the voices of mother and daughter; the only cue to indicate who authors each piece as one moves through the book is a difference in font (as indicated by an "Editor's Note" in the table of contents). One of the most frustrating and rewarding aspects of this textual feature is that the two fonts are nearly indistinguishable. The first time I read it, I obsessively flipped back and forth to the contents page to determine who was who until I reached the conclusion that such a labor was, perhaps, both futile and unnecessary. This text performs the deliberate labor required to separate one self from another, what Inmaculada Lara-Bonilla describes, in her sophisticated analysis of *Getting Home Alive*, as "an effect of constant interchangeability and mutation, of dynamism and spatial/subjectual simultaneity" (Lara-Bonilla 360). If we try to draw clear lines between its authors, we are reading against the grain of the book's ontology and epistemology.

Following the table of contents, the Introduction/Acknowledgments to *Getting Home Alive* is one piece, joined by a backslash, fusing the collection's point of departure with the authors' collective gratitude for past sources. In this backward-looking beginning, Rosario Morales describes their conjoined composition process in this way:

> It began because Rosario wrote rhymes at eleven and not again until she was in her forties and Aurora wrote poetic thoughts when she was seven and was a working writer and teacher when her mother started up again, each influencing the other willy-nilly, through the good times and the bad, the fights and the making up, the long sullen silences and the happy chatter cluttering the phone line strung between us like a 3000-mile umbilical cord from navel to navel, mine to hers, hers to mine, each of us mother and daughter by turns, feeding each other the substance of our dreams. (Levins Morales and Morales, *Getting Home Alive* n.p.)

"She" and "her" become indistinguishable as each steps in and out of the roles of mother, daughter, and writer. Strikingly, the phone cord that connects them virtually is a continuation of the umbilical cord that once tethered them to each other as a conjoined body. Not only is the maternal biologism of this passage radically trans-individual, but the physical manifestation of 1980s telecommunication seems as nurturing and uniting as the biological apparatus of pregnancy.

Yet it is not just the mother and daughter who share their selves in the text but also the diverse ancestors of each: grandmothers from Puerto Rico, New York, and the Ukraine; rhythms, scents, and genes from Jewish, African, and indigenous cultures. Lara-Bonilla's essay is helpful in pointing out that, though each piece in the collection seems to reflect an individual point of view (Aurora or Rosario), each individual bears the stories and the "genetic memory" of her predecessors (369, 366); each is thus more than individual. Lara-Bonilla regards the text, as well as its "space of writing" (the individual author's mind or desk), as points of intersection for multiple lives (364, 366). She uses the term "palimpsestic" to describe this dense web (366). The piece Lara-Bonilla regards as emblematic of an individual figure's internalization of history is Levins Morales's "Wolf," with which I opened this chapter. Yet the idea of internalizing multitudes within one palimpsest is defied by the shape-changing animal in "Wolf": a being that exceeds containment within any one body. Indeed, the idea of a palimpsest seems to domesticate and unify, while the collected pieces in *Getting Home Alive* (especially those authored by Levins Morales, if one differentiates) range across a wild variety of entities: magic, the earth, sugar cane, whales, an old medicine man, and an attic stuffed with other people's stories (38, 40, 66, 163, 177). This wildness pushes beyond the bounds of individual selfhood as well as anthropocentric Humanism.

To focus on the human obscures the ways in which relations among species drive the critical content of "Wolf." A human-centered approach would also miss the ethical issues Levins Morales raises at the broader level of the ecosystem. In an interview I conducted with Levins Morales in 2015, she explained that, given her childhood history of sexual trauma, connecting with her body "was like entering a minefield." To escape the minefield of her body, she turned to the wider "natural world" where she could feel "the ecological web extending out" ("Shared Ecology and Healing Justice" 190). Yet this is not a benign, romanticized nature. Nature is intimately related to her experiences of abuse, part of the structures of exploitation that sustained both the abusers and their victims. The abuse, according to Levins Morales, "had everything to do with it being the Puerto Rican countryside. And everything to do with the military and tourism presences in the country and the particular ways in which we were colonized" (189). In this way, abuse was part of the ecological web. The remote, mountainous location where her family lived was able to shelter international traffic in child pornography, and this economy of sexual abuse intersected with the presence of the U.S. military servicemen on the island as well as the number of industries mining the island's natural resources. Levins Morales describes her powerful relationship with rain as a byproduct of the abuse: the abusers would not come for her in the rain (190). Rain is certainly an unexpected source of shelter for human animals, highlighting the friction between conventional structures dividing humans from nature and the radical ecology in Levins Morales's work, an ecology in which nonhuman nature serves as both agent of abuse and protector. Telling her personal story, as in "Wolf," includes this broader ecology.

Another surprising instance in which human identity is routed through the nonhuman appears in "Sugar Poem" (also in *Getting Home Alive*). Unlike the refined poetry that shows up in silver bowls,

> I come from the earth
> where the cane was grown.
> I know
> the knobbed rooting,
> green spears, heights of
> caña
> against the sky,
> purple plumed. (*Getting Home Alive* 40)

The speaker here identifies with raw material, raw not just in its unrefined state but also in the potential damage its green spears might inflict. After the "cutting, cutting" of the *macheteros*, "sharp spikes . . . wound feet," and "rings of red fire" burn sugar into the wind (40). Likewise, "poems grown from the ground. . . . / heavy, raw and green" (40) might have the power to wound. This language gives agency to raw material and verbal power to the "plumed" cane/pen. The speaker of this poem is the poem itself, telling us its history of composition. The speaker of the poem is also the sugarcane, whose life story on a plantation emerges from a larger web that includes colonialism, slavery, and the colonizers' preference for tea sweetened with sugar. Consumption, greed, dehumanization, and abuse are the political content of sugar's personal story.

Food and ecology work their way through the text's much-anthologized "Ending Poem," too. This poem alternates between the voices of mother and daughter, accelerating the tempo of the interchanging voices in *Getting Home Alive*. The lines are drawn from earlier pieces in the collection, making this poem a gathering of echoes from the textual past. The form of the poem further problematizes differentiation between the authors: though the lines alternate between the different fonts associated with the two writers, the pattern of alternation and the assignment of fonts are inconsistent. Lines written by Rosario sometimes appear in the font associated with Aurora, and vice versa. "I am" clauses accumulate throughout the first stanza, blending Rosario's and Aurora's distinct identities ("I am New York Manhattan and the Bronx. / A Mountain-born, country-bred, homegrown jíbara child") with the very phrase that is supposed to assert individuation (212). The individual claim to being, "I am," becomes unreliable. "I" is replaced by "we" and "us" by the sixth stanza as the poem extends outward to include foremothers from around the world, taking Judy Chicago's famous installation piece *The Dinner Party* (1979) as a framework for inviting the "many mothers" of the Americas into the collective.[5] Here, too, it is not just the women but the objects upon which they eat that tell stories, stories of regional natural resources and the local handicrafts that emerge from the available minerals and vegetation:

> Each plate is different,
> wood, clay, papier maché, metal, basketry, a leaf, a coconut shell. . . .
>
> I am a child of many mothers.
> They have kept it all going
> All the civilizations erected on their backs.
> All the dinner parties given with their labor. (213)

As with "Sugar Poem," dehumanizing labor and the appropriation of raw materials are fundamental ingredients for dinner parties, but, in this case, the laborers are welcomed to sit at the table. The final lines form a "we" that incorporates the reader with direct address:

> Come, lay that dishcloth down. Eat, dear, eat.
> History made us.
> We will not eat ourselves up inside anymore.
>
> And we are whole. (213)[6]

The line "History made us" invokes all of the lives and labors involved with the production of food as well as with the production of the text that brings the authors and readers together.

Eating, especially in its relations to history and health, is a refrain that continues throughout Levins Morales's writing career, linking the mother and daughter's second coauthored work, *Cosecha*, to the shared voices published nearly thirty years earlier.[7] The opening section of *Cosecha* repeats the mother's dinner invitation from the 1986 "Ending Poem," with the added distancing clause "she would say" (presumably since Rosario Morales had passed away by the time Levins Morales was assembling *Cosecha*) and a shift from the intimate singular "dear" to an intimate plural community: "Come to the table, she would say. Eat, dears, eat" (*Cosecha* 2). Levins Morales follows this invitation with her piece "A Remedy for Heartburn," which describes the difficult process of digesting the insults of misogyny, racism, poverty, and environmentally caused cancer that impede healthy eating, "jaw-breaking language that gets pushed into our mouths every time we ask for a piece of bread" (3). As "Sugar Poem" and "The Dinner" suggest, eating cannot be divorced from the histories of food's production, and those histories often dehumanize laborers as much as grain and meat. The ultimate remedy proposed for the heartburn that comes with structural inequality is refusing to swallow it (9). Vomiting, in this case, is not a symptom to be remedied but a healing practice, a purging of toxic histories.[8] This story ends with a recipe, the "Remedy for Heartburn," which appropriates no agricultural ingredients, only attentive cooks organizing their own resources: "The Ingredients? You already have them. In your pockets, in your purses, in your bellies and your bedrooms. For this kind of broth, there can't be too many cooks. Get together. Stir the stuff around. Listen to your hunger. Get ready. Get organized" (10). What is the final product of this crowded cooking process?

The metaphor of eating invokes the homey image of a community of women gathered together in the kitchen, but the emphasis in "Remedy" is less on homeness than on sickness, the objects (and ideologies) that enter our bodies and inhibit their organic processes, the risky acts of absorbing and expelling, crossing back and forth over our bodies' boundaries. Eating is one of the most dramatic sites/events of corporeal permeability and reciprocal pollution. As feminist ecocritic Stacy Alaimo writes, "[P]erhaps the most palpable example of trans-corporeality is that of food, whereby plants or animals become the substance of the human" ("Trans-Corporeal Feminisms" 253). Alaimo's theory of transcorporeality helps us to imagine both the pleasures and the dangers that come with circulation between bodies: "[B]y underscoring that 'trans' indicates movement across different sites, trans-corporeality opens up an epistemological 'space' that acknowledges the often unpredictable and unwanted actions of human bodies, nonhuman creatures, ecological systems, chemical agents, and other actors" (238). The "space" where different entities meet, combine, and transform each other is, I would add, not just epistemological; different ways of being, different ontologies—human and nonhuman—intermingle here, too. Digestion mixes ontologies, negotiates between them, and responds with new forms. Levins Morales's poems in *Getting Home Alive* tell some of the life histories of these trans-species ontologies: the poems that come out of sugar plantations, the sexual abuse that comes from mining, and the feminist dinner parties that resist conventional consumption practices. Power dynamics circulate across species in each of these recipes.

My time in Levins Morales's home helped to clarify the potential intoxication that comes with eating. I use "toxic" here in its ambivalent sense, including both the chemical toxins that would trigger Levins Morales's chemical sensitivity disorder and potentially cause seizures as well as the tonic toxins, the tinctures and herbs stored in the bottles that lined shelves in her kitchen, dining room, and bathroom. For someone with a history of illnesses triggered by environmental factors, what goes into or out of the body is clearly a central preoccupation, and Levins Morales's need to eat or to drink tea formed part of the backdrop of our interview, along with a host of photographs, paintings, altars, plants, and other nonhuman participants in our conversation. Indeed, a lingering scent of jet fuel on my clothing delayed our conversation while I changed into some of Aurora's clothes. I include these details here to add materiality to the web of words I'm analyzing and to include my own body as a participant in the processes of shared authority I trace in this chapter.

These conversations among women recall another significant project of shared memoir that Levins Morales was involved with: the Latina Feminist Group was a collective of eighteen women, all of them Latina academics, who gathered together periodically from 1993 into the present to share stories and (in the later 1990s) to coauthor a collection of personal *testimonios* published in *Telling to Live* (2001).[9] The collaboratively authored introduction to that text describes this project as a way of expanding beyond the individualistic boundaries of memoir: "Departing from the heroic autobiographical tradition, we are not speaking from the voice of the singular 'I.' Rather, we are exploring the ways in which our individual identities express the complexities of our communities as a whole" (Latina Feminist Group 20–21). Accounting for complexity is always unwieldy, and the authors describe the clunky process of writing an introduction based on the consensus of eighteen different authors: dividing into subgroups for theorizing, debating, drafting, recasting, expanding, deleting, clarifying, tightening, line-editing, and polishing. "Having eighteen women in a room, collectively writing and editing a manuscript, is a sight to behold!" (15). *Telling to Live* includes within it a number of photographs of the authors assembled together around seminar tables with coffee cups (an academic sister image to *The Dinner Party*), sifting through stacks of papers, posed outdoors in the woods, and, in one shot, carrying what seem to be grocery bags, accounting for the material contexts and the mundane dailyness of sustaining a writing collaboration. Such work is difficult, and it should be. This is another remedy for heartburn. Accounting for heterogeneity within a group and the distinct labors of each member will never produce seamless stories, but these efforts might produce ethical visions for how to live in community, how to mobilize diverse individuals around shared causes, and how to build sustaining relationships across differences.

Posthuman Histories

> Ginger is ferocity and stubbornness. Ginger is aggressive and sharp. Ginger is the friend who drags you out of bed and makes you get up in the morning.
>
> —Aurora Levins Morales, *Remedios* 107

Between these collective memoirs, Levins Morales received a PhD in history from the Union Institute, where she decolonized her relationship to history.[10] She published both *Medicine Stories*—a "curandera's handbook of historical practice" (*Medicine Stories* 25–26)—and *Remedios: Stories of Earth and Iron from the History of Puertorriqueñas*—histories derived from her doctoral dissertation—in 1998. True to its subtitle, *Remedios* fuses history and story, earth and human, and wraps within its net a global history of women from the first mother in Sub-Saharan Africa to Levins Morales herself, the writer whose experiences of physical and emotional abuse as a young girl led her to seek healing narratives. She describes the text as "intertwining histories":

> One is the vast web of women's stories spinning out in time and space from the small island of Puerto Rico and encompassing some of the worst disasters to befall humanity: the Crusades; the Inquisition; the African slave trade; the witch persecutions; the European invasions of America, Africa, Asia, and the Pacific; and the enclosure of common lands in Europe itself, that sent a land-starved and dispossessed peasantry out rampaging in the wake of greedy aristocrats, merchants, and generals across the world—and all the plagues, tortures, rapes, famines, and killings that accompanied these events. (Levins Morales, *Remedios* xxiv)

The other story is about the ritual abuse of the author during her childhood in Puerto Rico, and she calls this story "exactly the same," though "smaller": "invasion, torture, rape, death, courage, solidarity, resistance" (xxiv). *Remedios* is thus both history and memoir. Its multiperspectival approach is unwieldy, impossibly comprehensive, and certainly more imaginative than empirical (since there are no written records for much of what Levins Morales wants to tell). This is, I think, the textual incarnation of what the "Remedy for Heartburn" asks for: it has "many cooks," and stuff gets "stirred around." It is lavishly excessive, full of lists. The numerous peoples, places, and events in *Remedios* wind on through 186 historical fragments, spanning the globe with a cast of thousands, including "Bantu women," the deer mother, piñon, Saint Teresa of Avila, gingerbread, the "Wild West," Queen Nzinga, Sor Juana, Nannytown, runaways, tuberculosis, Pura Belpré, needleworkers, the barrio, and milk thistle. In this context, ginger is as much an agent and ally (not just stimulating digestion but dragging you out of bed) as the twentieth-century Puerto Rican librarian and writer Pura Belpré.

As with *Getting Home Alive* and *Cosecha*, the acknowledgments of *Medicine Stories* and *Remedios* are intimately related to the philosophy of these texts. *Medicine Stories*, the collection of essays where Levins Morales describes her practice as a radical historian, begins with the claim that "political and creative thinking always takes place in community" and goes on to describe the various kinds of conversations, real and imagined, that contributed to the voice and vision in the book (*Medicine Stories* 1). *Remedios* likewise begins with a lush five-page "Agradacimientos," emphasizing that "writing a book like *Remedios* is something that happens only in community," followed by a list of multiple human sources that helped the author to move "back and forth between my own nightmares and revelations and the web of history" (*Remedios* xviii). An important aspect of both books is the relationship between the author's personal history and the larger histories she is charting. On the narrative level, the author is tapping into what she calls in *Kindling* "the healing properties of solidarity" (38), embedding her own experience within a collective context. This narrative plurality is also related to the testimonial process of the Latina Feminist Group. An individual story elevates and decontextualizes a singular life; a collectivity "nurtures utopian visions of social formations—families, work teams, social networks, communities, sexual relationships, political groups, social movements—that are formed on the basis of equality, respect, and open negotiation of difference" (Latina Feminist Group 20).

Remedios presents a cacophonous collectivity in which Levins Morales is embroiled as both subject and object. She explained in her interview with me: "I was conscious that I wasn't trying to be comprehensive; I was trying to be medicinal. And so I was researching those stories; I was creating a support group for myself across time" ("Shared Ecologies and Healing Justice" 191). *Medicine Stories* also emphasizes the therapeutic function of history: "I started graduate school and therapy within two weeks of each other because at some level I understood that the two processes were intimately linked" (*Medicine Stories* 3). History does not just describe the past: it enacts memories, performs value systems, and prescribes tested cures. It explains the world for us. A history with "many cooks" has enough different options embedded within it to heal multitudes.

The result of this philosophy and this methodology is a blending of genres: history, fiction, memoir, poetry, herbal. Levins Morales uses the term *testimonio* in her description of *Remedios*: "*Remedios* is testimonio, both in the sense of a life story, an autobiography of my relationship to my past, and, like the testimonios of Latin American torture survivors, in bearing witness to a much larger history of abuse and resistance" (*Medicine Stories* 25). Testimonio is a process of witnessing a life in conditions of collective oppression, revealing an individual story in order to illuminate larger patterns and mysteries. Testimonios revolve around one voice, often with the mediation of an editor or translator, but what Levins Morales takes on is a collective testimonio (unlike the multiauthored collection of individual testimonios in *Telling to Live*), in which she assumes equal authority over her own life story and those of the third-person others whose histories she presents as shared. The relationship between subject and object becomes even more complicated, then. Placing the author's childhood self alongside historical figures real and imagined estranges the author and embraces third-person women as intimate subjects. Indeed, in my conversation with her, Levins Morales described the subjects of *Remedios* as living beings who were actively involved in the author's life:

> AURORA: And so I was researching those stories; I was creating a support group for myself across time. You know, I was talking to Taíno women who were raped by the *conquistadores*. I was talking to West African women who were raped in the condition of slavery. I was talking to women across all of those groups coping with domination within marriage. They were my support group.
>
> SUZANNE: Can you clarify the "talking to"? Like, thinking? Writing?
>
> AURORA: I looked for their stories. I wrote to them and from them. I wrote in their voices. I imagined that they would understand me. And I felt like I understood them. ("Shared Ecologies and Healing Justice" 191–92)

Imagination is surely the primary source for each of the lives in this conversation, as "hard" evidence is difficult to come by in telling the stories of disenfranchised people (*Medicine Stories* 27). But how else does a Latina develop a personally relevant history? She must create her own archive. By combining her professional experiences as a poet, a feminist, and a historian Levins Morales is able to develop a transhistorical community that jettisons empiricism to form conversation and alliance across the generations.

It is not just humans who people these collective stories, either. In the preface to *Remedios*, where Levins Morales explains the relationship between her own body and the history of Puerto Rico, she explains:

> And people were not the only sufferers. Great forests, herds, flocks, and schools of creatures abundant beyond belief are gone, devoured by a frenzy of greed that killed five million pigeons, all but exterminated many kinds of seals, whales, and beavers, and clear-cut forests once many days journey across, leaving barren, eroded lands. All these events have immense consequences for our capacity to live with the earth and each other. (*Remedios* xxvii)

Interspersed throughout the human history in *Remedios* is a botánica of herbs, foods, and oils outlining their medicinal effects.[11] The stories of plants form a sort of refrain throughout the text, bringing the histories of colonialism and enslavement down to minute details of the nonhuman world. The plants that populate these histories are not simply objects of human manipulation; they, too, are agents, coauthors in the history of human/nonhuman evolution. For instance, the potatoes that have grown in Andean soil for thousands of years are—in their diverse colors, mutations, and adaptability to variations in sun, soil, and water—"small, round teachers of possibility" (21).

> Tuber of the three thousand forms, you remind us that there are always more choices, more unexplored paths, is always more potential than we can imagine from the present moment. Papita de los Andes, you roll into our hands shouting, "Diversify! Be colorful! Have fun!" You offer us the unknown, the multiple pathways, the different seasoning, the doorway to discovery, the unexpected bonus, the unqualified disaster, the privilege of making many fruitful mistakes. . . .
> Choosing safety, you say, with a wink, is not always safe! (22)

These winking potatoes,[12] half-hiding underground, adapting themselves into multishaped and multicolored forms, have the power to nourish *and* to instruct. They enter into our flesh when we eat them, they enrich the soil we move upon, and they teach us that each unexpected ecological problem creates not just new forms of potatoes but new biodiversities and new paths for solutions. The vulnerable human-potato ecosystem is not destroyed in a crisis; it is nudged into new forms of productivity. There is no safety in preserving the individual or resisting change; conjoined fluctuation is the path of health (and, I would add, the path to ethical living).

The preface to *Remedios* suggests that Levins Morales takes seriously what we have to learn from plants. She compares her work as a gatherer of global histories to an herbalist's "laboratory":

> One who gathers what is growing wild, and with the help of handed-down recipes, a little fire and water, and a feel for plants, prepares tinctures, concentrating faint traces of aromatic oils, potent resins capable of stopping a heart or healing it. . . . The plants that cure scurvy, tone the kidneys, purge parasites are buried in the tangle of weeds whose pollen sweetens the air but which do nothing for human bodies. I must taste the leaves, looking for that trace of bitterness, that special aroma of sweetness. I must let the plant act in my body in order to know what it is. (*Remedios* xxvi)

The job of the medicinal historian is radical indeed. In sifting through the forgotten stories of "women, poor people, workers, children, people of color, slaves, the colonized" (*Medicine Stories* 26), which are often left to grow wild among the weeds rather than stored away in official archives, the historian must determine which stories to pass on (to paraphrase the ambiguous ending of Toni Morrison's *Beloved*). She tests their healing powers by ingesting them herself, letting the plants work within her own body, internalizing trans-species chemical reactions.

The imagined community of people and plants formed in *Remedios* is clearly a helpful tool for Levins Morales's healing practice, since she controls the routes of each story and chooses which medicine to try based on the personal experience of abuse she is seeking to contextualize. But what lessons does this botánica offer for others? Shortly after the excerpt I quoted above from my interview with Levins Morales, she went on to say, "[I]f you look at the stories [in *Remedios*], I was creating my own medicine in the sure knowledge that what was medicinal for me would be medicinal for all of us. And that's something that somehow I've known all along. Like, you know, that the more personal and useful I made it to myself, the more universal it would be, the more accessible to other people" ("Shared Ecologies and Healing Justice" 192). How does the personal lead to the universal? Levins Morales's "sure knowledge" in the universal healing power of *Remedios* is likely a gesture of faith—or a political yearning—more than a certainty.

My intention, however, is not to measure the universal applicability of the text's healing powers. I am more interested in the mere fact of holding this goal for a text; I'm drawn to the broad idealism of the text's unique use of genre. *Remedios* captures the multitudes within one net, and the logic opening this net is driven by memoir: the author's personal experiences and needs. Like many memoirs, *Remedios* emerges from the imagination, which enables Levins Morales to make her memoir impossibly broad, an occasion to think globally. *Remedios* is utopian, ahistorical rather than grounded, arealistic rather than realistic. I say "ahistorical" and "arealistic" because the text is operating *outside the rules* of documentation and realism; it is more faithful to the author's aspirations than to reality. It has a "Medicine Cabinet" instead of a bibliography (*Remedios* 232). It refuses what AnaLouise Keating calls "status quo stories,"[13] calling us to try out new recipes and to change the world in the process. This kind of prescription could be applied universally.

But there is a horizon to this text's "vast web" of connections (*Medicine Stories* xxiv); its limits become apparent when compared to the other web medium that Levins Morales is now working with: the World Wide Web. Every story in *Remedios* is authored by one person, and one person controls the processes of inclusion and exclusion within the text, but Levins Morales's website is open to strangers who add comments and navigate the site on their own terms. Although the author selected which hyperlinks to include, and some of those links are closed circuits, it is ultimately possible to reach beyond the parameters she conceived. (The "Moon Phase" link, for example, leads to a variety of commercial sites, including Google.) While the fretwork of the textual web in *Remedios* is looped by the author's private designs, the digital frets that users spin out from the website are more ambiguous property (as I will discuss in greater depth in the next section). The website has no center and (virtually) no periphery. What seems utopian in *Remedios*, like global breadth and universal accessibility, the Internet makes more possible.

I'm taking these speculations about winking potatoes and websites as an opportunity to bring posthumanism into this conversation. Posthumanism is one of my favorite developments in critical theory because it tends to bring matter and agency back into the decentered epistemologies of postmodernism. Donna Haraway, who, as a biologist, a socialist, and a feminist, is friendly with the workings of a variety of organisms, is probably the most useful theorist for helping me to build this particular bridge.[14] Both Haraway and Levins Morales help us to imagine interspecies networks that decenter the human without sacrificing politics or embodied experience to theory.[15] Haraway's work displaces binaries with an orientation toward "the profusion of spaces and identities and the permeability of boundaries in the personal body and in the body politic" (*Haraway Reader* 30). Her career focuses on permeabilities and shared agencies through the conjoined relations of humans, dogs, and parasites as well as digital technologies.

It is in this vein that I find kinship between posthumanism and the work of Levins Morales. This is not a gesture that Levins Morales would necessarily embrace. In one of her better-known essays from the 1990s, "Certified Organic Intellectual: On Not Being Postmodern," Levins Morales asserts that "the ideas I carry with me were grown on soil I know"; "the intellectual traditions I come from create theory out of shared lives instead of sending away for it" (*Medicine Stories* 67).[16] She specifically rejects postmodernism's impenetrable packaging and its "unnecessarily specialized language [that] is used to humiliate those who are not supposed to feel entitled" (70). "I know that the complexity of unrefined food is far more nourishing than the processed stuff," she concludes, rejecting the (generalized, reified) products at Safeway in favor of the farmers' market. I agree with this critique of impenetrable packaging, and we do not need abstract theoretical language to shift our thinking from the autonomy and dominance of the human to the trans-species web of relations that both Haraway and Levins Morales attend to. Indeed, this web is as premodern as it is post-: it is a native plant that grows wild and comes to us covered in soil. But "organic" is an elusive ideal these days, involving such impurities as government certification, haute cuisine farmers' markets, and Whole Foods stores in urban food deserts where no one can afford their inflated prices. The organic is mediated by inorganic management. So where do we go, in the postmodern age, for healthy produce?

Life on the Web

I am a point of light in a web . . . I'm not actually
an individual . . . my skin is a formality . . . the air is
entering and leaving my body all the time, my skin
is shedding and things are coming in through the
pores . . . there are millions of filaments connecting
me to that maple tree. When I lose the individual
isolation and remember that I'm connecting to the
entire web, I can feel what's going on in the web, I
can feel my connections to everything.

—Aurora Levins Morales, "Shared Ecologies and
Healing Justice" 193

Levins Morales's website is, I would argue, a virtual farmers' market, a place for transcorporeal collectivity and exchange. It is not postmodern in the ways that the Internet was assumed to be in the 1990s (the disembodied, hyperreal territory of the military-industrial complex). Auroralevinsmorales .com emerges from the material needs of one particular body and its emplacement in a toxic ecosystem, and it lives in the activities of its embodied users. The networks the website forges in support of these lively matters use the tools of postmodernity in premodern fashion, with hyperlinks leading to anticapitalist barter and astrology. The various options to "Support Aurora" include contributing labor (like grant writing or web support), donating materials for the construction of the "tiny house on wheels" that enables her to live in a toxic-free environment and to travel for public lectures, and becoming a "*patreon*" or sustainer, which evokes both the premodern tradition of artistic patronage and the logic of an ecosystem that requires nurturance.[17] Each of these means of support will feed a community with blogs, poems, and public events. The certificate of patronage offered online (which is the work of Ricardo Levins Morales, the author's brother) gives sustainers the role of "villager," part of an ecological community where poems grow among the crops. The structures in this image, organic and inorganic, enfold each other, and the material processes that sustaining enacts reach beyond the digital signifiers to (dare I say it?) real bodies. (See figure 3.1.)

My understanding of posthuman ecosystems is influenced by the work of Stacy Alaimo, among others.[18] Alaimo's feminist ecocritical stance is based on a critique of human behaviors that have damaged our ecosystem and poisoned our own bodies, which implicitly keeps human concerns at the "heart" of her New Materialism. But these concerns are not just human; they revolve around larger questions of environmental justice that include nonhuman animals and plants. Since Levins Morales suffers from multiple chemical sensitivity disorder (MCS)—one of the conditions that motivates Alaimo's theory of "toxic bodies"—justice for her would entail broad environmental transformations.[19] (In a lecture she delivered at Loyola University Chicago in April 2017, Levins Morales critiqued my use of the label "chemical sensitivity" and claimed the term "environmental violence," instead. MCS is still the preferred term in disability studies, though, and I like the emphasis on "sensitivity"—as a form of vulnerability, connectedness, and perhaps even agency—embedded within it.) As Levins Morales writes in *Kindling*, "what isolates me is not my illness, but the widespread distress that prevents people from choosing non-toxic products" (*Kindling* 74). This "widespread distress" encompasses economic, cultural, and ethical matters: the for-profit industry of "personal care" products and their advertisements that persuade humans that smelling like perfume is bet-

FIGURE 3.1. Ricardo Levins Morales, Villager certificate.
(Reprinted with permission from Ricardo Levins Morales)

ter than smelling like humans, the individualistic belief that one person's choices are his/her "own business" rather than the business of us all, and the natural and artificial chemicals in which we unthinkingly soak our bodies. For Alaimo, MCS suggests an "ontological shift": it "dissolves something so basic to the sense of what it is to be human—a sense of being a discrete entity, separate from one's environs" (Alaimo, *Bodily Natures* 120). Healing Levins Morales, then, must include not just a cultural shift (rethinking our shared participation in a toxic narrative), but also an ontological shift in our perceptions of what it means to be human. We need to replace our belief in the human individual with an understanding of our transcorporeal relations within a collectivity.

What does memoir have to do with ecological relations? *Getting Home Alive, Remedios, Kindling, Cosecha,* and the website tell us about the life of the author in deep, personal detail, embedded in reflexive, metacritical analysis of the processes of memory and writing, but the details Levins Morales emphasizes also illuminate the collectivity of which she is a part.[20] Examining Levins Morales's writing as memoir highlights her critique of individualism, overturning the implied narcissism and representationalism of memoir. Though she returns again and again to her own memories and her own life experiences, the self around which Levins Morales's work revolves is humble and communal, intertwined with other humans, animals, and medicines in real and imagined ways. These qualities expand human ontology (reminiscent of Alaimo's insights about MCS) and reconceive memoir as an (eco)system of encounters.

Levins Morales describes this method we might call ecological memoir in *Kindling*: "If I write about our bodies I am writing about the land and what has been done to it" (7). This is not just because the body is present in the land, sharing air and water with it, but also because, particularly for someone with chemical sensitivities like Levins Morales, there is no clear distinction between a body and its environs. In an essay also published in 2013, titled "Guanakán," she borrows from indigenous Puerto Rican cosmology to describe the body as a radically permeable entity. Skin is not a wall or a barrier, she argues:

[I]t's a conversation, cells lined up in a smooth collaboration, a layered surface that is constantly exchanging molecules with everything else. What's more, a surface full of doors and windows, through which all kinds of wildlife passes. If skin is the wall of a house, that house is made of dried grass, is full of insects and small mammals and nesting birds, is its own habitat, constantly shedding stalks, or, to change the metaphor, is made of soft wood, growing mosses and mushrooms on its surface even as the shredded bark and wood fall away into the rich surrounding soil. ("Guanakán" 1)

That final sentence, like the body itself, is a lush compilation of materials joined loosely by commas in a shared habitat. Levins Morales uses the term "*guanakán*," drawn from the Taíno way of saying "our center," to reference "that cloudy gathering of denser particles and pulses in which our awareness exists"; guanakán is a less "bulky" way of saying "body-mind-nature-thing" (2). Guanakán is a premodern ontology, an organic alternative to the constraints of empirical reason and individual autonomy manufactured by Humanism. Life on the web holds every entity open to the fluctuations that come from relation; it is a continual process of coevolution. "We," our "guanakanes," are "full of unfinished stories, fragmented instructions, . . . new and ingenious responses to a changing environment" (3). In order to tell any body's story, in order to demand the social and environmental shifts that would protect a body from toxic infections, one must cast the net wider than conventional memoir. It's not that the demands on memoir have changed; the net has "always already" been wider than the boundaries of generic convention since the story of a self is transcorporeal by nature. But, having been schooled for so long in Humanism, we are not used to listening to all of the voices in an ecosystem.

How do we hear toxins, and how do we represent them? The larger movement toward healing justice with which Levins Morales has become involved makes the health of each individual body/environment/guanakán a communal matter since each inhales the exhaust of everyone and everything around her. From the perspective of contagious illnesses and environmental toxins, there are no individuals or boundaries; health is a state shared by all of us rather than the property of a few lucky individuals.[21] Levins Morales's website performs this insight: making her individual thriving a public concern by soliciting resources from across the Web. While we are used to thinking of infections and toxins as locally and materially shared, the website extends this sharing beyond regional boundaries. Auroralevins morales.com situates the single thread of its namesake's life and health within a larger (ecological and digital, premodern and postmodern) web.

Digital health and digital responsibility, however, are difficult to regulate. A website is a symbiotic network that links entities in sometimes healthful and sometimes unhealthful ways. The Internet might seem to like a "safe" environment for someone with chemical sensitivity: she can remain in the space of her own home (a space that she has constructed to minimize its toxicity toward her) while interacting with others. Indeed, in the interview I conducted with her, Levins Morales stressed the importance of being able to shop, to collaborate, and to conduct research online. When I asked her about what sort of environment the Internet is, she emphasized the intimate sorts of connections that develop in her Facebook group dedicated to people who are chronically ill and disabled: "For chronically ill people, it's the difference between life and death; it makes such a difference. . . . We're creating a system of support there" ("Shared Ecologies and Healing Justice" 197). There is reciprocal responsibility for members of an online community: sharing resources and advice, mobilizing local networks when someone is in trouble, and simply being witnesses for each other, ideally with love and respect. But there is also a great deal of shared vulnerability within such a web. Bad advice, anger, and judgment can circulate in unhealthful ways, just like credit card numbers that fall into the wrong hands. There are toxicities in a digital environment, though they are different from those one might find in a physical house, forest, or ocean. Indeed, the Internet has its own guanakán, which intersects with the guanakanes of everyone who goes there.

What is the difference between the indigenous idea of guanakán and the web formed by contemporary toxicity? The language of toxicity implies a polluting agent threatening the integrity of a body (a body we like to imagine as pure). Toxicity, according to modern understanding, is perverse because it involves nonhuman agents (like the hyperbolic smog monsters and killer tomatoes of science fiction). Under Enlightenment Humanism, only humans, with their dominating gift of reason, are proper agents. We are supposed to have lost our belief in animism and alchemy. Toxicity is like a resurgence of the primitive, a refusal of matter to abide by its supposed inanimate state. Yet Levins Morales's idea of the guanakán, like new developments in critical posthumanism and ecocriticism, reminds us that humans never were apart from nature. Though we might like to think of ourselves as transcendent, we have always been subject to/with other-than-human cohabitants in our ecosystem.

Contemporary toxic matters fall on both sides of the fictional organic/inorganic line: pollen, snake venom, infectious microbes, lead paint on a child's toy, cleansers meant to purify our bodies and homes, emails "phishing" for personal data all take on agency in their chemical activities. With a linguist's delight for the changing meanings of words, Mel Chen, in their brilliant book *Animacies* (2012), traces the shifting meaning of "toxic" from its association with poison in the 1600s to contemporary (metaphoric?) applications of the term to describe social atmospheres. The definition of toxin, then, "has always been the outcome of political negotiation" (Chen 191). Chen suggests that the "basic semantic schema for toxicity" is a real or assumed threat (of damage or alteration) posed to one body by another proximate body (191). It is important to bear in mind that neither of these bodies is static and that their shared relation intertwines them. Toxicity "meddles with" subject/object relations (195), which are at the heart of Humanism. This is true in two ways: First, supposed inanimate objects (like dioxin) are agentic in a way that objectifies the human recipient of their toxicity. Second, beyond this role reversal, the coherence of both "proximate bodies" is unstable as they infect and transform each other in a multidirectional manner: soap leaves residue on skin; skin leaves cells on soap.

We often focus on what the matter is *with* toxicity: its threat to the purity of systems, its breaching of our lines of defense, its undermining of our carefully guarded health. But it is also important to ask: What is the matter *of* toxicity? Is it a substance, like lead or mercury? In those examples, toxicity must be understood as a contextual valuation since mercury is not dangerous—is, indeed, part of a health management system—when contained within a thermometer. It's only when it leaks out that its toxicity is activated. Many substances are toxic only for certain people or only at certain points in their lives. So toxicity must be a matter of relation. This definition seems more useful when considering digital ecologies, for instance, where there is no material poison to trace or to eliminate. I want to raise a few important points about toxicity as relation. First, this relation must be understood as contextually situated, where context need not be based on embodied proximity but would also include digital or perhaps even metonymic association. One of the poisons in my guanakán is the United States' neo-imperial consumption of global resources. Its toxicity consists of vaporous matters like economics, culture, and social stigma: the availability of low-cost goods, the convenience of having the goods of the world brought to me, and the negative connotations associated with "my" country's global persona. The relative toxicity of these connotations waxes and wanes with fluctuations in U.S. foreign policy, pointing to a second important aspect of the toxic relation: it is temporally situated and thus changeable. In theory, because I am a part of U.S. foreign policy's guanakán, I have some influence over it, some ability to direct its fluidity. Yet the power of my vote comes nowhere near the scale of power of the leaders in international policy-making, which raises a third crucial point about toxic relations: unequal power within the web. The various bodies in relation within any guanakán coexist in terms of deep inequality and uneven circulation and communication. Compared to a presidential order my vote is tiny. Compared to an undocumented neighbor, whose voice is silenced by disfranchisement, my vote is large. Compared to the soils and plants of the environments subjected to military industrialization, whose voices are inaudible to or incommensurable with human conversation, my vote is gigantic.

What if we recast the negative valence of toxicity with affirmative (or at least neutral) notions of relational subjectivity and communal connectivity? In Nan Enstad's account, though it represents the triumph of global capitalism in insinuating itself into our very flesh, toxicity also leads us to recognize new subjectivities and new publics based on shared ecosystems, rather than the Humanistic medical model of individuated subjects sealed off from each other and the outside world (Enstad 62–64). In an account of her (non)solitary suffering in *Kindling*, Levins Morales describes the ambivalent simultaneity of vulnerability and distributed agency that comes with toxicity:

> In the steepest pitch, the darkest hour, in the ring of deadly wind, the only salvation is to expand, to embrace every revelation of my struggling cells, to resist the impulse to flee, and hold in my awareness both things: the planetary web of life force of which I am part, and the cruel machinery that assaults us: how greed strips and poisons landscapes and immune systems with equal disregard, how contempt for women, and the vastly profitable medical-industrial complex conspire to write off as hysterical hundreds of thousands of us bearing witness through decades in bed. (*Kindling* 6)

The same threads that carry contempt and poison and greed also link hundreds of thousands of people whose bodies dialogue with both illness and "planetary life force." The difficult question is: how do we amplify the positive connections that flow with toxicity? As Chen puts it:

> Although the body's interior could be described as becoming "damaged" by toxins, if we were willing to perform the radical act of releasing the definition of "organism" from its biological pinnings, we might from a more holistic perspective approach toxicity with a lens of mutualism. . . . Thinking of toxins as symbiotes—rather than, for instance, as parasites

which seem only to feed off a generally integral being without fundamentally altering it (which would perhaps be our first guess)—not only
captures some toxic affectivity but enables me to shift modes of approach.
(Chen 205–06)

Following this call to "shift modes of approach," perhaps instead of asking
"how might we eliminate toxins from our environment?" or "how might
we use toxins to our advantage?"—questions that reinscribe human moral
supremacy—we could ask, instead, "what outcomes might emerge from
participation in particular webs of toxicity?" or even "what do our partners
in infection have to teach us about communal responsibility?" This is not
merely a matter of looking on the "bright side" of a problem but, rather, of
noting who gains what from our symbiosis with toxins, who thrives and who
fails, and what possibilities for affirmative connection and shared vitality
circulate with toxicity. What would we see if we let go of our Humanist
claims to define what counts as "pollution" and opened our minds to the
lively ways that different species infect each other? What different forms
might thriving take?

With this shift of approach, I would like to return to Levins Morales's
website to examine healing relations of toxicity. Auroralevinsmorales.com
brings together humans, money, and scattered physical spaces of speaking
and witnessing. Though it is the author's page, it is also a communal space,
"the village it takes" to sustain a writer. When a trail of linkages takes one
outside the site, there is an option to "return to *our* website" (emphasis
added), welcoming viewers to a space where they are at home. The first
person plural "our" also makes viewers responsible for the connections and
content of the site. The menu options at the top of the page divide the site
into different neighborhoods that organize different webs of relation (my
terms, not Levins Morales's). If I click on "What We Can Do Together,"
the focus is on collaborative efforts to bring the author's words to wider
worlds. I can learn about how to bring the author to my hometown, what
her needs would be in terms of hosting and sponsorship. There is a hyper-
link for sending her a digital message if I would like to make arrangements.
I can also see her planned travel itinerary if I choose to follow her and
share guanakanes. Or I can pay to participate in a variety of webinars. If I
click on "Support Aurora," I can use my economic prostheses to become
a "sustainer" of the author and her work; I can donate labor or resources
to help maintain her house-on-wheels; or I can pay per blog post. Any of
these linkages opens writing and authority to larger communal processes

through the witnessing of embodied or digital audiences, through embodied or digital dialogue, through economic sponsorship, or through the back-and-forth reciprocity of paying for a blog and then posting a response on the website. And this web actually works! With donated money, goods, and labor, Levins Morales's house-on-wheels is done, and she has begun her cross-country travels, bringing her "Letters from Earth" into embodied public circulation.

Other "neighborhoods" of the website offer different kinds of relation. Under "Connect" I can follow the phases of the moon to chart my own cyclical energies. Under "Stuff I Love," I can learn about other authors who have influenced Levins Morales. I can join the mailing list, which promises "irregular" but "juicy" updates that "will not clog your in box," giving digital messages the material texture and heft of liquids or solids. Levins Morales enters the space of my email with content to consume on a schedule I cannot predict, opening my digital workspace to unplanned appearances of Aurora and her work. Other digital neighborhoods on the site are more reserved, allowing for conventional reading of literature and viewing of visual art. These different kinds of relation all come with different toxic matters, as well as different powers and pleasures, as the author and her followers (along with all of our guanakanes) coproduce an ecosystem.

What sort of a memoir is this? It seeps outside of Humanism and moves beyond the human subject; the self in the web loses herself in shared relations and finds her agency, vitality, and authority balanced against other actants. It's a virtual dinner party with everyone talking at once, a thrilling and terrifying experience of having one's body dispersed in tension throughout a community weighted with uncountable and unforeseen toxins. It's a global story that accounts for all of us, in noisy collaboration with our human and nonhuman neighbors. It's a political ecology wherein our every decision has implications that reverberate through like- and unlike-minded allies. (We are indeed all allies in our shared web, allies in a variety of possible projects and combinations, whether we like it or not.) The responsibility of each of us, not just writers and critics, is to make sure that our own voices aren't too loud for us to hear the others, to make sure our voices are modulated and directed in such a way that democratizes vitality, to sample the goods with careful reflection before injecting them into the web. As Karen Barad writes, in her increasingly influential vision of posthumanist ethics, "Intra-acting responsibly as part of the world means taking account of the entangled phenomena that are intrinsic to the world's vitality and being responsible to the possibilities that might help us flourish" (394). As I've already discussed, agency, in the other-than-Humanist sense, is not about individual responsibility or human morality; it is even more difficult. An agent does not simply rattle the web with her individual movements but actually participates—along with other human and other-than-human agencies—in the materialization of the web. Auroralevinsmorales.com makes this intra-active entanglement particularly palpable, but all of the phenomena I analyze in this chapter fall within this ethics: reading, writing, teaching, buying, eating. Since we are co-making the world together, we must "[take] account of the entangled materializations of which we are a part, including new configurations and new subjectivities, new possibilities" (Barad 384). The path is not clear, but when is anything difficult, any action of the trans-species multitude, clear? We are mired in the mud of it.

I close this chapter with Levins Morales's account of collective storytelling at the end of *Kindling*:

> Come into the clearing. Bring your tinder. Together, we will strike sparks and set the night ablaze. Come out of the forest, the woodwork, the shadows to this place of freedom, quilombo, swamp town, winter camp, yucayeque, where those not meant to survive laugh and weep together, share breath from mouth to mouth, pass cups of water; break bread—and let our living bodies speak. (Levins Morales, *Kindling* 165)

> We unwrap our tongues, we bind our stories, we choose to be naked, we show our markings, we lick our fingers, we stroke our bellies, we laugh at midnight, we change the ending, we begin, and begin again. (167)

> You, yes you. Take the cord of memory from my hands, and tie a knot to mark your own place. Each body knows its own exhausting journey, its own oases of joy, its belly-full of shouting, resilience and shame and jubilation. We mark the trail for each other, put lanterns by the door; scratch our signs in the dirt, make signals with fingers in palms, sing coded freedom songs. Strike the stick of aliveness on whatever will make a sound. Bind your stories together. This is how rope is made. Each strand is essential to the strength of the braid. Bring your body closer. Lean in toward the heat and the light. We are striking sparks of spirit, we are speaking from our flesh, we are stacking up our stories, we are kindling our future. (168)

These passages speak of power and vulnerability in intimacy with others; together, our exhausted bodies and all of their webs shape the narrative, the end of the story, and our collective future. This doesn't mean that we can simply choose happy or harmonious endings; from our place in the story's circuit, we "strike the stick of aliveness on whatever will make a sound."

Life

The Gloria E. Anzaldúa Papers and Other-Than-Humanist Ontologies

> She was both the chicken and the egg. Incubating.
> But what was she hatching?
>
> —Gloria Anzaldúa, "La serpiente que se come
> su cola" 103

My preceding chapter ends with a "stick of aliveness." This chapter uses the imaginative work of Gloria Anzaldúa to examine what sort of aliveness sparks ethical action. Anzaldúa is famous for breaking genre rules and rupturing fundamental intellectual categories, and there is a substantial body of criticism analyzing the ways in which her work transforms our ideas about language, race, gender, sexuality, and nation. Yet Anzaldúa criticism is currently in the midst of a sea change. When she died in 2004, and the massive archive she had saved in her home was moved to the Nettie Lee Benson Latin American Collection at the University of Texas at Austin, scholars encountered hundreds of unpublished stories, poems, essays, and even entire book manuscripts.[1] What we thought we knew about Anzaldúa has shifted as "new" works slowly enter public circulation. As academic executor to Anzaldúa's estate, AnaLouise Keating published *The Gloria Anzaldúa Reader* in 2009 (including previously unpublished works alongside some more familiar ones) and Anzaldúa's unfinished and never defended doctoral dissertation, *Light in the Dark / Luz en lo oscuro*, in 2015. A few articles written about unpublished archival documents have had time to make their way through the publishing pipeline and into print, as well, shifting the terms of the critical conversation. Though the majority of scholars still think of Anzaldúa as the author of *Borderlands / La Frontera* (1987) (or, really, the author of a few of the most anthologized essays from *Borderlands*), a somewhat different Anzaldúa is coming into view, with years of future transformation on the horizon. When we're talking about Gloria Anzaldúa, it's not always clear which Anzaldúa we're referring to. Of course, all authors vary depending upon who presents the interpretation and when, but as the Anzaldúa archive unfolds before us, we are presented with a unique example of the contingency and cacophony that make up an author and her life's work.

Anzaldúa's archive, itself, is something of a memoir: an accretion of memorabilia and manuscripts (often covered in edits, doodles, and notes from her writing comadres) that record not just the writing of Gloria Anzaldúa but also her personal relationships, her intellectual conundrums, and her experiences with a variety of illnesses and medical treatments. In addition to multiple drafts of poems, short stories, essays, talks, and a few plays, the archive includes ticket stubs from concerts she attended, I Ching predictions, candle holders with affirmations written on them, and logs recording her food consumption after she was diagnosed with diabetes. The fact that Anzaldúa saved, labeled, and stored these items in her own attic supports the idea of viewing the archive as a memoir since she deliberately preserved this collection of life records.[2] But it's a memoir whose construction relies on the activities of many agents. I have written at length already, in "Messy Archives and Materials That Matter," about how the life story contained in the archive is a product of not just the author but also of the various activities of the executors who determined which materials to make available to the public, the archivists who gathered and stored the materials, the scholars who read and write about these materials, and research processes that include the variable ordering of loose papers and the fluctuating ecosystem of the reading room at the Benson Latin American Collection.

Within the unwieldy "life" of the archive, I was delighted to find, in box 79, three folders containing an unpublished memoir entitled "La serpiente que se come su cola" [The snake that eats its own tail]. This title invokes the self-reflexivity (and potential self-destruction) of the process of life writing. The title page calls the work an "autocanción," or self-song (song to or about the self?), which adds a performative or ritual element to the idea of life writing. The manuscript is undated, but the events narrated suggest that Anzaldúa completed it (or, rather, set it aside somewhat incomplete, as I will discuss later) sometime in the 1980s.[3] Many of the episodes described in "La serpiente" are also included in *Borderlands* and her contributions to *This Bridge Called My Back* (1981),[4] publications where theory, poetry, and autobiography mix in what Anzaldúa later termed "autohistoriateoría," a genre that builds theory from life stories. The fact that Anzaldúa never published "La serpiente" might suggest that she ultimately preferred the mixed genres of *Borderlands* and *Bridge* to "pure" life writing. Or it might be that "La serpiente" was simply too personal to publish. (It does include details about intimate relationships with family members, collaborators, and other writers, details that those people might not want to see in print.) There is also the question of why Anzaldúa chose to write her life story when she was barely into mid-life. My speculation is that her interest in the contours of subjectivity (as demonstrated in *Borderlands*) turned her focus toward her own life in progress.

Life writing is also associated with disability studies. As David Mitchell and Sharon Snyder write, "[T]he discourse of disability has been largely defined by the genre of autobiography," "guided by the assumption that people with disabilities need to write their own stories in order to counteract the dehumanizing effects of societal representations and attitudes" (*The Body and Physical Difference* 9). Yet Mitchell and Snyder ultimately critique this generic focus: "The personal narrative expands the boundaries of our understanding of disability on an individual level, but its attendant social and political contexts tend to be overshadowed by the emotions of pity and/or sympathy evoked by the reader's identification with the narrator's personal plight" (11). The disability story in Anzaldúa's memoir, however, goes beyond the individual level, and the experiences she narrates are likely to evoke estrangement more than sympathy. The subject of "La serpiente" experiences pain and illness as well as hallucinations, travel beyond her own body, even death and rebirth—consistently pushing the limits of believability for what constitutes a life. Based on documents available in the archive, it seems that Anzaldúa was torn between different ways of addressing this fluid self in her writing: sometimes using the first-person pronoun, sometimes assigning herself a third-person semi-autobiographical persona, La Prieta, and sometimes splitting the subject by moving between different pronouns. There is no conventional "I" here. Recent scholarship has framed Anzaldúa's work in terms of emerging theories of posthumanism and speculative realism, foregrounding the ways in which Anzaldúa's subjects move beyond both Humanism and empiricism. Kelli Zaytoun, for instance, finds "a posthumanist capacity of subjectivity" in Anzaldúa's shape-shifting *naguala* figure: "La naguala, situated both in and beyond the body, shifts the shape and the boundaries of the subject beyond intellectual, humanist frameworks" (Zaytoun 2).[5] "La serpiente que se come su cola" offers an excellent place for examining subjectivity that extends beyond an individual life.

While disability studies focus on the heterogeneity of human life, some posthumanist and queer theorists have been positing the death of the human as the source of an alternative ethic. Claire Colebrook suggests that we must let go of the idea of human survival in order to imagine futurity. For Colebrook, as the Anthropocene leads to its own destruction, we must learn how to think past human agency in order to negate it: "ethics may have to be considered beyond discursive, human and political modes" (*The Death of the Posthuman* 60). She uses terms like "rupture," "cessation," "negation," and "refusal" in characterizing the posthumanities (61, 161). Similarly, but in the context of reconfiguring family and gender norms, Judith/Jack Halberstam turns to failure and self-destruction to break the cycle of constantly reproducing exclusionary visions of identity. In their critique of the teleological narratives of feminism, Halberstam proposes:

> Beginning with the injunction "Lose your mother" and building toward a conclusion that will advocate a complete dismantling of self, I explore a feminist politics that issues not from a doing but from an undoing, not from a being or becoming women but from a refusal to be or to become woman as she has been defined and imagined within Western philosophy. . . . This feminism, a feminism grounded in negation, refusal, passivity, absence, and silence, offers spaces and modes of unknowing, failing, and forgetting as part of an alternative feminist project, a shadow feminism which has nestled in more positivist accounts and unraveled their logics from within. (*The Queer Art of Failure* 124)

This dismantling of the self—which recalls Irene Vilar's central focus on suicide and abortion in *Impossible Motherhood*—resonates with the anti-Humanism of some posthumanist critiques. I appreciate these calls to rupture our "status quo" ways of thinking about gender, feminism, and selfhood, and I believe we do need radical transformation in the ways in which we envision life, but negativity does not seem to me like a sustainable approach.

I find in Anzaldúa's work, and in disability studies, ways of thinking beyond, but not necessarily post-, human agency. Her focus on illness as shape-shifting and her accounts of the altered consciousness produced by pain rupture Humanist narratives without negating human life. She accepted mystical encounters, ambiguous bodies, and interspecies minglings without judgment. She experienced her own disabling conditions, including Type 1 diabetes and hormone imbalance, in the epistemological fold between modern medical diagnosis (which enforces normative corporeality) and sacred Aztec figures (like the goddesses Coatlicue and Coyolxauhqui) that fall outside the shapes of Humanism and the requirements of empirical science.[6] In this sense, her ideas are prehuman, or simply outside the cultural-temporal evolution of Humanism, as much as they are posthuman; for this reason, I step aside from the chronological emphasis on the pre- and the post- to regard Anzaldúa's epistemology as simply other-than-Humanist and her imagery as other-than-human. Working outside the frameworks of Humanism enables Anzaldúa to imagine more capacious possibilities for being and to honor corporeal variability as an onto-epistemological tool, a tool that might help us to "change the sentience of the world" (Anzaldúa, "let us be the healing" 101). Breaking with the rules of reason that shape academic discourse enabled Anzaldúa to have a hopeful perspective: "I have this visionary experience where I'm flying in the sky as an eagle. . . . [W]e're going to leave the rigidity of this concrete reality and expand it. I'm very hopeful" (*Interviews/Entrevistas* 284–85). Whether or not one believes in the possibility of out-of-body experiences or shifting shapes into animal forms, these imaginative propositions take us beyond status-quo stories and beyond the seeming fatalism of negative critique. I would argue that other-than-human beings are a logical extension of the theories of permeable nations, genders, and cultures already associated with Anzaldúa, though these more imaginative ontologies might alienate some academic readers. These imaginative ontologies are also important for disability studies in their reconfiguration of life in affirmative and nonnormative ways. (It is important to distinguish this expansion of life from the neoliberal, biopolitical "incitement to life" as "regenerative reproductivity" or "market virility," that Jasbir Puar and others critique [Puar, *Terrorist Assemblages* xii–xiii].)

I begin my analysis by focusing on what "La serpiente" does to the perimeters of life itself, and then, in my second section, use recent frameworks from disability studies to analyze visual images that help us to imagine what other-than-Humanist life might look like. My third section views these permeable lives in conversation with others, focusing on imaginative and expansive kinships as the foundation for ethical relations. And I conclude with an analysis of some of the roadmaps for ethics that Anzaldúa's work provides.

Nonsingular Life

She wanted to be one with the non-human
world for if she was a tree or a sun or the wind
as well as human nothing could hurt her.

—Gloria Anzaldúa, "La serpiente que se come
su cola" 215

"La serpiente que se come su cola" is a 276-page manuscript with page numbers handwritten in the corners. It is a nearly complete text, but there are some unresolved revisions (with inserted edits and type-overs throughout) and some sections still written in note form (many of these take the form of strips of paper cut and pasted onto the backs of fliers and other recycled paper).[7] Throughout "La serpiente," references to the autobiographic self oscillate between the first person and the third (as La Prieta, in those cases), which might just be an effect of the process of constructing this draft of a book by compiling pieces written at various times in different voices. (Many pages in "La serpiente" have more than one page number on them—one from the original context of composition and another to fit within the pagination of the memoir—which places each page in more than one chronology.) Regardless of its origin, the movement between first and third person establishes simultaneous distance and intimacy with the central character and aligns the memoir with Anzaldúa's fictional works, which often revolve around a character named Prieta.

The subtitle of "La serpiente" is "The Death and Rites of Passage of a Chicana Lesbian." This is a life story in which the subject, herself, dies multiple times, so death is embedded in life, neither singular nor permanent.[8] She speaks of past lives and recurring out-of-body experiences ("La serpiente" 65–68, 88–89, 110), suggesting that life transcends the boundaries of individual human anatomy.[9] Toward the end of the memoir, she describes her body as a bridge to the region of the dead; to protect her vagina and belly, "sore from the traffic" between realms, she wants to install stop-and-go signals (198). This body is a locus for a range of activities, agencies, and processes—some of which she has no control over—rather than an individual property. Selfhood incorporates the environments and communities within which one is embedded as well as past and present experiences. Narrating the story of this kind of self would require accounting for more than an individual human life—or at least reconceiving what counts as life and what counts as a self.

Mel Chen's writing about different kinds of aliveness is helpful in thinking about Anzaldúa's expansive ontologies. Chen is surely influenced by posthumanism as much as Colebrook is, but, rather than turning toward negativity, they rethink life beyond anthropocentrism, posing "animacy" as a heterogeneous field cohabited by beings like stones, couches, toxins, and humans in their various scales and shapes of aliveness. Chen allies this multiplication of animacies with critiques of the exclusions that burden the concept of human life:

> Using animacy as a central construct, rather than, say, "life" or "liveliness" . . . helps us theorize current anxieties around the production of humanness in contemporary times, particularly with regard to humanity's partners in definitional crime: animality (as its analogue limit), nationality, race, security, environment, and sexuality. Animacy activates new theoretical formations that trouble and undo stubborn binary systems of difference, including dynamism/stasis, life/death, subject/object, speech/nonspeech, human/animal, natural body/cyborg. (Chen 3)

Anzaldúa's work follows this theoretical trajectory: her challenges to the boundaries of life upend race, gender, species, and other ontological categories.

Thematically, life is intertwined with death throughout the "La serpiente." Anzaldúa notes early in the manuscript that, on her birth certificate, not only were both parents' names and the baby's name misspelled, but the certificate also states that the baby was born dead (a case in which legal status literally negates the reality of the living child) ("La serpiente" 9).[10] One of the first stories Anzaldúa tells in the memoir is of the death of her father: in a section entitled "People Should Not Die in June in South Texas," she describes how his corpse quickly began to decompose in the heat and to smell like a cow, shifting in shape and species.[11] She later gazes at his body in the funeral home—"drained of blood, his entrails removed, his veins and arteries filled with embalming fluid" (24)—while contemplating the process of rotting. Is the body of the father still the father when it is has lost its entrails? What sort of life does the embalming fluid create for the father's last performance at his funeral? This experience, and the questions it raised about what constituted her father, placed death alongside the rest of Anzaldúa's life:

> At her father's death La Muerte had touched her with Her boney hand. And once again she had seen su hocico, once more she had smelled Her. Se habia tragado a su papa y un dia pronto se iba a comer a ella.[12] In India,

she learned, Death is called Kali and she is worshipped. Forever after that bright day in June, Death walked two paces behind her and the "other" world became part of the ground she walked on. (29)[13]

This death presents more gains than losses: Anzaldúa learned to live with death's immanence and to move through the "world" of the dead while she was still living. Personifying death as Kali and La Santa Muerte of Mexican tradition presents death as a sacred companion rather than the antithesis of life. This passage also resonates with Anzaldúa's embrace of Coatlicue, the serpent-skirted goddess who represented life and death, creation and destruction, for the Aztecs.

Much like Rosi Braidotti's assertion that death is central to thinking about life (as I discuss in chapter 1), Anzaldúa takes death as the starting point, rather than the terminus, of her life story. Braidotti lists a number of ways in which a body's life "goes on" after death. On the material level, nails and hair presumably continue to grow along with a number of other organisms, like worms and insects, that are not indigenous to but parasitical upon the human body. And, more broadly, "'Life' in me will go on in the memories of others, in the multiple webs of interrelations and connections one built up in one's life" (Braidotti, *Transpositions* 239). There is a kind of vitalism in death itself, "a point in a creative synthesis of flows, energies, and becomings"; death "is neither the significant closure, nor the defining border of human existence" (235). Death is one of many ruptures in a life/ body, and it produces its own set of creative reactions. The lives that follow death in "La serpiente" are even more animated then these empirically based vitalities that Braidotti points out.

Perhaps Anzaldúa begins her memoir with death in order to distance her story and her self from the normative view of life as linear and constructive. Following the model of Coatlicue, life, for Anzaldúa, is continually interrupted by processes of destruction. At around the same time that she was writing "La serpiente," Anzaldúa was developing her theory of the Coatlicue state: a process in which we relinquish self-control and habitual ways of living. Like a therapeutic deconstruction, "those activities or *Coatlicue* states which disrupt the smooth flow (complacency) of life are exactly what propel the soul to do its work" (*Borderlands* 46, original emphasis). Anzaldúa describes her experience of Coatlicue states as a rearrangement of her self, a process in which pain meets pleasure and death meets new life.

Suddenly, I feel like I have another set of teeth in my mouth. A tremor goes through my body from my buttocks to the roof of my mouth. On my palate I feel a tingling sensation, then something seems to be falling on me, over me, a curtain of rain or light. Shock pulls my breath out of me. The sphincter muscle tugs itself up, up, and the heart in my cunt starts to beat. A light is all around me—so intense it could be white or black or at that juncture where extremes turn into their opposites. It passes through my body and comes out the other side. I collapse into myself—a delicious caving into myself—imploding, the walls like matchsticks softly folding inward in slow motion. (*Borderlands* 51)

The self here is completely dismantled and, ultimately, recomposed—"all the lost pieces of myself come flying from the deserts and the mountains and the valleys"—in a different form, a different species—"my thousand sleeping serpent eyes blinking in the night, forever open"—taking the serpent eyes from Coatlicue's association with snakes (51).[14]

The title of "La serpiente" is undoubtedly meant to invoke Coatlicue, and various kinds of Coatlicue states occur throughout it. Anzaldúa describes her experience as a young adult with a mass growing in her uterus as "weaving death" within her womb ("La serpiente" 111), casting the process of "abnormal" growth in terms of artistry rather than pathology. The infections resulting from this mass led to an eventual hysterectomy, which Anzaldúa writes about throughout her *obra*. In "La serpiente," she describes the operation as a reconfiguration of her "old self": "For her, the dismemberment meant a breaking up of the old patterns, the death of the old self that had gotten fat and complacent. Descent and pregnancy—two feminine mysteries that have spawned myths in every existent culture. But she had been pregnant with Death, not Life. She had had to create her own mysteries for man had long ago outlawed women's mysteries" (134). Like Halberstam, Anzaldúa focuses on rupturing descent with her hysterectomy, subverting the reproduction of the heteronormative family by giving birth to death, mystery, and "outlawed" progeny. Yet, unlike Halberstam's emphasis on negation, death is productive for Anzaldúa. Rather than re-creating the old "women's mysteries," she creates her own.

Anzaldúa writes that, according to her medical chart, her heart had stopped beating for twenty minutes during the surgery and she had stopped breathing for twelve, had even been declared dead ("La serpiente" 137). She follows this account with a seemingly irrational proposition: "People treat dying as a disease, an illness. Resurrection—it could be learned. Lots of people died and came back to life and didn't even remember. Dying was learning to navigate in another element—different from air or water"

(139). The idea that dying is "learning to navigate in another element" renders death as an expansion upon life, or an alternative way of living, rather than its opposite. Anzaldúa's proposition not only refigures death as temporary and reversible. It also reclaims death from its association with unwanted pathology: it is implicitly *not* to be "treat[ed] as a disease." Invoking death and resurrection, along with dismemberment and the cessation of heartbeat, reconfigures the perimeters of life in very literal terms. The image created by this passage doesn't abide by conventional interpretations of death, resurrection, or the elemental requirements for human life.

In a section of "La serpiente" that appears after the account of the surgery, entitled "Something Is Trying to Burst Out," Anzaldúa describes feeling a tightness in her abdomen: something "alien growing in me still" that had "escaped the surgeon's knife." "*It* is my legitimate self, the real me," she writes. "It wants to break through all the masks and defenses, all the *personas* I've put over its face because I thought I should be this particular or that particular person. All that energy I've used to pull the wool over other people's eyes was energy I ripped off from her" (163, original emphasis). Not only does this "it" become a "her," but Anzaldúa also ultimately assigns the feeling a proper name and engages it in dialogue:

Crampness, you there just under my ribcage, what *are* you? And it speaks: I am the feeling, the yearning, the hunger to experience other realities, the spiritual realms and psychic spaces. I feel limited to this physical world. I want to stretch into "other" worlds. You need to open your third chakra, release the "baby" growing in your middle. It's not in your belly anymore.

I feel something trying to get out. Someone trying to get out. I need something to hold me in, tight pants, tight belt. "Crampness, what are you?" I ask. "Not what but who am I, it replies." (164, original emphasis)

The identity of "Crampness" oscillates throughout these passages. Though Anzaldúa initially describes it as her "legitimate self, the real me," it is clearly not singular. It is "it," "her," and "you"; it's a "something" and a "someone"; it's a self with a voice as well as an immaterial substance (a "feeling," a "yearning," and a "hunger" to experience other worlds beyond the physical). It's a "baby growing in your middle" but also "not in your belly." It's both "alien" and "self." It is either an embodiment of contradiction or a shape-shifter that need not abide by the laws of physics or biology. All of this indeterminacy, all of this irrational reproduction, disorders the life and body of Anzaldúa's memoir.

As with Irene Vilar's two memoirs, sickness and death form the primary plotlines of "La serpiente," but neither meets with any (healthful or moribund) finality. One metaphor that reoccurs in surprising ways throughout Anzaldúa's narrative is soup. There are homey images, like Cherríe Moraga bringing her "fiery chicken soup" to kill a virus (211), but ambivalence dominates; even in the cliché of healing chicken soup there is fire. In another reference Anzaldúa compares her belly to a "cauldron where the food of past experience cooked to become sustenance for the spirit which would engender the new work," but "occasionally the process fucked up" and "the soup went sour, turned poisonous" (195). The soup ultimately resolves into a figure of ambivalence in itself: ". . . she would vomit the half digested soup, it would flow out of her mouth like a rainbow. And out of the nausea and the fever, poetry" (198). The resolution to the fever is poetry and a rainbow, but it is poetry made of vomit, fluid bits of the self.

In the final section of "La serpiente," entitled "El Mundo Zurdo: The Vision,"[15] Anzaldúa is searching for a way "to renew her burnt out soul, her exhausted crippled body" (268). But what she proposes as a form of renewal is not focused on healing in any conventional way: "The bonds of netweavings must be of flesh and blood a crisscrossing and cross roading of bone. Anything less than this would not suffice for her. El cuerpo publico [sic] con el cuerpo privado" (267). This description is not posed in terms of improvement or resolution (emphasized by the fact that it is written in the conditional tense). "Netweaving" flesh and blood, private and public, and "cross roading" bone imagine material body parts to be strands of a larger network, strands that can be manipulated and fused in creative ways. "Netweaving" sounds organic—recalling the activities of spiders or fishermen—while "cross roading" is harder to visualize. The crossroads—like the bridge—is an important metaphor, throughout Anzaldúa's work, for a place of mixture, connection, and ambivalence, but turning this image into a verb—or, more precisely, making "road" a verb—shifts the focus to making the structures of the world themselves mobile rather than the individual human that navigates these structures. "Roading" evokes not just movement and travel, but the construction of places that enable movement and travel, so "cross roading" bone would mean using the material body to make places of meeting in the world, reorganizing femurs and arm bones in such a way that the body becomes a vehicle for public transit.

Though this reorganization sounds painful, recalling Aurora Levins Morales reminds us of the ways in which our bodies are already wrought within networks with other beings, moving through organic and inorganic webs.

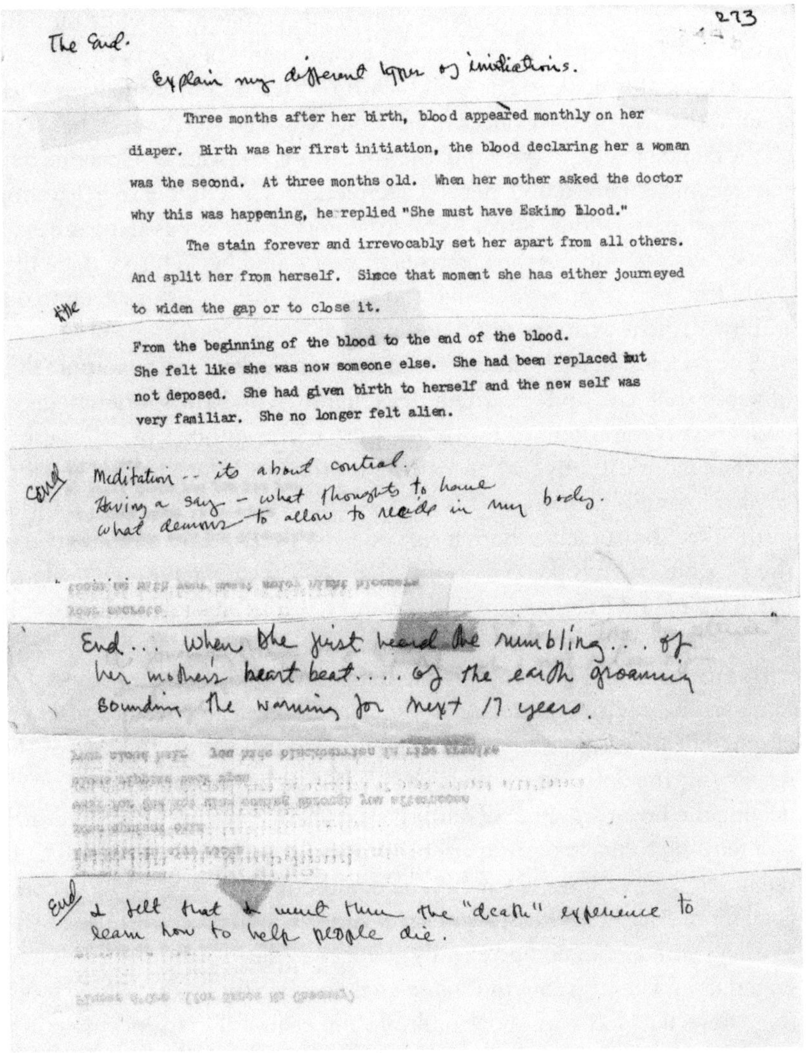

The End.

Explain my different types of initiations.

Three months after her birth, blood appeared monthly on her diaper. Birth was her first initiation, the blood declaring her a woman was the second. At three months old. When her mother asked the doctor why this was happening, he replied "She must have Eskimo blood."

The stain forever and irrevocably set her apart from all others. And split her from herself. Since that moment she has either journeyed to widen the gap or to close it.

From the beginning of the blood to the end of the blood.
She felt like she was now someone else. She had been replaced but not deposed. She had given birth to herself and the new self was very familiar. She no longer felt alien.

Meditation -- its about control.
Having a say - what thoughts to house
what demons to allow to reside in my body.

End... When she first heard the rumbling... of her mother's heart beat.... of the earth groaning sounding the warning for next 17 years.

End. I felt that I must thru the "death" experience to learn how to help people die.

FIGURE 4.1. Gloria Anzaldúa, "La serpiente que se come su cola" page 273.

Reorganizing the animacy of one self has effects that reverberate outward to others. "The Vision" incorporates the movements of an ecosystem: "She was writing this book so she could learn to breathe in through her open mouth, through all the orifices in her body, through the pores in her skin, so she could breathe in the wind, the air, the fire, the water—elements that had become estranged from her" ("La serpiente," 272). Rather than exerting agency as an individual force, Anzaldúa embraces agency as an openness, a porousness that inhales the elements that surround her. This vulnerability could lead us to a more inclusive and sensitive form of ethics: feeling our intertwinement with the world.

The conclusion to the memoir is literally unresolved, with multiple slips of paper that say "end" on them. (See figure 4.1.) How should memoirs end? Usually they don't end with the death of the author, since the author is presumably still alive when writing it (though Vilar's idea of suicides writing memoirs challenges this point). They also don't usually end with birth or feeling oneself unborn inside one's mother's pregnant body (two of the possible endings present on the final page of the manuscript). Blood, meditation, and helping others "learn how to . . . die" are other possible endings, all undead. It is likely that Anzaldúa did mean to finish this book with a "proper" conclusion, but she deferred completion of many of her manuscripts, revising and revising, sometimes even revising manuscripts after publication (as in the case of her story "Puddles"). In the case of "La serpiente," the deferred (or multipronged) conclusion seems appropriate, defying the linear structure of narratives, refusing to privilege life or death, and refusing to make one experience stand out with/as finality. Deferring publication also refuses to solidify the manuscript into any "correct" or official form. Anzaldúa's life story was still very much in process while she was writing this memoir, and it remains a process today, posthumously, as new materials and new interpretations emerge. It is like the "half digested soup" that "flows out" like a rainbow: multiple and beautiful in its incompletion.

Beyond Human Being

> Feminism's critique of man will not only transform humanity and its milieu but will open up a new thought of life.
>
> —Claire Colebrook, *Sex after Life* 9–10

What would this public/private, postdeath, transcorporeal life look like? The image of "cross roading" bone resonates with the Aztec moon goddess

Coyolxauhqui, whom Anzaldúa embraced later in her life as a model for rethinking human subjectivity and vulnerability. Coyolxauhqui, daughter of Coatlicue, was killed by Huitzilopochtli (her brother, the war god), decapitated and dismembered, the pieces of her body thrown into the sky to become the moon. A stone found at the Templo Mayor in Mexico concretizes her re-membered embodiment in a shape that has always reminded me of running. (See figure 4.2.) Life and death converge in this image that presents an alternative form of female wholeness, one that waxes and wanes as it runs through the sky. Not posthuman but outside the cultural-temporal framework of Humanism, not universal but explicitly female and particular to the histories and cultures of Mexico, Coyolxauhqui presents an alternative to Humanism with roots in Chicanx epistemology. "Let us be the healing of the wound," an essay Anzaldúa wrote in response to the September 11, 2001, terrorist attacks, develops the "Coyolxauhqui imperative" (building from her earlier model of the Coatlicue state) as a vision for reassembling the world in new shapes:

> Coyolxauhqui is my symbol for the necessary process of dismemberment and fragmentation, of seeing that self or the situations you're embroiled in differently. It is also my symbol for reconstruction and reframing, one that allows for putting the pieces together in a new way. The Coyolxauhqui imperative is an ongoing process of making and unmaking. There is never any resolution, just the process of healing. ("Let us be the healing" 100)

The fluidity of the moon, continually waxing and waning, models a state of permanent impermanence, "making and unmaking" without resolution or healing. As Felicity Amaya Schaeffer says of Anzaldúa's vision of Coyolxauhqui: "[T]he shrapnel pieces of the body literally and metaphorically shatter rational cognition, forcing us into other worlds, times, spaces, universes, and beings that splay open 'other alien perspective[s]'" (1016). The ideas of "splay[ing] open" our ways of seeing and "shatter[ing] rational cognition" perfectly capture the physical and mental vulnerability of Coyolxauhqui.

Coyolxauhqui's dismembered body—with its simultaneous fragmentation and mobility—resonates with insights from disability studies, though she is not conventionally disabled. She defies normative expectations for what a body must look like, but, as a mythic goddess figure whose lunar movements organize time and space on Earth, she is not exactly impaired. In my 2009 book, *Encarnación*, I focus at length on the relationship between Chicana feminist writing and disability studies and look to Coyolxauhqui as one example of premodern, indigenous corporeal sensibilities that embrace

FIGURE 4.2. Coyolxauhqui stone, Templo Mayor, Mexico City.
(Photograph by author)

permeability and pain as sacred ways of being. My argument about disability studies in *Encarnación* is that, in its relative lack of attention to cultural difference, the field is missing out on heterogeneous ways of valuing bodies and agency. Now, in the wake of ten years of posthumanist theorizing, new developments in disability studies, and access to Anzaldúa's archive, I would say that disability studies is not just too white: it is also too Humanist. Julie Avril Minich's *Accessible Citizenships: Disability, Nation, and the Cultural Politics of Greater Mexico* (2014) has helped to show how representations of disability in Chicanx art and literature expand identity beyond normative neoliberal individualism, and Robert McRuer's newest book, *Crip Times: Disability, Globalization, and Resistance* (2018), which I discuss below, makes similar moves in the context of European and Latin American disability art and activism. I would extend this expansion beyond the parameters of Enlightenment Humanism itself. Moving outside of Humanism—not just in her somewhat idealistic adaptations of Aztec cosmology but also in her imaginative visual and narrative speculations—enables Anzaldúa to challenge ideas that are hostile to disability, such as the false assumption that health and embodiment have natural and universal boundaries.

Valuing disability requires more expansive thinking about what counts as a viable life, resonant with the vision of "La serpiente que se come su cola."[16] People with disabilities sometimes see living in intimacy with death as a source of increased vitality and reject too easy an embrace of abortion or euthanasia as ways of negating lives deemed unlivable.[17] In one of her several memoir collections, A Troubled Guest: Life and Death Stories (2001), the late Nancy Mairs reflects on the likely proximity of her own death based on decades of living with multiple sclerosis. Throughout her work she emphasizes not just the physical degeneration but also the gifts and intimacies that come from living with her disability. In A Troubled Guest, she makes death central to life:

> Not merely our physical but our psychosocial selves rest in the reality that we don't have all the time in the world. We mold our fables into life's shape: beginning, middle, and end (death for tragedy, death deferred for comedy, but the reference point is the same). . . . Our relationships gain much of their piquancy from our awareness that every beloved is frail, imperfect, and subject to loss. . . . Death is what makes us who we are. (Mairs, A Troubled Guest 7)

Mairs's embrace of death, however, seems to be more about life than anything: death is valued to the extent that it shapes our lives. Indeed, many of the essays in A Troubled Guest end with uplifting messages, reflecting, for instance, on the homey proximity of Mairs's parents' ashes resting in boxes on her sideboard (redomesticated rather than entombed) and on the "sharpened" pleasure in her own grandsons that came with the untimely death of a friend's grandson (93, 113). I would suggest that this is not just looking "on the bright side" of death; it is understanding that we can't detach our feelings about life from death.

In stretching the boundaries of livable human life, many disability scholars, artists, and activists explicitly challenge the neoliberal (or neo-Humanist) expectations for self-reliant and productive individualism. McRuer's Crip Times advocates for "crip" sensibilities against neoliberal ones. According to McRuer, "[D]isability is currently not repressed but managed by neoliberal biopower," "domesticated" by questions of "identity, representation, and rights" (McRuer 36, 45). He critiques the ableist metaphors propagated by British "Thatcherism," such as the imperative for the children of the state to "grow tall" and compete in world markets; disability ethics demands images of other kinds of growth in order to reflect the true heterogeneity of corporeal development (188). McRuer turns to the earthwork of British performance artist Liz Crow, who made 650 small, squat clay figures out of brown river mud as part of her project entitled *Figures*:

> Each figure had a thick, crude base, wide enough so that it could be positioned upright without falling over. About three-quarters of the way from the bottom of the base, a slight indentation all around the figure suggested a neck, and two almost-but-not-quite identical cavities in the bulbous part of the figure of this "neck" suggested eyes in a head. (182)

McRuer analyzes these figures as hovering "somewhere between the 'natural' and the human-made" (182), but I would suggest that they challenge the very idea of the human. With a nod toward Jane Bennett's idea of "vibrant matter," I love McRuer's emphasis on the vitality of the figures' origins in the moving clay deposits of rivers (196), but he also describes the figures as nearly indistinguishable from "accidental" debris or even excrement (182). The tension between these two interpretations is what interests me most: what is radical about these "crip" figures is not just their challenge to normative human aesthetics but their indeterminacy on the boundary between vitality and excrement, valuable and nonvaluable being. Rather than aspiring to grow tall, these mud figures are mired in place. In distinguishing this vision from neoliberalism, McRuer writes:

> Our crip aspirations to totality, in contrast, are always necessarily, inescapably, disabled: attend to those who are not you, to those who are different from you (different embodiments, different minds, different behaviors), and attempt in that interdependent attending to apprehend the web of social relations in which we are currently located—social relations that can (of course) be figured, and that can (of course) be changed. (217)

McRuer's language of the web coincides exactly with my own thinking in *Shared Selves*. Crow's figures are about encounters with otherness—can we love a brown lump that resembles excrement?—and they also model the attachment between life and its ecosystems. These figures carry traces of the river (its water plus the incidental debris that flows with it) as well as of the longings and performances of their crip activist artist. They are ephemeral conglomerations rather than solo acts.

Crow's figures, Coyolxauhqui, and the incoherent images in "La serpiente" resonate with some of Anzaldúa's sketches that I found in the archive, all of which defy the Humanist logic of representation and identity. Anzaldúa was also a visual artist, and many of the drawings I found in her archive depict fantastical creatures: part human, part animal, part nonsense. She calls these drawings "doodles," a term I keep because it allows for lack of rigor and imaginative freedom. She probably did not intend the doodles I analyze here to be made public, but they provide evidence of the ways in which she used the visual to clarify some of her more abstract ideas. Her use of figure drawing is like her use of memoir: taking up a form associated with depictions of an individual and moving within and against those expectations. Some of these drawings seem inspired by the figure of Coyolxauhqui, but, unlike Coyolxauhqui, whose waxing and waning follow a set script, these playful doodles abandon all formal regularity. In an untitled sketch from 1977, a figure is emerging from, but still embedded in, an abstract background. (See figure 4.3.) The head and torso look human, but it is not clear how many arms the figure has, and there is no distinguishable body below the torso. One of the arms holds something that looks like a mask, on a string? It is not clear where the body ends and the background begins in the lower half of the drawing. Is there a curly tail in the middle? It's also not clear what exactly undergirds the figure: chair? animal? toilet? The curved shapes and parallel lines in the lower half are echoed in the figure, which suggests dialogue between figure and background. These lines and curves also suggest fluidity and movement (resonant with Coyolxauhqui). I see this as an image of environmental being (another insight from disability studies): the possibilities for individual thriving are found in the body's surrounding (physical and social) structures. Figure 4.3 incorporates elements from outside, injects elements into the outside, and moves in dialogue with the outside. There is no determinate form and no coherent story here (at least not one I can see!). This image literally trans-shapes (to use another Anzaldúan term) every shape within it and allows for many different stories to be told. It disrupts any one interpretation we might offer, at the same time that it provokes and invites interpretation. Another doodle is ambiguous in both its title—probably "Two Fishy Cats" but it could be "Fishy Two Cats"—and shape—conjoined animals that don't look like either fish or cat. (See figure 4.4.) But it does make us think about corporeal blending, species demarcation, and the possibilities of imagined creatures.

Though critics often don't see (or pretend not to see) the mystical and irrational elements of Anzaldúa's theories of mestiza consciousness and the borderlands, it is impossible to miss these elements in her visual art. A prospective title page I found in the archive, "Poems and Doodles by Gloria

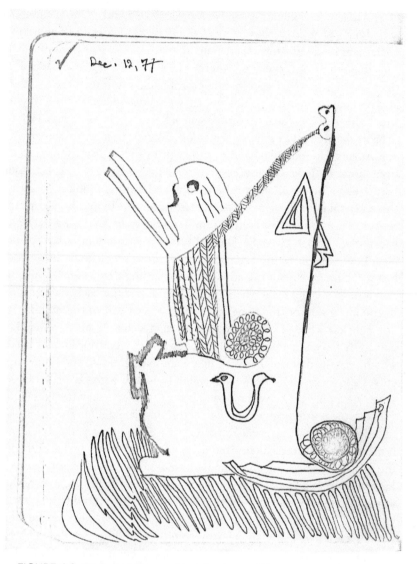

FIGURE 4.3. Gloria Anzaldúa, untitled sketch dated Dec. 12, 1977. (© by Gloria Anzaldúa and The Gloria E. Anzaldúa Literary Trust. By permission of Stuart Bernstein Representation for Artists, New York, NY, and protected by the copyright laws of the United States. All rights reserved. The printing, copying, redistribution, or retransmission of this content without express permission is prohibited.)

FIGURE 4.4. Gloria Anzaldúa, "Two Fishy Cats." (© by Gloria Anzaldúa and The Gloria E. Anzaldúa Literary Trust. By permission of Stuart Bernstein Representation for Artists, New York, NY, and protected by the copyright laws of the United States. All rights reserved. The printing, copying, redistribution, or retransmission of this content without express permission is prohibited.)

Anzaldúa," suggests that she wanted to link the work of the visual and the verbal. (See figure 4.5.) Though Anzaldúa's writing pushes against linguistic and generic conventions, using language is, in itself, is an exercise of human rationalism and cultural convention. The images, however, supplement our limited imaginations with shapes literally unknown, shapes that cannot be glossed over or translated into anything familiar. The doodle on the title page inserts what seem to be faces into a nonrepresentational maze, but it also makes us wonder how we recognize a face as such. How do we know that these are faces? They are all different shapes, so why do we put them into any single category? Is it because they seem to have eyes? But what makes us think they are eyes? (The dots in the apparent faces don't all come in twos.) How do we know which is figure and which is background, since the boundaries of each curve around the other? And were we even thinking about species? We have to jettison our normative frameworks in order to experience what this image has to offer.

Another doodle from the archive has a similar mazelike pattern with words embedded within and around it. (See figure 4.6.) The shapes tempt us to compare them to familiar terms and objects (like brains, titles, and calendars), but they are beyond recognition. We might assume that W. stands for "Wednesday" because it appears above "7:30." But it also appears next to a 4 and a letter I don't recognize and below "Home Girls" (which could be a reference to Barbara Smith's 1983 edited collection published by Kitchen Table Press or could be something else). The butterfly-like image at the bottom defies symmetry with "Wed" in one wing and "Thur" in another, and the small head with catlike ears has what looks like an "M" inside it rather than anything resembling a cat face. Perhaps the clearest and most resonant point in this drawing is "caramba"—surprise, exasperation, or wonder. Wow: what do we have here, and what assumptions are we bringing to it?

In looking at abstract visual images, it is customary to try to find a figure, to discern a plotline. These doodles were found among Anzaldúa's writings, and one could probably come up with plausible connections between the drawings and her life. They invoke enough of the human to lure us into these sorts of interpretive moves, but they so insistently thwart Humanist interpretation that they force us to reexamine our suppositions. These images ask us to jettison our expectation that a figure (human, animal, or plant) should be at the center of our epistemologies or our ontologies; we can think and be without "man" (recalling my epigraph to this section from Colebrook).

Poems and Doodles

by

Gloria Anzaldua

FIGURE 4.5. Gloria Anzaldúa, "Poems and Doodles by Gloria Anzaldúa." (©
by Gloria Anzaldúa and The Gloria E. Anzaldúa Literary Trust. By permission
of Stuart Bernstein Representation for Artists, New York, NY, and protected
by the copyright laws of the United States. All rights reserved. The printing,
copying, redistribution, or retransmission of this content without express
permission is prohibited.)

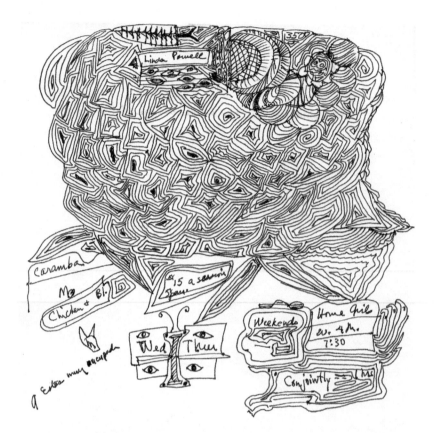

FIGURE 4.6. Gloria Anzaldúa, untitled sketch. (© by Gloria Anzaldúa and The
Gloria E. Anzaldúa Literary Trust. By permission of Stuart Bernstein Representation
for Artists, New York, NY, and protected by the copyright laws of the United States.
All rights reserved. The printing, copying, redistribution, or retransmission of this
content without express permission is prohibited.)

In her call for a truly posthuman posthumanism, Colebrook suggests that feminists need to question not just the male subject at the heart of Humanism but the ways in which life under Humanism has been configured around human thriving. (One should extrapolate from this that questioning any dominant identity under Humanism, like white or able-bodied people, would not be sufficient either.) As Colebrook speculates: "[T]he very question that enabled women to challenge the rights of men, will lead to a full-scale destruction of any assumed right whatsoever. . . . Feminism's critique of man will not only transform humanity and its milieu but will open up a new thought of life" (Colebrook, *Sex after Life* 9–10). Colebrook notes the turn to life in general (versus gender, race, or species) in ecofeminism and concludes that "what needs to be thought today is that which cannot be thought, lived, retrieved, or revitalized as the saving grace of man or woman" (17). I would argue that Anzaldúa's archival doodles enact just this sort of "thought experiment" that Colebrook would call for ten years after Anzaldúa's death. Although one might be inclined to read these images as derivations of the human figure, they not only resist being pinned down by one life form but lead us to question the reductionism of finding a figure in the drawing. And, importantly, these are not images of destruction or negation; they enact multiplication rather than cessation. I could find nine or ten eyes in figure 4.5 and two heads in figure 4.4, but why? Why reduce these compilations of forms to individuated human (or animal) figures? Indeed, one might ask these same questions about "La serpiente que se come su cola." Though its designation "autocanción" does cue readers to look for self-reference, the life at the "center" of this narrative challenges our assumptions about what constitutes a life.

Imagination is an important tool for Anzaldúa in her attempts to probe the limits of human life.[18] In the memoir, she uses imagination to challenge the narrative forms of human life; in the doodles, she challenges its visual coherence or recognizability. In this way, she prefigures Donna Haraway's assertion, in 2016, that "If there is to be multispecies ecojustice, which can also embrace diverse human people, it is high time that feminists exercise leadership in imagination, theory, and action to unravel the ties of both genealogy and kin, and kin and species" (*Staying with the Trouble* 102). In her undefended doctoral dissertation, Anzaldúa discusses imagination as a creative force that generates life forms: "The imaginal's figures and landscapes are experienced as alive and separate from the dreamer" (*Light in the Dark* 36). Works of the imagination are not therefore "fantasy, not reality"; rather, "we must redefine the imagination not as a marginal nonreality nor as an altered state, but as another type of reality" (37). The works of one's imagination help to create the reality one lives in; they give form to our feelings and mold our perceptions. Creating alternative life forms requires us to suspend not only our disbelief (in the "reality" of imagination) but also our belief in the reality we perceive ourselves as inhabiting: "To change or reinvent reality, you engage the facultad of your imagination. You must interrupt or suspend the conscious 'I' that reminds you of your history and beliefs because these reminders tie you to certain notions of reality and behavior. . . . We must empower the imagination to blur and transcend customary frameworks and conceptual categories reinforced by language and consensual reality" (44–45). If reality is "consensual," it is continually being enacted and configured by all of its participants (human and nonhuman). Choosing to alter one's relationship to reality would challenge those with whom one shares the world to shift in response. If we believe, for instance, that there is a spike in violent crime in our city, we will react out of fear, avoiding contact with others and thereby creating disconnections and hostilities. If we believe that our world is a safe place, we will approach all that we touch with greater sensitivity and openness. If we open our imaginations to other modes of relating, our relationships will change—as will the entities with which we relate.

As AnaLouise Keating writes in her 2012 essay on Anzaldúa's "poet-shaman aesthetics,"

> While it might seem to be common sense to dismiss this discussion as "simply" metaphoric and thus limited exclusively to the power of disembodied, intangible words, to do so overlooks the possibility that language's causal power can provoke additional material levels of transformation. According to Anzaldúa, these linguistic images, when internalized, can trigger the imagination, which then affects our embodied state—our physical bodies—at the cellular level. ("Speculative Realism" 53)

Keating derives her argument from indigenous theories of the causality of language (theories with which Anzaldúa was familiar), and she describes writing and reading as enacting a form of alchemy, citing her own experiences of transformation in response to reading Anzaldúa's work (59). These experiences are difficult to measure, too personal to be objective, and they challenge the bounds of rational academic discourse. And this is precisely what Anzaldúa wants to do: to make us question the limits we impose upon knowledge and upon life (our own and that of our entire ecosystem). She is able to do this by looking forward—to unseen horizons—as well as looking back to traditions that predate Humanism.

Animals and Reimagined Kinship

> Anzaldúa locates in the queer interface the promise of a future uncontained in the repertoire of present possibilities. This "bridging" of entities, their hybridization, enables an evolutionary deformation of current existence and a becoming-other of what is presently available.
>
> —Mikko Tuhkanen, "Mestiza Metaphysics" 271

One of the more "practical" outcomes of this rethinking of human life is that it leads us to reimagine the kinds of relationships we form in the world. Though we might not actually experience states of shape-shifting or boundarylessness, perhaps we should practice our relations with others as if we did. Returning to the work of Mel Chen, replacing our perception of human subjects with an ontologically diverse field of animacy shifts the basis of our interactions with others: "In its more sensitive figurations, animacy has the capacity to rewrite conditions of intimacy, engendering different communalisms and revising biopolitical spheres, or, at least, how we might theorize them" (Chen 3). In this section I focus on forms of engagement (intimacy, community, and kinship) that emerge from the imaginative ontologies I discussed above.

In the acknowledgments to "La serpiente," Anzaldúa thanks not only friends but also Macey the cat, books (including the I Ching), and places, saying, "All these flesh and paper friends caused earthquakes in my psyche and have been catalysts for my growth in one way or another" ("La serpiente" v). The memoir thus opens with the agency of animals and paper (indeed, imagines a sort of equality among these by putting "flesh and paper" into the same category of "friends"); it also provides a vision of the human self as an ecology subject to reorganization by outside influences. The earthquakes in her psyche caused by relations with others are not viewed as disasters but as catalysts for growth, presumably growth of imagination as well as extension of self through others.

Anzaldúa addresses her relationship with animals explicitly throughout "La serpiente." She explains that she used to fear horses' "wildness" until she learned to ride them (180). "Wildness" implies an otherness, the uncircumscribed difference of animals from humans, but riding them makes them domestic, converts them from wildness to human vehicle. There is also a poem in "La serpiente," "El tigre," that resists domesticating this wildness:

Me voy a volver tigre	[I am going to come back as/ return to being tiger]
voy a correr por los bosques	[I am going to run through the woodlands]
y las selvas hullendo a la luna	[and the jungles fleeing by the moon]
en la media noche. Ese tigre soy yo	[in the middle of the night. I am this tiger]
y lo que yo soy yo le tengo miedo.	[and that which I am I fear] (180, my translation)

Even as the speaker blends with the tiger here, the tiger remains a thing to fear, along with the speaker herself. The use of the verb "volver" [to return] implies that tiger is a habitual, or at least a previously inhabited, form. Rather that engaging the animal in a Humanist act of domestication, this poem engages the human in an expansive act of wilding. A similar sentiment emerges in the next section of the memoir:

She was not as she appeared to be to others. She was the wolf in the woods, the vulture circling overhead. She was the hemlock pine, the wood wind and the night. Beneath the human mask was the animal face and under the animal was the "thing," the non-human face. And she was terrified of that third face. . . . The only way not to fear the non-human world was to embrace the non-human in herself. If she let her being flow into the white pine and the spider and the night wind and if she allowed their spirits to come into her, then nothing supernatural could harm her for she too would be supernatural. (182)

This blending between self and wild(er)ness is presented as a form of safety. Reconfiguring the human to include the nonhuman removes the barrier between the self and the "thing" and positions various forms of animacy in a field of horizontal equality. There is no supernatural power over the human because the human, too, is supernatural. The ethical conclusions of this sentiment are wonderful, but this blending is generally demonized in modern cultures, regarded as madness. Embracing such madness places Anzaldúa's worldview distinctly outside of rational political discourse.

Although Anzaldúa's desire to blur national and cultural borders has been embraced by many involved in Chicanx studies and Chicanx activism, her trans-species boundary crossings are not so readily embraced. Toward the end of "El serpiente," Anzaldúa worries about her ability to live up to the ideal envisioned by Chicano politics: "For all that animality made her a grotesque person, the sweat and the bleeding and the shitting. She was so organic so connected with the processes of nature how could she become a cosmic person as the Chicano is supposed to be la raza cosmica [sic] when the forces inside her were polarized and paralysed" (219). In Anzaldúa's account, the mestiza ideal borrowed from José Vasconcelos's *La raza cósmica* (1925) must be disembodied, while Anzaldúa/Prieta in "La serpiente" is connected to "processes of nature"—shit, blood, and sweat, corporeal elements often deemed "animal" and grotesque.

What does "animality" represent in these passages? There is clearly a symbolic element to the animal as the undomesticated and organic other, but what would it mean to read these engagements with animals literally, too? For Haraway, rather than humanizing animals, it is important that we recognize their "'otherworldly' subject status" to learn about the "radical otherness at the heart of relating" (*Haraway Reader* 143). Part of the appeal of companion species for Haraway is the ways in which beings whose language and subjectivity are completely unlike each other (as in the case of dogs and humans) maintain mutual and constructive relationships across this gap of incomprehension. In this light, being "animal" is not just a matter of being less "civilized" but of being *other*worldly or engaging with worlds differently. For Cary Wolfe,

> [T]he full force of animal studies—what makes it not just another flavor of "fill in the blank" studies on the model of media studies, film studies, women's studies, ethnic studies, and so on—is that it fundamentally unsettles and reconfigures the question of the knowing subject and the disciplinary paradigms and procedures that take for granted its form and reproduce it. (Wolfe, *What Is Posthumanism?* xxix)

While I might object to this apparently dismissive attitude toward women's studies and ethnic studies (which certainly do take on fundamental questions of subjectivity and Humanism), it is worth noting Wolfe's implication that animals are somehow *more* other than these others, fundamentally disruptive to conventional ways of thinking. Animals, for Wolfe, further challenge "the liberal justice tradition and its central concept of rights, in which ethical standing and civic inclusion are predicated on rationality, autonomy, and agency" (127). Based on this argument, Wolfe sees animal studies and disability studies as allied (posthumanist) critical approaches. By claiming that she is an animal, Anzaldúa steps outside this liberal Humanist tradition herself and faces us with embodied otherness that is difficult to process within our accustomed perceptions of agency and selfhood. (I would add that this other-than-human orientation is allied not just with animals or disability but also with the insights of feminism, queerness, and ethnicity, whose critical value Wolfe undervalues.)

In an interview with AnaLouise Keating in 1999, for instance, Anzaldúa discussed her experiences shape-shifting into animal forms: when she's "trancing," she becomes her totem animal, a jaguar, a serpent, or an eagle looking down at the ground from above (*Interviews* 284). When Keating asked how literal she was about these transhuman embodiments, Anzaldúa explained that a second or third body can leave the physical body to become a jaguar, can even lose the flesh-and-blood body and "stay in the jaguar reality, in the jaguar form" (284). The implications of these propositions are tremendous, laying the foundation for a radically expansive understanding of the self, corporeality, and reality. Even if there isn't literally a parallel animal universe, Anzaldúa asks us to believe that tapping into jaguar ontology gives her access to other ways of perceiving and being in the world.

She fleshes out some of these alternative visions in her extensive body of fiction, most of which is unpublished and can be found in the archive. Since we are accustomed to speculation in fiction, other worlds are more easily digested there than they might be in memoir, where we expect the content to conform to empirical "data" about the author herself.[19] "Werejaguar" is an unpublished story Anzaldúa was likely working on up to her death.[20] The most recent draft in the archive is a version sent to Keating in June of 2002, titled "La Werejaguar in the Woods of the Dream—9." In this story, Prieta is the heroine, and she has an encounter with a jaguar that challenges the boundaries between human, animal, and environment. The other central human in the story is Prieta's cousin Teté; the two primos, lesbian and gay man, are roommates, described as "kissing cousins" ("Werejaguar" 5). Teté is a "cyber vato," searching for "digital love" online, but he also jokes about being Prieta's "wife" (with the masculinity of the slang term "vato" conflicting with the presumed femininity of "wife"). This queerness pushes at the conventional forms of family, gay and straight.

The jaguar first appears as a vision in a dream, with a "musty cat smell" and the face of a woman (2), but ultimately leaps out of the dream and into "this world," "bring[ing] the wild with it, the woods and everything" (4). Prieta later tells Teté, "'I think the jaguar represents a disruptive force beyond human control'" (7). This claim captures the material and intellectual eruption that the jaguar presents in this story; it is a force beyond reason that challenges Prieta's perceptions of reality and ultimately transforms both individuality and kinship, including her relationship with Teté. The jaguar appears in boundary states where dream and reality meet. (These states, interestingly, seem to be triggered by both housecleaning and erotic fantasies.) In one instance, while vacuuming, Prieta oscillates between the dream world and her housecleaning until the jaguar draws her into the woods, taking her across a portal where the material boundaries between things begin to blur: her hair catches in the trees, and the ground loses its solidity beneath her when "leaves in various stages of decay give under her feet como un piso hueco" (11). When she tells her primo about this experience, he warns her, "'Prietita Linda, it's dangerous to walk in two realities'" (12). Dangerous walking, to be sure.

A subsequent excursion with the jaguar occurs when Prieta is lying on the couch, her breasts becoming aroused as she feels a jaguar licking her hand (16–17). Looking out the window moves her in space (and, apparently, in time) to a small village where the jaguar paces, waiting for her. Prieta follows her until she gets tangled up in some low-lying braches. She then feels her body expanding, assuming the size and shape of a tree. The limbs of the tree become the nerves in her body, and she keeps expanding until she is filled with the woods (18). Teté warns her, perhaps jealously, "'You're getting carried away with this nostalgia for mythical indigenous origins'" (20), invoking the pre-Humanist sensibility of indigenous shamanism and the interrelationship of human and nonhuman nature. Prieta even conducts research about Olmec nagualism to help her to understand her experience, suggesting that perhaps shape-shifting includes assuming the forms of not just nonhuman animals but trees, too (9).[21]

Prieta's relations with the jaguar become increasingly sexual, with detailed descriptions of whiskers on lips and fur touching human buttocks (20).[22] Toward the end of the story, when Prieta is in bed, in a dreamlike state, the jaguar leaps through the window, sinks her teeth into Prieta's flesh, and licks her "donde quiera" with her "incredibly long tongue" (23). "You want to feed on me, don't you?" Prieta asks, and the cat "growls" in response, "let's **both** be the beast" (23, original boldface). Eroticism here blends fear and pleasure, sex and destruction. It also fuses allo- and auto-eroticism by blending both animals (human and non-) into a singular beast. Upon waking, Prieta finds orange hairs and scratches in her bed, whisker marks on her own face (23–25). She explains, "There's even a word for her kind, therianthrope, a being that is part animal and part human," but it's not clear which "her" she means: jaguar, Prieta, or both of them fused.[23] "'Now that's giving hybridity a new spin,'" Teté tells her; "'I wonder how Chicana high theorists would theorize that'" (26–27). This self-reflexive jab at Chicana theory highlights the ways in which Anzaldúa is pushing beyond her celebrated ideas of the borderlands and mestiza consciousness. Does the werejaguar push trans identities too far beyond reason to have utility in the real world?

I would argue that a clear ethical vision follows from "Werejaguar," one that reminds us of our responsibilities to nonhuman nature and of our responsibility not to repeat the violence of the past. When Teté tells Prieta "'you're supposed to slay the beast, not get seduced by her'" (16), we see Anzaldúa reaching for a new script for animal–human relations. The jaguar in Anzaldúa's story is disconnected from the militarism and blood sacrifice associated with Aztec jaguars (and sometimes adopted by Chicano nationalists in their invocation of the Aztec warrior as a model of resistance to Anglocentrism). Anzaldúa's jaguar is associated, instead, with desire. And desire in "Werejaguar" is truly polymorphous, imagining modes of sexuality with powerful feminist and queer potential. (Challenging prohibitions against cross-species sexuality also resonates with efforts to undo the stigma surrounding disabled sex.)

Beyond her attachment to the jaguar, throughout the story, Prieta also has an erotic attachment to Teté, calling him "mi amor" and fingering his private parts. This relationship challenges the incest taboo as well as the gender binary, taking it outside hetero- *and* homoerotic norms. As the story progresses, Teté becomes jealous of the jaguar, resists its intrusion upon their queer domesticity. Prieta assures him, "'You're not going to lose me. I'll still be here. And you'll be here. The only difference is that there'll be a third addition to our happy home'" (25). Ultimately, Prieta gives birth to a baby with a cleft forehead, tiny incisors, and jaguar eyes. In the end, she, Teté, and the werejaguar child enter the wilderness in a literal and metaphorical way.

The branches of the trees enter her body, become her bones. Awareness of the woods, the sounds of the rustle of leaves and of the scurrying of animalitos flows through her, like a river leaves her open. Teté follows holding the were-jaguar child in his arms. The light shining through the misty rain polarizes into hundreds of tiny rainbows. Prieta llama al jaguar. As the three pass under the arc of trees [sic] branches, they step out of time. (27–28)

This idyllic resolution is, despite being located in the woods, implicitly domestic as the "family" is contained by an arc of trees, the idea of a "happy home," and the blessings of rainbows (an iconic symbol for queer family).[24]

But the jaguar lover is still out there, somewhere in the woods, a third "parent" to the mixed-species child. Teté asks "'What good does it do you to have a wife in the woods? Will she help you to keep house, be here when you need her?'" Prieta replies: "'I don't think I could tolerate a full-time lover—know I need my space. A lover in the woods. And you here,' Prieta says. 'Now that would work.'" Teté's response to the proposition that he share Prieta "with a part time lover who's a spirit cat from a mythic time" is "'Can't get queerer than that. Maybe we'll set a presidence [sic] for the new alternative family'" (27). This challenging kinship defies the assimilationism of "gay marriage" and "gay family" by including members within and without of the house, within and without of the wilderness, within and without of reality, and within and without of biological bloodlines. Indeed, the bloodline connections here are the ones that would be deemed the most perverse (illegal, in fact, in the contemporary United States): the cross-species embodiment of the baby and the incestuous "marriage" of Prieta and Teté. Perhaps this is why they must step outside of time at the end of the story, refusing domestication within that reality.

Kinship is the system that has conventionally trapped women in roles of heteronormative subservience, subjecting them to the positions of mother and wife and alienating them from the productivity of their own bodies. This is why kinship has been a central component of Donna Haraway's feminist challenge since her earliest publications, just as family has been central to Anzaldúa's elaborations of race, class, gender, and sexuality since the 1980s. In *Staying with the Trouble*, one of Haraway's mottos is "make kin, not babies!"—emphasizing "something other/more than entities tied by ancestry or genealogy" (*Staying with the Trouble* 102–03). For Haraway, "kin is an assembling sort of word," a term that includes "stretch and recomposition." Rather than privileging the implications of sameness and heredity embedded within reproduction, Haraway argues that "kin are unfamiliar (outside what we thought was family or gens), uncanny, haunting, active," and incorporating this difference within our kinship involves "being part of increasing well-being for diverse human beings and other critters" (103). (This view of kinship, I would add, might allow Halberstam to sidestep their injunction to "lose" the mother.) "Werejaguar" expands kinship to include nonhuman animals and trees, to cross beyond single time periods, and to bring together "real" beings with those that emerge from the alternative realities of dreams and fantasies.

In Anzaldúa's other, more autobiographical, writings (especially "La Prieta" and *Borderlands*), we see her family disparaging her for being dark-skinned, forcing her to conceal her early menstruation, calling her a "throw-back" to native ancestors, and refusing to accept queer sexuality. But the imagined kinship produced in "Werejaguar" does not lead to these critical judgments, building family through difference rather than resemblance, boundary-breaking rather than obedience, recomposition rather than heredity. The genre of "Werejaguar" allows Anzaldúa to create speculative relations that don't fit so easily into her memoir (where shape-shifting and eroticism are linked to pathology, shame, pain, intoxication, and abandonment). The framework of fantasy rather than autobiographical realism allows her to imagine ways of being that do not abide by species divisions, time divisions, or the requirements of empiricism.

Behind the "outside of time" quality to the queer family Anzaldúa invents is a distinct way of relating. The rainbows that follow Prieta, Teté, and the werejaguar baby are not just an obvious symbol for LGBTQ pride; they are literally a product of diffraction. Anzaldúa's theory of "yoga of the body," which she describes in a 1983 interview with Christine Weiland, similarly imagines that one could open up the cells of the body and expand, ultimately recomposing the molecules to overcome barriers to mobility: "If I could expand, open up my cells and expand them, I'd go through this wall because there would be nothing. The molecules in my body would be flexible enough for me to go through the wall. It's like watching Star Trek when they energize; they decompose the molecules and recompose them in the place that they want to be. . . . I believe this can happen by doing yoga of the body" (*Interviews* 99). What "Werejaguar" does to bodies, families, species, and sexualities is like diffraction or *Star Trek* "energizing." Prieta recomposes herself in other worlds and creates new beings in the process.

Ontology and Ethics

What is the cost of kinship, of category making
and unmaking, and for whom? The content
of any obligation is dependent on the thick
and dynamic particularities of relationships-in-
progress, that is, of kin and kind. The common
matrix for these diverse claims on us is an ethics
of flourishing.

—Donna Haraway, *When Species Meet* 134

This epigraph from Haraway joins making and unmaking as part of the process of kinship. What kin and kind share in their relationships is an "ethics of flourishing." Flourishing is not, however, just on the side of life. Plagues can flourish. Cancer cells flourish to the benefit of the tumor and the detriment of the host. Flourishing is active, forceful, agentic, but not individual. It is an effect of the unequal relations of growth and decay within an entire ecosystem. Anzaldúa's work helps us to imagine how to think ethically within an other-than-Humanist framework. By taking seriously a variety of kinds of flourishing, her work queers hierarchies of race, gender, nation, ability, and species. She requires us to rethink not just kinship but also ontology and relation.

The writing of self as/in relation is extended by the use of the second person in Anzaldúa's 2002 essay "now let us shift," where she both addresses herself from outside ("you've chosen to compose a new history and a self . . . ") and forces readers to walk in her shoes ("you walk across lighthouse field . . .") ("now let us shift" 540, 558). There is an ethical dimension to this second-person interface: looking at oneself through the eyes of others and sharing points of view. There is also a certain amount of discomfort in being lead through not just the second-person protagonist's growing spiritual activism but also her experiences of diabetes, mugging, earthquake, and a number of out-of-body experiences. Yet I don't think this relational self is simply a way of engaging readers. It is based on Anzaldúa's insistence that we are intertwined with the other beings with whom we share our world: "Your identity has roots you share with all people and other beings—spirit, feeling, and body make up a greater identity category. The body is rooted in the earth, la tierra itself. You meet ensoulment in trees, in woods, in streams. The roots del árbol de la vida of all planetary beings are nature, soul, body" (560). She develops a theory called "new tribalism" out of this commonality between the different entities in our ecosystem.[25] We inhale and exhale the same air as the trees and animals around us. We leave traces of ourselves (like skin, hair, sweat, ideas, and prints) on all that we encounter. Our bodies and movements emerge within and shape the material context that shapes us (recalling Stacy Alaimo's theory of "transcorporeality," which I discussed in chapter 3). These phenomena show how community and environment carve our very bone.

In an essay about "decolonizing the heart" through indigenous understandings of spirituality, Laura E. Pérez reaches a similar conclusion, but focuses on an idealized transcorporeality with more friendly-seeming life forms:

> Based on the spiritually discerned understanding of the nature of the interrelationship of all planetary life forms, nonviolent being performs not as repetition of the status quo, nor only as disidentification with dominant, oppressive orders, but as identification, as reharmonization with respect to a different, wilder, undomesticated, natural, lush, rich, plural, multiple, transformative, continually hybridizing and interconnected reality. (Pérez 29)

It's worth noting that this inclusive ontology of interconnectedness, according to Pérez, is based not only on "disidentification" with the dominant but also on an expansive identification—in the affirmative—with "different, wilder, undomesticated" stuff. Mikko Tuhkanen similarly locates a "metaphysics of interconnectedness" in Anzaldúa's work, which, as he describes it, "assumes an ontological approach that sits uncomfortably with our dominant epistemological paradigms. Anzaldúa's queer throwbacks and monsters cannot be done justice from the epistemological perspective of the Butlerian theory of power and performativity" ("Ontology and Involution" 43).[26] One of Tuhkanen's primary points is that the involution of unrealized pasts within the present, the resurgence of "resources once abandoned for their dangers and consequently unactualized," are not Butlerian citations of existing discourses (escaping the seeming fatalism of Judith Butler's early work). These "unactualized" possibilities—like the premodern goddesses and monsters in Anzaldúa's work—have the power to help us think with radically different tools about the present and the future.[27]

It seems relatively easy to imagine (if not so easy to live out) an ethics built upon shared substance: if we share substance with other beings, we must respect them. Tuhkanen would call this a "hemophilial ethics," an affection between blood relations that he describes in a later essay ("Mestiza Metaphysics" 273). Yet Anzaldúa's new tribalism goes beyond blood and kin to include entities that are bloodless and conventionally regarded as inanimate (like rocks and streams). Though Tuhkanen does remark on the "increasing deprioritization of *the human* in Anzaldúa's ethics" (279, original emphasis), he doesn't follow up with any specifics or explain how the participation of the nonhuman (or alternate animacies, to recall Chen) could fit within an ethics based on such Humanist notions as affection and blood relation. It is less easy to imagine an ethics based upon shape-shifting, kinship with trees, and the intertwinement of life and death. These literally and figuratively incoherent beings do what Anzaldúa calls for in "now let us shift": they "pick holes in the paradigms currently constructing reality" (560).

What is it like to find holes in one's reality? What does it mean to share blood with trees? To die and live and die again? Anzaldúa's work has consistently asked us to embrace seemingly irrational states (like the Coatlicue state or the Coyolxauhqui imperative).[28] By orienting her memoir toward illness, pain, and death, she is likewise positing intimacy with alienation as the defining feature of (her) life. This might evoke terror in some, but we could also view vulnerability as establishing the "groundwork" for posthumanist/disability/queer/ecofeminist ethics. If being implies permeation, our selves should tend toward uncertainty and otherness as much as harmonious relation. Anzaldúa's encounters with illness subjected her body to surgical knives, medications, vomiting, the love of friends, and soup—each of which re-formed her body in distinct ways, just as she re-formed them (turning soup into vomit, for instance, or vomit into poetry). This life lesson isn't necessarily comforting, but it seems to me to be more realistic (and more necessary) than the idea of an autonomous human subject dictating anthropocentric terms for ethical action.

Many of the posthumanist ethics I've seen have trouble accounting for power differentials and histories of oppression (since power and oppression are usually attached to human actions and human agency). Karen Barad's intra-active ethics, for example, revolve around "apparatuses" in the most general terms (versus people, animals, toxins, or ideologies), and her "agential cut" seems like a universal aspect of every apparatus in every phenomenon (in a deliberately nonspecified sense), as in: "the apparatus specifies an agential cut that enacts a resolution (within the phenomenon) of the semantic, as well as ontic, indeterminacy" (Barad 148). How do we account for the disproportionate influence of humans without returning humans to the center of our ethics? I think Anzaldúa sidesteps this question by appealing to premodern, other-than-human, and mystical foundations—epistemologies in which the human was not (yet) reified as a singular, superior, and overpowering actor and in which all life included gradations of death. Are these other-than-Humanist ontologies accurate ways of accounting for our interrelatedness, or are they imaginative ideals? I would say that it does not matter. Anzaldúa invites us to value ethics over empiricism and to open our minds to ways of being that move beyond the competitive, defensive human we have been taught to prioritize. Letting go of life, health, and personal boundaries is a threat to the tenets of Humanism but not a threat to life itself. Life goes on beyond the human. If we imagine ourselves to be a "two fishy cats" or a werejaguar, we are clearly involved in other-than-Humanist kinships. But even if we simply open our eyes to the being around us, we will likely notice relations we are already embroiled in, relations in which power and agency matter but are not necessarily human. Rather than love or hate (Humanist terms), relations would proceed through sentient and transformative encounters with difference.

> She wanted to re-connect her bonds of kinship with all life. She wanted a bridge of communication to the non-human world. . . . And when she succeeded, as now, she set her third heart to beating. She went into a state of ecstasy. ("La serpiente" 268–69, original emphasis)

Diffraction, diffusion, and pulsation have their own pleasures and dangers, but their ethics are far more enabling and democratic than Humanism.

Conclusion

Selflessness?

A poem,
like a studio,
is an ecosystem,
a diverse society.
Enter full face into
a crush of shapes.
Each pose its own animal.
Light bounces from the walls
of each, breathing space
between the nouns and bones.
The poses together kaleidoscope
in place. Arms and elbows
everywhere. Self. Incoherence. Yoga.

—Suzanne Bost, "Practicing Yoga /
    Embodying Feminism / Shape-
    Shifting" 195

This conclusion raises many questions that I don't intend to answer, including its title. In choosing the term "selflessness," I'm thinking about what it means for a self to dissolve into a community or ecosystem. I'm also thinking about the supposed virtue of selflessness—putting others before oneself—but this idea presupposes a central self that is usually given priority, a hierarchical order that selflessness inverts. Thinking outside of Humanism enables us to view selflessness not as an inversion of hierarchies but as a state that defies hierarchies. The distinctions assumed by Humanism dissolve in a web of connections.

This might be a lovely ideal to imagine. It might also be terrifying, and not just for those who prefer anthropocentric and hierarchical orders. Humanism has worked hard to protect us from the terror of being subject to others. Corporeal integrity and individual responsibility are so deeply engrained for people in modern Western societies that living without these defense mechanisms is literally unthinkable. Gloria Anzaldúa shows us the power of imagination to conceive worlds and relations apart from the "status quo stories" we have internalized. But even for those who embrace alternatives to Humanism, work like Anzaldúa's often looks like nothing but an aesthetic and intellectual exercise. Anzaldúa believed in the power of image and word to enact material transformations, but this view is not popularly held. Her method borders on utopianism, as in her early claims that mestiza consciousness could, "in our best dreams," bring about a "massive uprooting in dualistic thinking" and lead to the end of rape, violence, and war (*Borderlands* 80–81). These claims are good tools to think with because they allow us to imagine our world without the hierarchies that perpetuate the status quo, without hatred and bigotry. Empiricism leads us back to the domesticated world; imagination takes us elsewhere.

I confess that, comfortable as I am without Humanism, I have a difficult time thinking outside of rationalism. I would truly love to believe in alternative realities, spirits, or shape-shifting between species, but the most I can summon at this point is a belief in the power of imagination to help us along in our ethical thinking. I wouldn't say that Anzaldúa's more mystical ideas are just metaphors, though, because their utter difference from our conventional orientations to the world stimulates us to move in new directions. New tribalism, opening up to vulnerability, and other-than-human kinships do provide, in my view, a roadmap to real ethical world-building, much like Aurora Levins Morales's radical historiography or John Rechy's guides to queer/outlaw underworlds.

But these maps might lead us right back to our selves. One of the points I hope I have made in *Shared Selves* is that Humanism itself is a fiction imposed upon the messy intertwinements of the material world. The challenge might not be to create new worlds (as Anzaldúa claims with her repeated references to "haciendo mundo nuevo").[1] Maybe it's just a matter of recognizing interconnections we have been trained to overlook—or to fight off with alarm systems, border wars, and antiseptics—within the world we already inhabit. Various pathways have brought me to this recognition, among them, most obviously, posthumanist theory, but also Latinx literature, precolonial Latin American studies, ecofeminist New Materialisms, disability studies, and my personal experiences as a practitioner of yoga. (Though yoga as it is practiced in the United States today is often dismissed as narcissistic consumerism, my epigraph is meant to show how yoga moves beyond anthropocentrism and individualism.)

Since I've been using memoir as a vehicle for thinking about the parameters of the human subject, it seems only appropriate that I conclude with some reflections about my own movements through selfhood (self-indulgent as this might seem). First, I need to acknowledge that my perspective throughout *Shared Selves* rests on the tremendous and often unearned privilege I enjoy as a white-skinned, middle-class, nondisabled human. I would not say that my sense of self has ever been solid or comfortable, but I have not been forced by racism, poverty, or proximate violence to question the status of the human in our world. Indeed, it is my immense privilege as a highly educated academic that has exposed me to alternatives to Humanism.

The personal level at which these ideas resonate with me is based less on cultural resemblance than on a more visceral sense of permeability I've felt all my life. I've always been surprised by what is supposed to be my own image in the mirror or the sound of my own voice, which I don't feel any ownership toward, and I've always been prone to pick up the accents, emotions, and hand gestures of those around me. (I also have terrible proprioperception—awareness of one's physical boundaries in space—which makes yoga, or even walking through doorways, both physically and mentally challenging.) As a young girl, I felt invisible and often talked to myself in order to be sure I was there. When my family moved from Chicago to New Mexico, I, an adaptable ten-year-old, set out to be a shape-shifter, imagining myself as different kinds of girls moving through a strange mountainous environment. Long hair and roller skates? Short hair and a sports car? I learned Spanish, Spanglish, and how to pronounce English with a New Mexican accent. Even my skin—after a few blistering sunburns—thickened and adapted itself to the high-altitude sunshine, browning more easily. I learned the direction east from my view of the Sandia mountains and grew to accept spiders in the house. When I wandered into academia from middle-class suburbia, I was explicitly told that I needed to change my wardrobe and my "folksy" way of talking; my faculty advisors taught me how to "pass." My fluency in blending smoothed the way for me, but this "me" is so fluid that I'm not sure I'm the same person. Permeability is sometimes embarrassing, like when I start to cry when someone near me cries or echo words someone else has just said, as if I didn't have any unique ways or feelings all my own. Yet when it comes to trying to chip away at white privilege and ethnocentrism, I have few "core" beliefs or turfs to defend. Again, my privilege makes this selflessness tolerable; it would certainly be less so for people whose selfhood is threatened by systemic inequalities. What feels like moving through air to me might be experienced as a violating trespass to others.

I took up Latinx literary studies with the passion of a student in love, fueled by a sense of aesthetic attachment, political urgency, and regional identification as well as naiveté about my own complicity with racialized structures of power (like SAT tests, university admissions, biased curricula, and hegemonic vocabulary). As I rise through these structures (with publications, tenure, promotion), I realize that it is my responsibility to challenge structures that sustain me at the expense of others. I write this conclusion during a time when the rhetoric of our federal government is unabashedly racist and specifically anti-Latinx. Though this rhetoric isn't literally about me, it's about what matters to me, and it reinforces my un-earned power as a white-skinned native English speaker. I am less likely to be dismissed, more likely to be heard by the dominant culture. How do I use my voice and my privilege without asserting power, without referring back to myself all the time? I am generally uncomfortable with power and often undermine my authority with self-deprecating jokes. If only I could speak as an ecosystem, write with all my guanakán. But that would make for exceedingly dense sentences.

Birthed by texts like *This Bridge Called My Back*, and keenly aware of the ways in which white women's voices have dominated the conversation and defined its terms, my feminism has aimed toward something like self-effacement. At a recent promotional event for the new edition of *Bridge*, Cherríe Moraga proclaimed that the kind of writing that brings down institutions is personal, hard, and usually makes people uncomfortable. I agree, and I embrace discomfort as a sign of productive transformation, but what does this means for white people, like me?[2] If I make people of color uncomfortable, aren't I reproducing racial aggression? If I am intimate about my own experience as a white woman, aren't I reinforcing the hegemony of white experience? This paragraph was very difficult to write.

I have been asking myself these kinds of questions with increasing frequency since I was promoted to full professor and find myself institutionalized as the Latinx studies "expert" in my department. In an effort to examine what it means to bear such authority as an "outsider" within Latinx studies, I now approach the field from a self-reflexive angle that includes my own experience intra-acting with the materials I study, reflecting on my time in the archives, my conversations with other scholars, my shifting ways of using texts. Simply focusing on my unearned privileges as someone with white skin would keep white privilege and myself at the center of the conversation, which is why I have generally avoided Whiteness studies. What interests me more than myself—or any of the structures and identities I represent—is reflection between self and other, dialogue across differences, and shared encounters. This doesn't involve effacing my self so much as focusing on what tethers it to others.

Gloria Anzaldúa and AnaLouise Keating help me to theorize these tethers. Anzaldúa's late idea of "inter-planetary new tribalism" moves beyond her earlier writings on mestiza consciousness and overflows the fetishized demarcations between not just races, sexes, and genders but also species, to embrace trees, rocks, and spirits. She explains how we get to this inclusive understanding of identity: "[I]f you hold opposites long enough without taking sides a new identity emerges" ("now let us shift" 548); "you 'grow into' . . . the new tribalism by propagating other worldviews, spiritual traditions, and cultures to your árbol de la vida" (560). If I were to attach other cultures and worldviews to my own "tree of life," would that be appropriation? Or might attachment to others be indigenous to selfhood—before competitive individualism and ethnocentrism led some of us to deny these connections?

AnaLouise Keating's idea of post-oppositional consciousness (in her 2013 book *Transformation Now!*) emerges from a critique of ontological frameworks that posit "a distinct separation between human beings" and that divide reality into "discrete parts" (6). She poses, instead, a connectionist framework oriented toward thresholds rather than borders, openings rather than rigid lines of demarcation. With her "metaphysics of interconnectedness," she proposes that we start "with the presupposition that we are intimately, inextricably linked with all human and all nonhuman existence. Each individual being is interrelated with all that exists—on multiple levels and in multiple ways, ranging from economics and ecology to language, social systems, and energy" (11). Like Anzaldúa, Keating works from a ground of shared existence—she doesn't use the term "identity" here— but she gives specific pathways (economies, ecologies, socialities) for the shared matter Anzaldúa idealizes. Rather than the "substance monism" one finds in Anzaldúa, a belief in a single substance at the root of all things, Keating's idea of the threshold focuses on relations among entities that are (implicitly) separable. Though these entities are linked through an open threshold, a threshold is not a nothing: it is a subtle reminder of structures that demarcate, of different orientations and different powers here versus there. Thresholds create friction, places where our feet trip if we drag them, but we can move through. We don't need to gape at them helplessly.

In her earlier work, Keating makes a direct statement about identity: "I am not suggesting that we should dismiss all identity categories and declare ourselves from this day forward 'color-blind,' 'gender-blind,' and so forth. . . . My point here is that educators, scholars, and others who are concerned with social justice need to become more aware of how these categories function to prevent us from recognizing our interrelatedness" (*Teaching Transformation* 3). Identity matters because it has mattered; it has been used both as an organizing principle for structures of inequality and as a source of pleasure and pride. Keating does not suggest that we jettison identity. What she does call for is an act of "recognition," a choice to see interrelatedness between differences where the rhetoric of identity has trained our focus on the differences themselves. Interrelations are not based on sameness, and they don't require any shared substance. They ask us to witness the open doorways and the exchanges that occur there: the air that moves between beings in a shared environment, the violence that cuts across differences, the resources that change hands.

Fear of tripping (or trampling) over my connections with others has led me to embrace Trinh Minh-ha's idea of "speaking nearby"—"a speaking that reflects on itself and can come very close to a subject without, however, seizing or claiming it" (Trinh 87). Speaking near, as an ally and a listener, is an alternative to the authoritative academic voice that objectifies its subject and overpowers it with the author's own tenor. Speaking near (rather than about) a subject presumes a distance, a gap I long to bridge even as the bridge highlights the gap between us. Intimacy with others involves recognition of our shared ecosystem as well as our distinct orientations to that ecosystem. As I sit nearby the subjects of Latinx studies, what movements are set into play by my neighborly relations? Though I will never love a border wall, and don't believe that "good fences make good neighbors," perhaps my neighbors fear that I will begin to encroach upon them. Donna Haraway's proposal that "the relation" is the smallest unit of analysis (which emerges in her discussion of human-dog coevolution) is helpful here;[3] it forces us to focus on how we live with "significant others" rather than individual identities. Relations are based on shared boundary-making, reciprocal but not necessarily equal, as power leads to asymmetrical exchange. With relation as the subject, I am not looking at myself alone; I am looking at *us* in contact, at the multitudes of entities we touch and multitudinous ways of touching.

In order to move past the academic stance of assertion, which is an exercise of power, I have been experimenting recently with more relational modes of scholarship. I published a creative piece about yoga—"Practicing Yoga / Embodying Feminism / Shape-Shifting"—in which I laid down my own words alongside Gloria Anzaldúa's without offering an interpretation of either. The idea was to emulate the ways in which people in a shared yoga practice embody different variations of the same postures at the same time, in a shared ecosystem made up of shared breath, sweat, music, and movement. My words were sharing a page with Anzaldúa's, moving alongside them in our distinct incantations. As physical and mental space, yoga studios are inevitably crowded with others in various states of intertwinement and (mis)alignment. The goal is to notice different shapes and feelings without judgment. Yoga has taught me to attend to this messiness rather than searching for truth, agreement, emulation, or praise.

Another recent experiment in multivocality as an alternative to the self-effacing (and implicitly self-asserting) empiricism of a conventional essay is "Identity and Cross-Cultural Empathy: Writing to Sister Mary Agnes Curran, O.S.F.," a letter I wrote to a missionary nun, a deceased white woman, who, like me, worked in and with Latina communities. I imagine letters—especially letters to the dead—as a symbol of the missionary's effort to reach across difference *toward* an other that one will never be. A problem with missionaries is that their faith leads them to see one truth, which becomes a barrier to reciprocity. But it's not an insoluble barrier. One of the disciplinary differences made palpable for me when reading the archived letters of Sister Mary Agnes is that, unlike scholars, who write about their subjects from a distance, missionaries live with and among their subjects, sharing food, water, and telephones along with stories, sewing, political conflict, and eruptions of violence. Mary Agnes prayed alongside her community in Spanish. I wrote my letter to share my ideas about cross-cultural work alongside her words, to reach towards the woman I will never meet and the colonía I have never been to. Letters are like empathy: though we will never literally walk in an other's shoes, we can send our feelers out toward them. Plus, letters always invite the possibility of response.

Talking about my own methodological experiments—dialogic though they may be—puts my self back at the center of the conversation. So I'll turn to another scholar of Latinx studies who works to decenter the power of whiteness (his own and that of the nation) and then to some questions that open outward. Lee Bebout asks, in a 2014 article on whiteness in the classroom, "How might teachers, particularly those who occupy positions of privilege, help foster a socially engaged and justice oriented classroom?" (344). I would add, how might scholars, particularly those who occupy positions of privilege, help maintain the "political commitment" that both he and I believe must be central to Latinx studies? Bebout's proposition is to keep "skin in the game," to study the function of not only the race our skin seems to wear but also the historical entity our skin seems to enclose, a self that moves through social interaction and political structures. I'm attracted to this focus on skin because it's not just a marker of racial identity; it's the place where we touch one another, where different selves meet. Skin is rigid enough to hold us in pretty consistent shapes but fluid enough to shed cells, to stretch and bend with our movements, and to absorb dirt, water, or toxins from the world around us. Though it is subject to variation, skin also marks the limits of our flexibility: the circumference of what we think of as ourselves. It's a threshold whose crossing involves pain or pleasure. We don't forget it's there; we tend to it ritually or compulsively; we study its transformations and leavings. It defines our selfless selves.

Does the permeability of skin eclipse the (inertial, nostalgic, and structural) workings of identity? Viewed from the lenses of pre-, post-, or other-than-Humanism, how do categories like "Latinx" function? Are identity categories inevitably tied to Humanism and its defense of human particularity? Or, if identity is inseparable from shifting environments, economies, communities, power structures, and ideologies (which I believe it is), is identity itself other-than-Humanist? Certainly the fluidity and inclusivity of the term "Latinx"—along with its allied developments in queer theory, ecocriticism, disability studies, black studies, digital media, and speculative fiction—transcend the individual objectivity assumed by Humanism. Returning again to Karen Barad, our ideologies and tools of measurement, including identity categories, intra-act with material bodies, setting multiple entities in motion, reverberating with the movements of others. "Latinx" is an ontological and epistemological "apparatus" that circulates in a variety ways with rights and privileges, love and community, inclusion and exclusion.

One of the insights my experience has to offer is how Latinx studies circulates outside its apparent boundaries and wraps other elements (like myself) into its web. Its ethical, intellectual, and aesthetic products resonate widely and ask us to be attuned to the complexity of our webs. If we believe in the lessons and obligations of posthumanism (or the lessons and obligations of feminism, queer theory, antiracism, ecocriticism, or disability studies), we need to account for the many structures and beings with which we intra-act: our economies, our shared toxins, our distinct privileges, our lives and deaths, you, me, this book, and everything. How do we coordinate our efforts and mobilize our various selves in ways that minimize violence and domination and maximize respect and love? We need each other to answer these questions.

Notes

Introduction. Beyond the Self

1. See Moraga's *A Xicana Codex of Changing Consciousness* (2011), Castillo's *Black Dove: Mamá, Mi'jo, and Me* (2016), Cisneros's *A House of My Own: Stories from My Life* (2016), Corpi's *Confessions of a Book Burner* (2014), and Behar's *Traveling Heavy: A Memoir in between Journeys* (2013).

2. Beltrán worries that "Latino pan-ethnicity has been fostered by a climate of xenophobia": "Homogenizing depictions of Latinos continue to be invoked by those who fear the rapid growth of the United States' Latino population." These depictions, for her, reinforce the xenophobic sense of Latinos as "monolithically 'foreign'" and a threat to the country's "unity and civic values" (Beltrán 7).

3. See Saldaña-Portillo as well as Anzaldúa's own "Speaking across the Divide."

4. See Halberstam's *In a Queer Time and Place.*

5. There have been a few recent articles published comparing Gloria Anzaldúa's work to developments in posthumanism, particularly Kelli Zaytoun's 2015 essay "'Now Let Us Shift' the Subject: Tracing the Path and Posthumanist Implications of La Naguala / The Shapeshifter in the Works of Gloria Anzaldúa" and my own 2013 essay "Diabetes, Culture, and Food: Posthumanist Nutrition in the Gloria Anzaldúa Archive."

6. I use "posthuman" to describe formations that exceed human autonomy. Posthumanism is a broader term that includes critiques of Humanism inspired by poststructuralism as well as empirical approaches derived from the technologies of "hard" science.

7. Haraway's theories of filiation and kinship are built, in part, upon the "bridges" constructed by Cherríe Moraga and Gloria Anzaldúa's groundbreaking collection *This Bridge Called My Back: Writings by Radical Women of Color* (1981). In "A Manifesto for Cyborgs"(*Haraway Reader*) Haraway proposed new tools for feminist theory in the 1980s, and she turned not only to the military-industrial command, control, communications, intelligence networks that link us all to structures of power but also to the ideas of intersectionality, hybridity, and coalition developed by women of color feminisms. Though I wish Haraway had gone into deeper analysis of the ethical and cultural distinctions between cyborgs and feminist of color coalitions, the resonance remains.

8. Alison Kafer presents an extended "close crip reading" of Haraway's cyborg in *Feminist, Queer, Crip* (105), first providing a necessary critique of the ways in which Haraway romanticizes (as embodied utopias or provocative monsters) prosthetic intertwinements that are material realities for many people with disabilities. Yet Kafer finds Haraway's cyborg to be an ally in her search for a vision of "crip futurity"—a future not dependent upon resolving corporeality into individual "wholeness."

9. In her famous essay "How to Tame a Wild Tongue," from *Borderlands* (1987), Anzaldúa writes: "In the 1960s, I read my first Chicano novel. It was *City of Night* by John Rechy, a gay Texan, . . . For days I walked around in stunned amazement that a Chicano could write and could get published. . . . I felt like we really existed as a people" (59–60).

10. To my knowledge, no one else has written about this text, which cannot be copied or photographed due to pending possibilities for future publication.

Chapter 1. Writing Latinx Memoir: Fragmented Lives, Precarious Boundaries

1. Presumably the title *A Message from God in the Atomic Age* was changed because it was deemed not to be an accurate reflection of Vilar's memoir. Gregory Rabassa, who translated the original text from Spanish to English, worried that the first title "smacked too much of a devotional homily from the likes of Billy Graham or some other bible-whacker" (Rabassa 152). Vilar would likely reject this pathologization of religious devotion given her own apparent open-mindedness about her grandmother's visionary writings. The original title certainly puts the famous Lolita Lebrón at the center of the narrative. Though the revised title also revolves around Lolita to an extent, naming the location within the Capitol building where she opened fire, the "Ladies Gallery" invokes a space that a plurality of "ladies" may occupy.

2. Lolita (as she is known in popular discourse as well as throughout *The Ladies Gallery*) was accompanied by three men, Irving Flores, Rafael Cancel, and Andrés Figueroa, who were actually responsible for all of injuries inflicted that day—Lolita reportedly having lost control of her weapon, firing at the ceiling instead. Yet the image of the beautiful Puerto Rican woman, wrapped in a Puerto Rican flag, pulling

a gun out of her purse in the Ladies Gallery of the U.S. Congress and firing down at the legislators discussing the status of Mexican farmworkers, with its more obvious drama and symbolism, has been passed on as of greater historical significance.

3. Discussions about *The Ladies Gallery* often revolve around the famous Lolita Lebrón more than Irene Vilar herself. Aurora Levins Morales's review of the text (written when it was still titled A *Message from God*) is no exception: beginning and ending with Lolita's heroism.

4. In her analysis of Ortiz Cofer, Jacqueline Doyle critiques Friedman for this tendency: "Friedman paints her picture of female selfhood and group identities with broad strokes, without considering the complexity and range of collective affiliations that women might embrace" (Doyle 169).

5. As Aparicio notes in her analysis of *Silent Dancing*, "One of the more interesting issues regarding the reception of this and other Latina autobiographical narratives is the degree to which they are more often appraised for their sociological or anthropological value and overlooked in terms of their aesthetic merit" (64).

6. Albizu refers to the Puerto Rican nationalist Pedro Albizu Campos (1891–1965), who influenced Lolita's choice to leave behind her family and dedicate herself to the nation.

7. Operation Bootstrap was a mid-twentieth-century industrialization program enforced by the U.S. government in Puerto Rico, with the assistance of then governor Luis Muñoz Marín, which shifted the Puerto Rican economy from agriculture to reliance upon U.S. corporations. The use of the term "bootstrap" is (unintentionally) ironic in that, rather than encouraging the island to "pull up" its own economy, the new industrial economy was tethered to U.S. economic interests.

8. To complicate genres further, the first Library of Congress category assigned to *Silent Dancing* on its copyright page is "Biography—Youth."

9. In the interview with Stephanie Gordon, Ortiz Cofer explains that "the actual event is not as important as the memory of it, to me. It may be to a historian, and I probably shock people when I say that. But the place of poetry is what interests me" ("Ensayos: Essays of a Life" 13).

10. The death of the narrator's father, for instance, which should be a significant event in her life, does not appear in the chronology of the text; it shows up only as a past-tense clause in the final chapter, in a sentence that refers to her mother's affection for the father, "dead in a car wreck now for over a decade" (*Silent Dancing* 163).

11. Throughout the preface, Ortiz Cofer establishes her ideas about memoir in dialogue with Virginia Woolf's essay "A Sketch of the Past," in which Woolf talks about not just her work on memoir writing but also her experience with sexual abuse and the shame she feels about her own body after being abused. Ortiz Cofer includes no reference to this aspect of Woolf's essay, forming another erasure of violence.

12. In "¡La Verdad?" Ortiz Cofer describes her realization that, when her relatives' accounts of an event differed from each other, they were not lying; they were simply preserving their own unique version of reality. Ultimately, she "understood that

memory is relative, and that [her] relatives were practicing their particular theory of relativity" (29). The plays on "relativity" and "relatives" here situate variable perspectives within the heart of the family and relation in general.

13. I never imagined myself writing a sentence that includes the phrase "the function of the literary," since any function posed would obviously be debated. Indeed, some might say that the literariness of the literary derives from its lack of function. (Though even "art for art's sake" has a function: art.) But my point is to differentiate literature from empirical disciplines, and I do see literature as inevitably having some (though often unacknowledged) ethical or aesthetic impact.

14. The text of the Three Sirens reappears with a different tone in the epilogue of *The Ladies Gallery*, where the narrator states her intention of writing a book about her family: "Mother has died, therefore I am. Not a nation, it is true, but a presence that remains. A book" (323). These sentences are clearer, more orderly. "Therefore I am" reinstates the vitality of the "I," though it comes at the cost of the mother's death. The book itself takes on a presence (indeed, its own two-word sentence) linked to the narrator's self-assertion in a way that seems more healthful here. Yet, as I discuss later in this section, in *Impossible Motherhood* Vilar renounces this attitude toward her mother's death, claiming that her husband suggested she end *The Ladies Gallery* in this way (*Impossible Motherhood* 100–101). (It is for this reason that I reserve my analysis of this passage for the notes.) The optimism and rebirth in this ending defy the tone of the rest of the book, especially the disembodiment that comes with the miscarriage in the final chapter (the page immediately preceding the epilogue).

15. Vilar explicitly links these crops to the stories of Puerto Rico's human inhabitants, invoking the loss of the island's agricultural economy in which her family had achieved some stature: "coffee doesn't grow all by itself, and its story, like that of many other things, before it became a nostalgic subject of conversation, paralleled the lives of people, those of my grandparents and great-grandparents and of so many who one day would cheer themselves with the memory that they had really known how to grow coffee" (*The Ladies Gallery* 70).

16. This idea could be taken from Jacques Lacan. In her 1988 essay "Authorizing the Autobiographical," Shari Benstock draws from Lacan and Georges Gusdorf to point out the conventional thought that "psychic health is measured in the degree to which the 'self' is constructed in separateness, the boundaries between 'self' and 'other' carefully circumscribed"; autobiography is supposed to maintain these psychic walls and act as a "linguistic fortress" for the autobiographical subject (Benstock 15). Benstock, of course, notes how women are, because of their alienation within the Symbolic law, excluded from this linguistic protection (19). The variety of permeabilities that Vilar depicts, however, defies any essentialist conclusions based solely on gender.

17. It is not coincidental that both Vilar and Ortiz Cofer invoke Virginia Woolf, who radically disrupted both the form and the subject of memoir throughout her career.

18. I wanted to say that pregnancy conjoins two "selves" of unequal power and stature, making it a sort of microcosm of the "master–slave" relationship Vilar suggests she had with her first husband. But the more I thought about it (and G.W.F. Hegel would probably agree), the more apparent it became that the power imbalance is unstable as the two selves exert different sorts of power over the other. Though the fetus seems more limited in its ability to express its will, it also has the power to terminate the potential mother's life and to act upon her body in ways that she cannot control. Perhaps the fetus is the master of the host; if this is the case, it is an inversion of the dynamic envisioned by those who demonize the "mothers" of abortions.

19. Here is an elaboration of this point in Barad's dense language: "From the perspective of agential realism, the fetus is not a preexisting object of investigation with inherent properties. Rather, the fetus is a *phenomenon* that is constituted and reconstituted out of historically and culturally specific iterative intra-actions of material-discursive apparatuses of bodily production" (217, original emphasis).

20. I appreciate the criticism that empathy too often resembles appropriation; as feminist philosopher Lorraine Code puts it, "it is dangerous in affirming the center's capacity to coopt, appropriate, own the experiences and situations of Others" (270). It is also important to consider Sneja Gunew's critique of the lack of attention to cultural particularity in most affect theory and her proposition that there is more than one variety of empathy based on the culture from which this feeling is derived.

Chapter 2. Community: John Rechy, Depersonalization, and Queer Selves

1. Several critics have focused on this autobiographical tendency. Juan Bruce-Novoa (in 1979 and 2001) teases out the distinction between the autobiographical and the fictional elements in Rechy's writing, and Kevin Arnold focuses on the tension between the truth value (or textual realism) of Rechy's work and the construction of fantasy. Rather than trying to separate fact from fiction, David Vázquez links the "conscious blurring of fiction and autobiography" to a desire for community efficacy (109), echoing the feminist practice of using personal narrative to illuminate political problems.

2. There is far less criticism published about Rechy's non-autobiographical works—like *Marilyn's Daughter* (1988), *The Miraculous Day of Amalia Gomez* (1991), or *Our Lady of Babylon* (1996)—which suggests that critical interest in Rechy revolves around the author himself and the hustling or cruising male persona at the center of his autobiographically oriented works.

3. The singular "kept woman" of the memoir's title refers to Marisa Guzman, the mistress who lives in Mexico, but the second woman is just as important to the memoir as a model of self-estrangement. The author/narrator meets Alicia Gonzales at the same moment when he first watches Marisa Guzman smoke a cigarette

in a room alone at his sister's wedding; both John and Alicia seem to be obsessed with the romantic image of Marisa Guzman, and they both strive to leave behind their drab families in El Paso in order to simulate such romance in their own lives.

4. Casillo describes Rechy's obsession with beauty as a product of a deep aesthetic sensibility and his love of watching movies. He links Rechy's identity to that of the movie actresses he loved on the screen (Joan Crawford, Rita Hayworth, Hedy Lamarr): by combining the images of the "desirable, catered-to woman and the lusty, powerful man [who coveted them], Rechy eventually created his persona as a hustler" (Casillo 48–49). This latter claim suggests that Rechy's persona was both imitative and, despite his butch façade, based on a combination of masculine and feminine performance.

5. As Juan Bruce-Novoa described it in 1979, Rechy's work presents "life aestheticized through the artistic-critical eye of the self-conscious novelist" ("In Search of the Honest Outlaw" 45).

6. In *About My Life*, Rechy addresses the implicit violation involved in telling a community's story: "I was whipped into a frenzy of doubt and guilt—and self-recrimination—doubt that I could recapture those unique times, which I was still living; guilt that if I did, I would be plundering real lives, sealing them into a book while the actual lives would go on beyond our shared experiences, far beyond me, without me, secure in a new life" (303). In this language, recalling Irene Vilar, writing both violates and preserves a life, with the life preserved having been altered in the process of writing.

7. Masking and opacity are linked to Sedgwick's "epistemology of the closet," in which homosexuality is organized around hidden selves and open secrets.

8. David Vázquez and Rafael Pérez-Torres both call *The Sexual Outlaw* a novel in their analyses of it, but I think it is important to emphasize how the authorial essays, interviews, newspaper accounts, and other apparently empirical details that fill the text take it beyond the realm of fiction.

9. Frederick Luis Aldama argues that this "self-reflexive," "multiform" representation in *The Sexual Outlaw* conveys "the many lives and voices that make up a total vision of a city," "solidifies in the reader's mind the role of the literary text to capture such a world," and "also reveal[s] the real forms of power, located in the state apparatus and executed by a real ruling class, that dominate and exploit ethnoqueer subaltern subjects through police force, legislation, and judicial institutions" (61). The dissonance of forms and voices realistically captures the saturation of discourses through which structures of power organize, enable, and inhibit social-sexual behavior.

10. This complicates the use of identity terms when referring to Rechy's *obra*. I use "Chicano" to refer to the earlier, patriarchal manifestations of the Chicano movement and "Chicanx" to refer to more gender-inclusive manifestations.

11. This tension between sexuality and ethnicity marks much criticism of Rechy's work. For Ricardo Ortiz, Rechy's body of work is crucial in the development of queer

identities and queer publics because his graphic representations of sex between men resist the "ideological and libidinal repression" of the dominant culture (Ortiz 123). Yet this intense, nearly obsessive, focus on sexuality is, according to Ortiz, linked to the "existential trauma" resulting from Rechy's "unwillingness to explore the 'Mexican side' of his own psyche" (115). David Johnson worries over the degree to which queer themes have placed Rechy's books outside most genealogies of Chicanx literature, and David Vázquez analyzes the ways in which Rechy's identity as a gay Chicano leads to a "triangulated" sense of self divided between ethnic and sexual communities. I would point out that each of these approaches assumes that race, nationality, or ethnicity is separable from sexuality rather than intersectional.

12. The loss of the dog Winnie forms the opening scene of *City of Night*, defining the young boy's sense of loss and his disillusionment with a world in which dogs aren't admitted to heaven: "Soon Winnie will blend into the dirt. There was no soul, the body would rot, and there would be Nothing left of Winnie. That is the incident of my early childhood that I remember the most often" (*City of Night* 12). References to this event recur throughout *City of Night* and throughout Rechy's *obra* overall.

13. See, especially, Tim Dean's argument about barebacking in *Unlimited Intimacy*.

14. This same depersonalizing quality that facilitates communal formations is the basis for some negative reviews of Rechy's writing: Gary Indiana criticized Rechy's mid-career books by saying that his characters "have hardly any dimension, being mainly defined by their physical appearances—indescribably 'beautiful' if they're young, distinguishable only by height, hair color, muscle density, and the exact nature of their sexual wishes. If they're old, fat, or plain, they're 'trolls.' Both types lack the kind of interiority a fictional character needs for the reader to care about his or her fate" (qtd. in Casillo 274). Casillo defends the flatness of these characters by saying "these are simply the social realities of the worlds Rechy inhabits," and he quotes Rechy himself as embracing stereotypes as "a source of great strength. Sissies, drag queens, bull dykes—these are our heroes. They are the ones who step out into the world and say, 'We are here'" (Casillo 274). If we view these qualities as a rejection of individualism and an overdramatization of artifice (along the lines of camp), then these characters could be seen as enacting a deliberate ethical stance against identity norms.

15. Rechy's naming of "Jim" is overtly depersonalized. On the third page of *The Sexual Outlaw*, Rechy writes, "Jim—he calls himself that sometimes, sometimes Jerry, sometimes John," suggesting that all names are pseudonyms. Yet this depersonalized person is also closely identified with the author; immediately following this passage about the interchangeability of his names, "Jim" is described as having "a mixture of Anglo and Latin bloods," like Rechy himself (23), and one of the nonfictional interludes inserted within Jim's story blurs Jim and Rechy when the author (John Rechy) arrives at a man's apartment to be interviewed only to discover that the man is a former partner from the "sex-hunt."

16. Rechy drops apostrophes throughout *City of Night*—either as a blurring of

words and identities or as a way of communicating the youngman's resistance to the laws of grammar.

17. One of the earliest critical essays published about *City of Night*, Stanton Hoffman's 1964 "The Cities of Night," focuses on how the "gay world"—with its play of stereotypes and "obsessive consciousness of effeminacy and masculinity"—overwhelms particular individuals seeking love within it (Hoffman 195–96). Though there is an individual "I" that emerges at points throughout *City of Night* (especially at the beginning of the novel when the youngman is a child and at the end of the novel when he withdraws from the masquerade of Mardi Gras), this "I" is explicitly "removed from the context of the other elements of the novel," argues Hoffman (203), especially the "gay world" in which the youngman functions as a mute cipher for the stories of the drag queens and hustlers he encounters on his journey. In a 2009 essay, Kenneth E. Roon Jr. similarly argues (without citing Hoffman) that, "without the City," the narrator in *City of Night* "could not exist": "Rechy's hustler-flâneur is literally part of the crowd. . . . Whenever he leaves the crowd, whether it is to return to El Paso or to get a regular job, he almost ceases to exist" (Roon 182).

18. Ricardo Ortiz reaches a similar conclusion in his analysis of Johnny's physical training regimen in *Numbers*, arguing that "[t]his program clearly functions as an image of literal self-composition easily translatable into textual terms" (114).

19. Vázquez also argues that Jim's sexuality keeps him from experiencing the community envisioned by Chicano nationalists and that his race "estranges him from mainstream gay liberation" (114), suggesting that intersectionality itself complicates communal affiliation.

20. In *Light in the Dark* (her never defended doctoral dissertation that AnaLouise Keating published in 2015), Anzaldúa writes: "To change or reinvent reality, you engage the facultad of your imagination. You must interrupt or suspend the conscious 'I' that reminds you of your history and beliefs because these reminders tie you to certain notions of reality and behavior. . . . We must empower the imagination to blur and transcend customary frameworks and conceptual categories reinforced by language and consensual reality" (44–45).

21. I borrow Freud's masculine engendering of the ego with my singular pronouns in the first part of this sentence.

22. In *The Sexual Outlaw*, Rechy talks about the claiming of space that occurs with gay communities across specific locations: "Board [up] one place, we'll find two more. Block park roads into sexual arenas, and we'll discover better ones below. And we'll do it in Los Angeles, New York, Atlanta, El Paso, Dallas, New Orleans, St. Louis, San Francisco, Denver, Chicago—and Brownsville, MacAllen, Prairie Ridge, Waukegan, Morganfield, Twenty-Nine Palms" (300). This list imagines a trans-spatial community or, rather, a use of space that transcends particular locations.

23. In the memoir, Rechy tells of Don Allen, "the elegantly dressed classy gentleman editor from New York," wanting to see "the scene": "I took him to ChiChi's,

the toughest bar in downtown Los Angeles. It was as if, for him, it had prepared to display itself in all its tawdry splendor amid intimations of dangers. Ratty pushers lingered outside, tough queens cursed and shoved their way in, rough hustlers gathered in tight conspiratorial groups. They all seemed to spot Don at the same time. Everything and everyone froze. Don, too, froze. 'I think it's perhaps too noisy,' he said, already heading back to the car" (*About My Life* 284). Though this account might be exaggerated, it does highlight the chasm between the world of professional commerce (book publishing, elegant clothing) and the world of outlaw commerce.

24. If we extend this model to the level of the nation, dirt is also a helpful metaphor for Chicanx studies since Mexicans in the United States are often deemed matter out of place; whether they are immigrants or their belonging in the United States dates from the earlier order in which the southwestern United States was northern Mexico, they are marked, in the new world order, as an alien presence thwarting sterile modes of national belonging. The paranoid nation firms up its border to differentiate the United States from Mexico, interior from exterior, and it resists infection by deporting, stigmatizing, and denying public services to those who inhabit its interior in a Mexican way.

25. When Jeremy asks the youngman his name (after they first made love on the white sheets of Jeremy's New Orleans hotel room), "following the rules of that nightworld which tacitly admits guilt while seldom openly acknowledging it," he tells only his first name. When Jeremy replies "My name is Jeremy—Jeremy Adams," the narrator states, "I told Jeremy Adams my own last name" (*City of Night* 345). This name thus becomes known to the fictional Jeremy, but the youngman remains nameless to readers.

26. David William Foster has a far more pessimistic take on the "dirty realism" of Rechy's work, describing the Los Angeles of *Bodies and Souls* as a "nightmare of American corruption and injustice . . . in which perfumed fragrances are really putrid stenches." Foster interprets the decay of Los Angeles as a symbol of the bleak opportunities for love and salvation offered there: "just as sexual love can never be ennobling for lost angels and must always be violently dysfunctional, Nature in Los Angeles can never be innocent and will always only thinly veil the putrid" (Foster 205). He concludes that homoeroticism has "no context of legitimation" in this text and "therefore must be viewed as strange and abnormal" (206). This interpretation, however, assumes one standard of what counts as "putrid" rather than critiquing the hierarchy of substances maintained in the symbolism of heteronormative romance.

27. This performance is part of Youd's "100 Novels Project," which has also included retyping the works of Hunter S. Thompson, Walker Percy, and William Faulkner.

28. Rechy describes this event in the introduction to *City of Night* (viii).

29. I use *actant* in the sense that Bruno Latour does, to describe action in a non-individualistic and non-anthropocentric way. While "actor" conventionally suggests a "human intentional individual" who "extends his power" by doing something,

an actant "can literally be anything provided it is granted to be the source of an action" (Latour 372–73).

30. The Chicano movement's 1969 "El Plan Espiritual de Aztlán" affirms: "In the spirit of a new people that is conscious not only of its proud historical heritage but also of the brutal 'gringo' invasion of our territories, *we*, the Chicano inhabitants and civilizers of the northern land of Aztlán from whence came our forefathers, reclaiming the land of their birth and consecrating the determination of our people of the sun, *declare* that the call of our blood is our power, our responsibility, and our inevitable destiny" ("El Plan" 1, original emphasis). In this language, Aztlán is not just the mythical homeland of Chicanxs' Aztec ancestors but a present and future place that they inhabit. By referring to the U.S. Southwest as "Aztlán," writers of the *movimiento* deny the U.S. colonizers' claims on the land and assert continuity with precolonial indigenous ways of occupying the land. In her 1993 work, *The Last Generation*, Cherríe Moraga echoed the 1969 nationalist gesture by penning her own manifesto, of sorts, "Queer Aztlán: The Reformation of Chicano Tribe." The re-reclamation has obvious relevance for Rechy's reclaiming of stigmatized spaces as queer homelands.

Chapter 3. Webs: Aurora Levins Morales's Animal, Vegetable, and Digital Ecologies

1. Donna Haraway's work is helpful for thinking about the significance of the wolf's "wildness": for Haraway, animals should not be thought of in terms of human emotions or human rights. Instead, we must recognize their "'otherworldly' subject status" in order to learn about the "radical otherness at the heart of relating" (*Haraway Reader* 143).

2. In my 2000 *MELUS* article, for instance, I simply claim that, in *Getting Home Alive*, Levins Morales affirms the United States' multiracial heritage and decenters European authority (Bost, "Transgressing Borders" 202). Rina Benmayor describes *Getting Home Alive* as a model for emerging calls to build coalitions and multicultural alliances based on the authors' "multiple relationships as mother/daughter and to their various communities of identity" (Benmayor 116). The text, Benmayor argues, "foregrounds the issue of identity in order to break the confines of unidimensional paradigms" (107). Monika Wadman likewise describes *Getting Home Alive* as an affirmation of multiculturality, a "confluence of diverse ethnic ancestries and cultures," that ultimately favors solidarity, connection, and "peoplehood" over any exclusive ethnic identity (Wadman 224, 227). For Wadman, the broad reach of Levins Morales's multiple, "unlimited" identifications is a strictly literary creation, an ideal invention rather than an actual identity (232–33). Wadman's claim is prescient for the transgenerational, trans-species community mapped out in Levins Morales's later work, *Remedios*, which is a literary manifestation more than an empirical account;

the author's website might actually enable these unlimited networks in ways that seemed impossible before the global circulation now made possible on the Internet.

3. In one of the only articles published about *Remedios,* Efraín Barradas is somewhat critical of the blurring of history and imagination in the text, comparing Levins Morales's method to Virginia Woolf's creation of Shakespeare's sister in *A Room of One's Own.* In her search for roots for Puerto Rican feminism, Levins Morales invented figures when there were none, based on speculation about what those imagined figures' lives might have been like (as in her imagined Puerto Rican "copy" of Mexico's Sor Juana Inés de la Cruz [*Remedios* 125]). In these instances, according to Barradas, Levins Morales, "deja de ser historiadora y se convierte en poeta y crea la realidad que busca y que no halla en los archivos ni en los libros de historia. . . . Quizás como escritora, pero no como historiadora, Aurora Levins Morales tiene todo el derecho a crearse su pasado. (Ella diría que la historiadora tiene el mismo derecho; no sé si esté de acuerdo) [stops being a historian and becomes a poet and creates the reality she searches for and does not find in archives or history books. Maybe as a writer, but not as a historian, Aurora Levins Morales has every right to create her past for herself. (She would say that the historian has the same right; I'm not sure if I am in agreement)]" (Barradas n.p., my translation). Barradas describes this construction of history as "dangerous" in his article's abstract. Both this claim and his worry that historians might not have the right to create their pasts seem to assume the possibility and desirability of truthful, empirical history. But Levins Morales's intention, as Barradas even notes, is to create not history as much as remedy: to establish new sources for Puerto Rican women to draw upon as feminists. When viewed in relation to posthumanism, cultural activism, and the genre of memoir, the fantastical stories of *Remedios* make good sense, and the documented sources that get called history must be seen as amputations from the vast web of events that constitute our past, present, and future.

4. When I use the word "radical" to describe Levins Morales, I mean it in both the political and the intellectual sense. Her political affiliations with socialism, feminism, and the disability justice movement demand structural reconfiguration of our institutions and our environments as well as valuing community over individual success. Her works are intellectually radical, too, in that they challenge some of the most basic ways of thinking (especially about the human self and the distinction between nature and culture) underlying modern Western thought.

5. Judy Chicago's installation *The Dinner Party* is a symbolic history of women, a table set with place settings representing women who were (conscious or unconscious) foremothers of contemporary feminism (or, at least, the artist's somewhat limited conception of feminism in the 1970s). The three wings of the triangular-shaped table feature women from "Prehistory to Classical Rome," "Christianity to the Reformation," and "American Revolution to the Women's Revolution," including Ishtar, Kali, Sappho, Eleanor of Aquitaine, Christine de Pisan, Sacajawea, Mary

Wollstonecraft, Sojourner Truth, and Virginia Woolf. This pluralism prefigures the preponderance of lists in Morales's and Levins Morales's writings.

6. In this excerpt, Rosario Morales's short prose piece "The Dinner" is the source of the allusions to Judy Chicago's *The Dinner Party*; most of the history references come from Aurora Levins Morales's "Child of the Americas."

7. In the preface to *Cosecha*, "Before Words," Levins Morales opens with saying that she cannot yet write about her mother's death because it is "too vast and disorderly within me. I have vivid scraps, but they don't make a pattern. There's no quilt" (1). The cover of the 1986 book is, indeed, a picture of a brightly colored quilt (made by Rosario) whose scraps come together to form a house perched on a verdant mountaintop. The cover of *Cosecha* is a black-and-white photograph of Rosario Morales, from 1953, when she was pregnant with Aurora. This image, looking up at the round-bellied mother standing with the foliage, tinges this collection with nostalgia as well as affirming the power of collective subjects.

8. It is difficult to mention vomiting in a feminist discussion of eating without invoking bulimia. The subtlest analysis of the simultaneous rebellion and self-destruction involved in self-induced purging is still, in my mind, Susan Bordo's account in *Unbearable Weight* (1993).

9. The genre of *testimonio* was originally associated with Latin America, and most famously with the controversial testimony of the Guatemalan indigenous woman Rigoberta Menchú. Latinx storytellers have taken up the genre in the United States, arguing that conditions of oppression here are comparable to structural hierarchies in Latin America and the work of "testimoniando" just as important for uncovering the operations of power and violence in the United States. The Latina Feminist Group defines *testimonio* as "a form of expression that comes out of intense repression or struggle, where the person bearing witness tells the story to someone else, who then transcribes, edits, translates, and publishes the text elsewhere. Thus, scholars often see *testimonios* as dependent products, an effort by the disenfranchised to assert themselves as political subjects through others, often outsiders, and in the process emphasize particular aspects of their collective identity. . . . These texts are seen as disclosures not of personal lives but rather of the political violence inflicted on whole communities" (Latina Feminist Group 13).

10. In *The Writing of History*, Michel de Certeau argues that the "intelligibility" of "modern Western culture . . . is established through a relation with the other . . . the Indian, the past, the people, the mad, the child, the Third World" (de Certeau 3). Feminist and Latinx historiography often deny this "progress" narrative, claiming immanence with the repressed past, the "Third World," and "the Indian." Chicana feminist historian Emma Pérez's "Third Space" or "decolonizing" historiography, for instance, critically recovers the indigenous, female, and queer voices that were marginalized by Eurocentric patriarchal histories for centuries and, then, by Chicano patriarchal histories for decades. From a Latina feminist perspective, the past is not an ideal to return to but a contested terrain of competing truth claims and

biased authors, all inflected by the power dynamics of sex, race, and nationality. By rejecting Eurocentric and patriarchal historical narratives, Levins Morales is following in a tradition of decolonial and feminist historical practice that has changed the rules for evidence gathering, challenged ideas of authority, and developed new ways of making meaning from the past.

11. "Botánica" is used to describe both a catalogue of medicinal herbs as well as a store in which one might buy these herbs.

12. Winking, here, is not necessarily anthropomorphizing; potatoes have their own sorts of eyes that wink in nonhuman ways.

13. In *Transformation Now!* Keating describes "status quo stories" as "worldviews that normalize and naturalize the existing social system, values, and standards so entirely that they prevent us from imagining the possibility of change" (35). The unexamined assumptions that underlie many of our conventional beliefs and research methods perpetuate hierarchies of power: "[T]hose of us raised and/or educated in western systems of thought have been trained to read and evaluate ourselves and others according to status-quo stories. We have been indoctrinated into a supremacist worldview—an overreliance on rational thought, scientistic empiricism, and hierarchical binary thinking that creates a restrictive framework that labels, divides, and segregates based on socially defined difference and sameness" (36).

14. While Haraway does not explicitly identify as a posthumanist, her engagement with feminism through interspecies relations is certainly other-than-Humanist, and her 1980s cyborg manifesto has been taken up as an icon of posthumanism.

15. Haraway works with animals rather than plants, but her analysis of liminal organisms like the microscopic *Mixotricha paradoxa* reveals lessons like those of Levins Morales's potatoes: odd alliances and adaptations between integrated organisms can be traced back "to the earliest bacteria" and forward to any trans-species recombinations that are "fundamental to life's history" (*Haraway Reader* 146–47).

16. This essay was also published in *Telling to Live* (*Latina Feminist Group*).

17. The details I discuss in this section are based on my encounter with the website in 2015.

18. Also see Jane Bennett's *Vibrant Matters* and Nancy Tuana's "Viscous Porosity: Witnessing Katrina" for analyses of the environmental agency of nonhuman matter. Karen Barad's *Meeting the Universe Halfway* proposes a universalizing ethics for the intra-action among the human and nonhuman "relata" in any spatiotemporal environment; I cite this ethics at the end of the chapter.

19. The National Institute of Environmental Sciences uses the term "idiopathic environmental intolerance" (IEI), a term that casts doubt on the origins of the illness and poses the sufferer as one who is "intolerant." In opposition to this framing, the terms MCS and environmental illness (EI) place the onus on chemical environments. Alaimo's *Bodily Natures* notes how the medical industry has dismissed MCS as psychosomatic. Yet "psychosomatic" (which is certainly not the same thing as "imagined") might actually be the best way to understand the intersection of mind

and body in our experience of illness as an assault on the self by exterior factors; indeed, the terms used by institutions to dismiss the disease aptly capture the unruliness and diffuseness of individual health. To "cure" diseases like MCS/EI, we would need to embrace an understanding of health that is by nature unruly and diffuse.

20. "Forget Me Not," the final story in *Cosecha* (2014), presents a good example of this self-reflexive approach to memoir. The story opens with a photograph of Jane Speed (a former friend of the author's family) holding an infant Aurora Levins Morales in Puerto Rico in 1954, seeming to offer empirical evidence of a past encounter. But Levins Morales insists four separate times that the story is not about the Speed family and that "the feelings I attribute to them come purely from the wild interior of my own mind. . . . Imagination run riot, blooming over and around the tiny pebbles of fact" (*Cosecha* 149). The story ends with the image of a fictionalized Aurora writing in the overgrown ruins of the Speed house while rain washes down around her:

> Well, she had come here to unearth the mysteries of memory, to dig in the neglected burial ground of her inheritance, to water these lost seeds and make them bloom. . . . She pulled the typewriter close. . . . The dark was full of whispers and rustlings, and the endless downpour of years, striking tin and flowing away, down the mountains of the cordillera, toward the sea, drenching her imagination. She began to write. (160–61)

Seeds and roots and rain and typewriter come together here not to preserve their particulate memories (as the story's title, "Forget Me Not," implies) but to "drench" the imagination with a flood that erases the boundaries between the various actants in the ancestral garden. Memory is represented as mystery and buried seeds, which crack open with water and a drenched imagination.

21. Though the environmental justice movement highlights the ways in which underprivileged people are disproportionately exposed to environmental pollutants (because of the politics and economics surrounding the location of highways, dump sites, and factories), disorders like MCS/EI focus on exposure to toxins present in household products like perfumes, detergents, and plastics, products that people with economic privilege are more likely to accumulate. (See Alaimo's *Bodily Natures* and Tuana's "Viscous Porosity.")

Chapter 4. Life: The Gloria E. Anzaldúa Papers and Other-Than-Humanist Ontologies

1. According to the eighty-four-page catalogue, the Gloria Evangelina Anzaldúa Papers measure 115 linear feet and consist of more than 200 file boxes of materials.

2. See AnaLouise Keating's "Archival Alchemy" for more information about the history of the archive.

3. There is another brief version/excerpt stored elsewhere in the archive that is dated 1984.

4. Accounts that appear in both "La serpiente" and *Borderlands* include the stories about Anzaldúa's early menstruation, about killing a snake in the fields, about her cousin who was a woman for six months and a man for the other six, and about looking at herself in the mirror and finding her face divided into layers of masks and cubist fragments (a vision that, according to "La serpiente," occurred while she was tripping on mushrooms). "La serpiente" also contains preliminary thoughts on mestiza consciousness and the shamanistic writing of "Tlilli Tlapalli" plus a longer version of the prose poem "Cervicide." Her experiences with uterine cysts and hysterectomy, which receive extended attention in "La serpiente," are discussed more briefly in "La Prieta," which was published in *This Bridge Called My Back*.

5. In a 2018 essay published in *Signs*, Felicity Amaya Schaeffer also explores the ways in which Anzaldúa rethinks ideas of the human, agency, and justice. Schaeffer proposes that, to re-create the world, Anzaldúa turns to "nonlife": "Perhaps by entering into states of nonlife, we can collectively heal. . . . Becoming nonlife just might be another queer crossing into the long state of stillness and silence necessary to hone ancient and future vibrations and voicings that collectivize a rhythm from far and deep—from the dead ancestors of the past that commune from the earth to the universes that travel back from beyond" (1026). I would say that even death, for Anzaldúa, is a form of life; rather than creating an opposition between life and "nonlife," I see Anzaldúa's work as a continual expansion and re-creation of life itself.

6. Anzaldúa has been critiqued—most notably in Josefina Saldaña-Portillo's 2001 essay "Who's the Indian in Aztlán?"—for what seem to be her (mis)appropriations and romanticization of pre-Columbian indigenous cultures. Anzaldúa wrote an essay addressed to Native studies scholars, "Speaking across the Divide," in which she responds to these critiques directly. AnaLouise Keating argues that "Anzaldúa was deeply concerned by the possibility that her references to indigeneity (which occur at various points throughout her work) could be misconstrued as an invitation to appropriate, distort, misuse, or in any other ways disrespect Native peoples, philosophies, and/or cultures" ("Speculative Realism" 55). As I have written, in *Encarnación* and elsewhere, I interpret Anzaldúa's invocations of indigenous epistemologies (like those of Cherríe Moraga, Ana Castillo, and other Chicana writers) as an imaginative repurposing, a borrowing of pre-Humanist thought in an effort to think about the future without the limiting parameters of Humanism. Anzaldúa's representations of Aztec goddesses are, in my view, no more grounded in empirical claims than are her doodles. These representations are grounded in ethics, imagination, and a deep commitment to expanding our intellectual toolkit.

7. I talk about this literal version of "cut and paste," which Anzaldúa employed even after adopting a word processor, in "Messy Archives and Materials That Matter."

8. The exact number of deaths varies depending upon how one defines life and how one interprets the text, but there are at least four. (Chapter 5 of "La serpiente," narrating her experience of having tumors growing in her womb and her subsequent hysterectomy, is called "Death Four.") The first death is recounted at

the beginning, when her birth certificate erroneously reported that she was born dead. Anzaldúa claims the onset of menstruation at three months as a second death ("La serpiente" 271).

9. In a 1975 journal entry incorporated into the manuscript of "La serpiente," Anzaldúa writes of tripping on magic mushrooms in order to tap into a larger "spirit-body thing" (68): objects in the room began to glow and to smell, taking on a kind of vitality of their own. She began to hear sounds from far away and to see the unconscious thoughts and fears of others (88–89). While examining her own image in the mirror, she saw her face as layers of masks. From this experience, she developed her idea of "La Gloria Multíplice" (also discussed in Borderlands 44), a "Cubist-like" self with multiple angles and many orientations at once ("La serpiente" 88–90).

10. The actual birth certificate with this misinformation is available in the archive.

11. This story is also published separately in Growing Up Latino (edited by Augenbraum and Stavans).

12. The accent marks are all missing in the original manuscript, which was composed on a typewriter.

13. To honor the politics of Anzaldúa's linguistic code-switching, I do not translate mixed-language passages like this one. See "How to Tame a Wild Tongue" in Borderlands/La Frontera.

14. In a 2013 essay about Anzaldúa's potential relationship to disability studies, Aurora Levins Morales writes about the Coatlicue state, describing it as "a shattering that lets in light" (Kindling 5). Levins Morales reframes Coatlicue states in terms of Puerto Rican storm goddesses, "the Guabancex and Oyá state," and compares the "creative destruction" of these states to hurricanes (5), which unmake and remake ecologies.

15. The final section in This Bridge Called My Back bears the same title, "El Mundo Zurdo: The Vision."

16. In more recent work, Mitchell and Snyder similarly call for affirmative recognition of "the active transformation of life that the alternative corporealities of disability creatively entail" (The Biopolitics of Disability 2).

17. See, in particular, Nancy Mairs's writings in Waist-High in the World.

18. Anzaldúa was a fan of science fiction, and many of the stories in her archive engage with this genre. As a student of Donna Haraway's, Anzaldúa was surely aware of her professor's belief in the generative power of science fiction (or speculative fiction). Yet, as a scientist, Haraway's fabulations always remain attached to something empirical. In the beginning of her newest book, Staying with the Trouble (2016), Haraway uses "SF" to refer to "science fact and speculative fabulation," claiming that each needs the other (Staying with the Trouble 3). Anzaldúa seems more willing to push the boundaries of "fact."

19. In a 1982 interview with Linda Smuckler, Anzaldúa acknowledges that her personal experiences with illness and hormone imbalance resemble science fiction

more than conventional reality: "I mean, the stuff that was going on with me is like seeing a movie or reading a science fiction book, you know?" (*Interviews* 35).

20. "Werejaguar" seems like an Aztec version of the mythic werewolf (since jaguars were sacred to the Aztecs, associated with warriors as well as the shape-shifting god Tezcatlipoca). In "La serpiente," Anzaldúa recalls an encounter with a wolf-dog that looked straight into her eyes. "Years later in the midst of painting this episode with her oils she realized that this animal, half wolf, half dog, was her *nagual*, what the Aztecs call the animal-companion that each person has and with whose destiny she is closely aligned" ("La serpiente" 19–20). I found a drawing of a werewolf affixed to red felt in the Anzaldúa archive, presumably the one drawn for her by her close friend Randy Conner. (Anzaldúa recalls Randy painting a portrait of her animal-companion: "It was an animal—a sort of wolf or werewolf or wolf-bird, it's [sic] fur looked like feathers. But it *was* her portrait. That was exactly how she saw herself in the mirror whenever she had dropped acid. But how had *he* known? She had never told anyone about it. Randy had her *Nagual*" [247, original emphasis].) She wore this picture as a mask on Halloween and then framed it and carried it with her on long trips (248).

21. Naguals are animal companions; nagualism is a sacred form of shifting shapes between human and animal often associated with shamanism.

22. In "La serpiente," Anzaldúa writes about her black cat performing oral sex on her while she lies in bed at night, suggesting a possible autobiographical source for the speculative story: "The cat. Wow. Maybe she thought it was a fish. Prieta opened her legs wider. Amazing, the feel of the raspy pink tongue. She wanted to say, 'But I hardly know you.' Maybe the cat was ~~th~~ Bast [sic], the cat goddess" ("La serpiente" 200). (The "th" before "Bast" is crossed out in the original manuscript in the archive.) Both "La serpiente" and "Werejaguar" describe the cats' tongues and refer to the cat as a beast.

23. In the 1999 Keating interview I cite above, Anzaldúa references this story and explains that "Prieta literally transforms from a woman to a jaguar and becomes caught in between: She's half human and half jaguar, a were-jaguar" (*Interviews* 284).

24. In her 1991 essay "To(o) Queer the Writer," Anzaldúa also defines the rainbow in terms of racial heterogeneity and coalition: "A rainbow is a bridge. The word is used politically by Native Americans—it derives from Native American people symbolizing the way different people communicate and relate with each other. It's the vision that Native Americans have of the red and the white and the black and the yellow being able to communicate and make alliances" ("To(o) Queer the Writer" 174). The rainbow in "Werejaguar" might also be meant to signify communication across different species.

25. Mikko Tuhkanen sees Anzaldúa's ontology as a form of monism, a belief that all beings are connected through shared substance and shared spirit ("Mestiza Metaphysics" 270). "[H]er thinking of life's interconnectedness brings her system close to Deleuze's reading of Spinoza's single substance," he writes (279). I wouldn't

regard this ontology as kin to Deleuze and Spinoza as much as I would trace it to her philosophical grounding in premodern indigenous cultures. Monism also seems a bit too seamless to account for the friction—not to mention the shocking monsters—that accompany Anzaldúa's transcorporeal connections.

26. It is a bit ironic to talk about Anzaldúa in terms of Butler, when, in her *MELUS* interview with Ann Reuman, she claims to have theorized about performances of identity before Judith Butler ("Coming into Play" 13).

27. In *Encarnación*, I argued a precursor to this idea, that the premodern Aztec cosmologies Anzaldúa invokes in *Borderlands* help us to imagine a feminist future based on permeability rather than individual self-defense.

28. See Anzaldúa's "Let us be the healing of the wound" for more on the Coyolxauhqui imperative.

Conclusion: Selflessness?

1. In advocating for building connections with others, Anzaldúa develops a model of "nepantleras," "boundary-crossers, thresholders who initiate others in rites of passage, activistas who, from a listening, receptive, spiritual stance, rise to their own visions and shift into acting them out, haciendo mundo nuevo [making new worlds] (introducing change)" ("now let us shift" 571).

2. Identifying as "white" means owning up to the unearned privileges that have been given to me based on my skin color; it is not a racial identity I claim with any pride.

3. See Haraway's *The Companion Species Manifesto* and *When Species Meet*.

Works Cited

Acosta, Oscar "Zeta." *Autobiography of a Brown Buffalo*. 1972. Vintage, 1989.

———. *The Revolt of the Cockroach People*. 1973. Vintage, 1989.

Ahmed, Sara. *The Cultural Politics of Emotion*. Edinburgh UP, 2004.

Alaimo, Stacy. *Bodily Natures: Science, Environment, and the Material Self*. Indiana UP, 2010.

———. "Trans-Corporeal Feminisms and the Ethical Space of Nature." *Material Feminisms*, edited by Stacy Alaimo and Susan Hekman. Indiana UP, 2007, 237–64.

Alcalá, Rosa. *Undocumentaries*. Shearsman Books, 2010.

Alcalá, Rosa, Eduardo Corral, and Aracelis Girmay. "Interviews: Latino/a Poetry Now: 3 Poets Discuss Their Art." *Poetry Society of America*, www.poetrysociety.org/psa/poetry/crossroads/interviews/roundtable_talk/, 29 Mar. 2018. Accessed 20 Mar. 2019.

Aldama, Frederick Luis. *Brown on Brown: Chicano/a Representations of Gender, Sexuality, and Ethnicity*. U of Texas P, 2005.

Anzaldúa, Gloria. *Borderlands / La Frontera*. Aunt Lute, 1987.

———. "Coming into Play: An Interview with Gloria Anzaldúa." By Anne E. Reuman, *MELUS*, vol. 25, no. 2, 2000, 3–45.

———. *Gloria Evangelina Anzaldúa Papers, 1942–2004*. Benson Latin American Collection, University of Texas at Austin.

———. *The Gloria Anzaldúa Reader*. Edited by AnaLouise Keating, Duke UP, 2009.

———. *Interviews/Entrevistas*. Edited by AnaLouise Keating, Routledge, 2000.

———. "Let us be the healing of the wound." *One Wound for Another / Una herida por otra: Testmonios de Latin@s in the U.S. through Cyberspace (11 de septiembre de*

2001–11 de marzo de 2002), edited by C. Joysmith and C. Lomas, Universidad Autónoma de México, 2005, 92–103.

———. *Light in the Dark / Luz en lo oscuro*. Edited by AnaLouise Keating, Duke UP, 2015.

———. "now let us shift . . . the path of conocimiento . . . inner work, public acts." *This Bridge We Call Home: Radical Visions for Transformation*, edited by Gloria Anzaldúa and AnaLouise Keating, New York: Routledge, 2002, 540–78.

———. "La Prieta." *This Bridge Called My Back: Writings by Radical Women of Color*, 4th edition, edited by Gloria Anzaldúa and Cherríe Moraga, SUNY P, 2015, 198–209.

———. "La serpiente que se come su cola: una autocanción." *Gloria Evangelina Anzaldúa Papers, 1942–2004*. Benson Latin American Collection, University of Texas at Austin.

———. "Speaking across the Divide." *The Gloria Anzaldúa Reader*, edited by AnaLouise Keating, Duke UP, 2009. 282–94.

———. "Speaking in Tongues: A Letter to Third World Women Writers." *This Bridge Called My Back: Writings by Radical Women of Color*, edited by Cherríe Moraga and Gloria Anzaldúa, Kitchen Table, 1983.

———. "To(o) Queer the Writer—Loca, escritora y chicana." *The Gloria Anzaldúa Reader*, edited by AnaLouise Keating, Duke UP, 2009.

———. "Werejaguar." *Gloria Evangelina Anzaldúa Papers, 1942–2004*. Benson Latin American Collection, University of Texas at Austin.

Aparicio, Frances. "Judith Ortiz Cofer, *Silent Dancing: A Partial Remembrance of a Puerto Rican Childhood*." *Reading U.S. Latina Writers: Remapping American Literature*, edited by Alvina Quintana, Palgrave, 2003, 61–70.

Arnold, Kevin. "'Male and Male and Male': John Rechy and the Scene of Representation." *Arizona Quarterly*, vol. 67, no. 1, Spring 2011, 115–34.

Augenbraum, Harold, and Ilan Stavans, editors. *Growing Up Latino: Memoirs and Stories*. Houghton Mifflin, 1993.

Barad, Karen. *Meeting the Universe Halfway: Quantum Physics and the Entanglement of Matter and Meaning*. Duke UP, 2007.

Barradas, Efraín. "El recuerdo como remedio: historia y memoria en Aurora Levins Morales." *La Nueva Literatura Hispánica*, vol. 15, 2011.

Bebout, Lee. "Skin in the Game: Toward a Theorization of Whiteness in the Classroom." *Pedagogy*, vol. 14, no. 2, 2014, 343–54.

Behar, Ruth. *Traveling Heavy: A Memoir in between Journeys*. Duke UP, 2013.

Beltrán, Cristina. *The Trouble with Unity: Latino Politics and the Creation of Identity*. Oxford UP, 2010.

Benmayor, Rina. "*Getting Home Alive*: The Politics of Multiple Identity." *The Americas Review*, vol. 3–4, 1989, 107–17.

Bennett, Jane. "Powers of the Hoard: Further Notes on Material Agency." *Animal, Vegetable, Mineral: Ethics and Objects*, Oliphant Books, 2012, 237–69.

———. *Vibrant Matter: A Political Ecology of Things*. Duke UP, 2010.

Benstock, Shari. "Authorizing the Autobiographical." *The Private Self: Theory and Practice of Women's Autobiographical Writings*, edited by Shari Benstock, U of North Carolina P, 1988, 10–33.

Bordo, Susan. *Unbearable Weight: Feminism, Western Culture, and the Body*. U of California P, 1993.

Bost, Suzanne. "Diabetes, Culture, and Food: Posthumanist Nutrition in the Gloria Anzaldúa Archive." *Postnational Appetites: Rethinking Chicana/o Literature Through Food*, edited by Meredith Abarca and Nieves Pascual, Palgrave Macmillan, 2013, 27–43.

———. *Encarnación: Illness and Body Politics in Chicana Feminist Literature*. Fordham UP, 2009.

———. "From Race/Sex/Etc. to Glucose, Feeding Tube, and Mourning: The Shifting Matter of Chicana Feminism." *Material Feminisms*, edited by Stacy Alaimo and Susan Hekman, Indiana UP, 2007, 340–72.

———. "Hurting to Change the World: My Grandmother, Faith, and Gloria Anzaldúa." *Bridging: How and Why Gloria Evangelina Anzaldúa's Life and Work Transformed Our Own*, edited by Gloria González-López and AnaLouise Keating, University of Texas Press, 2011, 191–96.

———. "Identity and Cross-Cultural Empathy: Writing to Sister Mary Agnes Curran, O.S.F." *Feminist Formations*, vol. 29, no. 2, Summer 2017, 177–99.

———. "Messy Archives and Materials That Matter: Making Knowledge with the Gloria E. Anzaldúa Papers." *PMLA*, vol. 130, no. 3, May 2015, 615–30.

———. *Mulattas and Mestizas: Representing Mixed Identities in the Americas, 1850–2000*. U of Georgia P, 2003.

———. "Practicing Yoga / Embodying Feminism / Shape-Shifting." *Frontiers: Journal of Women's Studies*, vol. 37, no. 2, Summer 2016, 191–210.

———. "Transgressing Borders: Puerto Rican and Latina Mestizas." *MELUS*, vol. 25, no. 2, Summer 2000, 187–211.

Bost, Suzanne, and Frances Aparicio, editors. *The Routledge Companion to Latino/a Literature*. Routledge, 2012.

Braidotti, Rosi. *The Posthuman*. Polity Press, 2013.

———. "Posthuman, All Too Human: Towards a New Process Ontology." *Theory, Culture, & Society*, vol. 23, nos. 7–8, 2006, 197–208.

———. *Transpositions: On Nomadic Ethics*. Polity Press, 2006.

Brodzki, Bella, and Celeste Schenk, editors. *Life/Lines: Theorizing Women's Autobiography*. Cornell UP, 1988.

Bruce-Novoa, Juan. "In Search of the Honest Outlaw: John Rechy." *Minority Voices*, vol. 3, no. 1, 1979, 37–45.

———. "Rechy and Rodriguez: Double Crossing the Public/Private Line." *Double Crossings = Entrecruzamientos: Antología de artículos presentados en el Noveno Congreso Internacional de Culturas Latinas en América del Norte*, edited by Mario Martín Flores and Carlos Von Son, Ediciones Nuevo Espacio, 2001, 15–34.

Butler, Judith. *Frames of War*. Verso, 2009.

———. *Giving an Account of Oneself*. Fordham UP, 2005.

———. *Precarious Life: The Powers of Mourning and Violence*. Verso, 2004.

Caminero-Santangelo, Marta. *On Latinidad: U.S. Latina Literature and the Construction of Ethnicity*. U of Florida P, 2007.

Casillo, Charles. *Outlaw: The Lives and Careers of John Rechy*. Advocate Books, 2002.

Castillo, Ana. *Black Dove: Mamá, Mi'jo, and Me*. Feminist P, 2016.

———. *Massacre of the Dreamers: Essays on Xicanisma*. Plume, 1994.

Chen, Mel Y. *Animacies: Biopolitics, Racial Mattering, and Queer Affect*. Duke UP, 2012.

Christian, Karen. *Show & Tell: Identity as Performance in U.S. Latina/o Fiction*. U of New Mexico P, 1997.

Cisneros, Sandra. *A House of My Own: Stories from My Life*. Vintage, 2016.

Code, Lorraine. "Rational Imaginings, Responsible Knowings: How Far Can You See from Here?" *Engendering Rationalities*, edited by Nancy Tuana and Sandra Morgen, SUNY P, 2001, 261–82.

Colebrook, Claire. *Death of the Posthuman: Essays on Extinction*, vol. 1. Open Humanities Press, 2014.

———. *Sex after Life: Essays on Extinction*, vol. 2. Open Humanities Press, 2014.

Corpi, Luca. *Confessions of a Book Burner: Personal Essays and Stories*. Arte Público P, 2014.

Couser, G. Thomas. *Recovering Bodies: Illness, Disability, and Life-Writing*. U of Wisconsin P, 1997.

Dean, Tim. *Unlimited Intimacy: Reflections on the Subculture of Barebacking*. U of Chicago P, 2009.

de Certeau, Michel. *The Writing of History*. Translated by Tom Conley, Columbia UP, 1988.

Delany, Samuel. *Times Square Red, Times Square Blue*. NYU P, 1999.

Deleuze, Gilles, and Félix Guattari. *A Thousand Plateaus: Capitalism and Schizophrenia*. Translated by Brian Massumi, U of Minnesota P, 1987.

Douglas, Mary. *Purity and Danger: An Analysis of Concepts of Pollution and Taboo*. 1966. London: Routledge, 1988.

Doyle, Jacqueline. "The Coming Together of Many 'I's': Individual and Collective Autobiography in Judith Ortiz Cofer's *The Latin Deli*." *Rituals of Movement in the Writing of Judith Ortiz Cofer*, edited by Lorraine M. López and Molly Crumpton Winter, Caribbean Studies Press, 2012.

Enstad, Nan. "Toxicity and the Consuming Subject." *States of Emergency: The Object of American Studies*, edited by Russ Castronovo and Susan Gillman, U of North Carolina P, 2009, 55–68.

Epstein, William, editor. *Contesting the Subject: Essays in the Postmodern Theory and Practice of Biography and Biographical Criticism*. Purdue UP, 1991.

Erevelles, Nirmala. *Disability and Difference in Global Contexts: Enabling a Transformative Body Politic*. Palgrave, 2011.

Fischer, Michael. "Ethnicity and the Post-Modern Arts of Memory." *Writing Culture: The Poetics and Politics of Ethnography*, edited by James Clifford and George Marcus, U of California P, 1986, 194–233.

Foster, David William. "John Rechy: *Bodies and Souls* and the Homoeroticization of the Urban Quest." *Studies in Twentieth-Century Literature*, vol. 25, no. 1, Winter 2001, 196–209.

Fowlkes, Diane. "Moving from Feminist Identity Politics to Coalition Politics Through a Feminist Materialist Standpoint of Intersubjectivity in Gloria Anzaldúa's *Borderlands/La Frontera: The New Mestiza*." *Hypatia*, vol. 12, no. 2, Spring 1997, 105–24.

Friedman, Susan Stanford. "Women's Autobiographical Selves: Theory and Practice." *The Private Self: Theory and Practice of Women's Autobiographical Writings*, edited by Shari Benstock, U of North Carolina P, 1988, 34–62.

Grusin, Richard, editor. *The Nonhuman Turn*. U of Minnesota P, 2015.

Gunew, Sneja. "Subaltern Empathy: Beyond European Categories in Affect Theory." *Concentric*, vol. 35, no. 1, March 2009, 11–30.

Halberstam, Judith/Jack. *In a Queer Time and Place: Transgender Bodies, Subcultural Lives*. NYU P, 2005.

———. *The Queer Art of Failure*. Duke UP, 2011.

Halperin, Laura. *Intersections of Harm: Narratives of Latina Deviance and Defiance*. Rutgers UP, 2015.

Haraway, Donna. *The Companion Species Manifesto: Dogs, People, and Significant Otherness*. Prickly Paradigm, 2003.

———. *The Haraway Reader*. New York: Routledge, 2004.

———. *Modest_Witness@Second_Millennium.FemaleMan©_Meets_OncoMouse™*. Routledge, 1997.

———. *Staying with the Trouble: Making Kin in the Chthulucene*. Duke UP, 2016.

———. *When Species Meet*. U of Minnesota P, 2008.

Hayles, N. Katherine. *How We Became Posthuman: Virtual Bodies in Cybernetics, Literature, and Informatics*. U of Chicago P, 1999.

Hoffman, Stanton. "The Cities of Night: John Rechy's *City of Night* and the American Literature of Homosexuality." *Chicago Review*, vol. 17, nos. 2–3, 1964, 195–206.

Johnson, David E. "Intolerance, the Body, Community." *American Literary History*, vol. 10, no. 3, Autumn 1998, 446–70.

Kafer, Alison. *Feminist, Queer, Crip*. Indiana UP, 2013.

Kanost, Laura. "Re-Placing the Madwoman: Irene Vilar's *The Ladies' Gallery*." *Frontiers*, vol. 31, no. 3, 2010, 103–15.

Keating, AnaLouise. "Archival Alchemy and Allure: The Gloria Evangelina Anzaldúa Papers as Case Study." *Aztlán*, vol. 35, no. 2, Fall 2010, 159–71.

———. "Speculative Realism, Visionary Pragmatism, and Poet-Shamanic Aesthetics in Gloria Anzaldúa—and Beyond." *WSQ: Women's Studies Quarterly*, vol. 40, nos. 3– 4 Fall/Winter 2012, 53–72.

———. *Teaching Transformation: Transcultural Classroom Dialogues.* Palgrave Macmillan, 2007.

———. *Transformation Now! Towards a Post-Oppositional Politics of Change.* U of Illinois P, 2013.

Kingston, Maxine Hong. *The Woman Warrior: Memoirs of a Girlhood among Ghosts.* Knopf, 1976.

Kristeva, Julia. *Powers of Horror: An Essay on Abjection.* Translated by Leon S. Roudiez, Columbia UP, 1982.

Lara-Bonilla, Inmaculada. "*Getting Home Alive* (1986): Urgency and Polyphony in the Figuration of the 'Diasporican.'" *Latino Studies*, vol. 8, no. 3, 2010, 355–72.

Latina Feminist Group. *Telling to Live: Latina Feminist Testimonios.* Duke UP, 2001.

Latour, Bruno. "On Actor-Network Theory: A Few Clarifications." *Soziale Welt*, vol. 47, no. 4, 1996, 369—81.

Levins Morales, Aurora. *Aurora Levins Morales: Writing That Other World That Is Possible.* www.auroralevinsmorales.com. Accessed 10 Jan. 2015.

———. "From Self-Sacrifice to Self-Preservation: A Message from God in the Atomic Age." *Women's Review of Books*, vol. 14, no. 8, May 1997. www-jstor-org.flagship.luc.edu/stable/4022690?sid=primo&origin=crossref&seq=1#metadata_info_tab_contents. Accessed 2 June 2017.

———. "Guanakán." *nineteen sixty nine: an ethnic studies journal*, vol. 2, no. 1, 2013, 1–3.

———. *Kindling: Writings on the Body.* Palabera Press, 2103.

———. *Medicine Stories: History, Culture, and the Politics of Integrity.* South End P, 1998.

———. *Remedios: Stories of Earth and Iron from the History of Puertorriqueñas.* South End P, 1998.

———. "Shared Ecologies and Healing Justice in the Work of Aurora Levins Morales: An Interview [with Suzanne Bost]." *MELUS*, vol. 42, no. 1, Spring 2017, 186–203.

Levins Morales, Aurora, and Rosario Morales. *Cosecha and Other Stories.* Palabera Press, 2014.

———. *Getting Home Alive.* Firebrand Press, 1986.

Lorde, Audre. *Zami: A New Spelling of My Name.* Persephone P, 1982.

Mairs, Nancy. *Carnal Acts.* Beacon, 1996.

———. *Plaintext: Essays.* U of Arizona P, 1992.

———. *Remembering the Bone-House.* Beacon, 1995.

———. *A Troubled Guest: Life and Death Stories.* Beacon, 2001.

———. *Waist-High in the World: A Life Among the Non-Disabled.* Beacon, 1997.

McRuer, Robert. *Crip Times: Disability, Globalization, and Resistance.* NYU P, 2018.

Minich, Julie Avril. *Accessible Citizenships: Disability, Nation, and the Cultural Politics of Greater Mexico.* Temple UP, 2014.

Miranda, Carolina A. "Artist Tim Youd Retypes John Rechy's novel *City of Night*." *Los Angeles Times*, 1 July 2016, https://www.latimes.com/entertainment/arts/miranda/87754674–132.html. Accessed 1 Aug.2016.

———. "'I've Been Flashed. I've Been Mooned': The Hollywood Boulevard Adventures of Tim Youd, Who Is Spending July Retyping John Rechy's *Numbers* at Griffith Park." *Los Angeles Times*, 5 July 2016, https://www.latimes.com/entertainment /arts/miranda/la-et-cam-tim-youd-city-of-night-20160628-snap-story.html. Accessed 1 Aug. 2016.

Mitchell, David, and Sharon Snyder. *The Biopolitics of Disability: Neoliberalism, Ablenationalism, and Peripheral Embodiment.* U of Michigan P, 2015.

Mitchell, David, and Sharon Snyder, editors. *The Body and Physical Difference: Discourses of Disability.* U of Michigan P, 1997.

Moraga, Cherríe. *The Hungry Woman and Heart of the Earth.* West End, 2001.

———. *The Last Generation.* South End P, 1993.

———. *Loving in the War Years: lo que nunca pasó por sus labios.* South End P, 1983.

———. *Waiting in the Wings: Portrait of a Queer Motherhood.* Firebrand, 1997.

———. *A Xicana Codex of Changing Consciousness: Writings, 2000–2010.* Duke UP, 2011.

Moraga, Cherríe, and Gloria Anzaldúa, editors. *This Bridge Called My Back: Writings by Radical Women of Color,* 4th ed. SUNY P, 2015.

Moreman, Shane. "Memoir as Performance: Strategies of Hybrid Ethnic Identity." *Text and Performance Quarterly,* vol. 29, no. 4, October 2009, 346–66.

Morrison, Toni. *Beloved.* Knopf, 1987.

Muñoz, José Esteban. *Cruising Utopia: The Then and There of Queer Futurity.* NYU P, 2009.

Negrón-Muntaner, Frances, Ramón Grosfoguel, and Chloe S. "Introduction: Beyond Nationalist and Colonialist Discourse: The *Jaiba* Politics of the Puerto Rican Ethno-Nation." *Puerto Rican Jam: Essays on Culture and Politics,* edited by Frances Negrón-Muntaner and Ramón Grosfoguel, U of Minnesota P, 1997, 1–36.

Nussbaum, Felicity. *The Autobiographical Subject: Gender and Ideology in Eighteenth-Century England.* 2d ed. Johns Hopkins UP, 1995.

Ortiz, Ricardo. "Sexuality Degree Zero: Pleasure and Power in the Novels of John Rechy, Arturo Islas, and Michael Nava." *Journal of Homosexuality,* vol. 26, nos. 2–3, 1993, 111–26.

Ortiz Cofer, Judith. "Ensayos: Essays of a Life" [Interview with Stephanie Gordon]. *Rituals of Movement in the Writing of Judith Ortiz Cofer,* edited by Lorraine M. López and Molly Crumpton Winter, Caribbean Studies Press, 2012, 11–18.

———. *Silent Dancing: A Partial Remembrance of a Puerto Rican Childhood.* Arte Público, 1990.

———. "¿La Verdad? Notes on the Writing of *Silent Dancing: A Partial Remembrance of a Puerto Rican Childhood* (A Memoir in Prose and Poetry)." *Truth in Nonfiction: Essays,* edited by David Lazar, U of Iowa P, 2008, 26–30.

Pedwell, Carolyn. *Affective Relations: The Transnational Politics of Empathy.* Palgrave Macmillan, 2014.

Pérez, Emma. *The Decolonial Imaginary: Writing Chicanas into History.* Indiana UP, 1999.

Pérez, Laura E. "Writing with Crooked Lines." *Fleshing the Spirit: Spirituality and Activism in Chicana, Latina, and Indigenous Women's Lives*, edited by Elisa Facio and Irene Lara, U of Arizona P, 2014, 23–33.

Pérez-Torres, Rafael. "The Ambiguous Outlaw: John Rechy and Complicitous Homotextuality." *Fictions of Masculinity: Crossing Cultures, Crossing Sexualities*, edited by Peter F. Murphy, NYU P, 1994, 204–25.

"El Plan Espiritual de Aztlán." *In Aztlán: Essays on the Chicano Homeland*, edited by Rudolfo Anaya and Francisco Lomelí, U of New Mexico P, 1989, 1–5.

Puar, Jasbir. *The Right to Maim: Debility, Capacity, Disability*. Duke UP, 2017.

———. *Terrorist Assemblages: Homonationalism in Queer Times*. Duke UP, 2007.

Rabassa, Gregory. *If This Be Treason: Translation and Its Dyscontents: A Memoir*. New Directions, 2005.

Rechy, John. *About My Life and the Kept Woman*. Grove Press, 2008.

———. *After the Blue Hour*. Grove Press 2017.

———. *Bodies and Souls*. Grove Press, 2001.

———. *City of Night*. Grove Press, 1963.

———. "Common Bonds and Battles." *Beneath the Skin: The Collected Essays of John Rechy*, Carroll & Graf, 2004, 70–73.

———. "Interview: John Rechy" [with Debra Castillo]. *Diacritics*, vol. 25, no. 1, Spring 1995, 113–25.

———. *The John Rechy Collection*. Howard Gotlieb Archival Research Center, Boston University.

———. *Marilyn's Daughter*. Carroll & Graff, 1988.

———. *The Miraculous Day of Amalia Gomez*. Arcade, 1991.

———. *Mysteries and Desires: Searching the Worlds of John Rechy*, edited by the Labyrinth Project, USC Annenberg Center, 2003. CD-ROM.

———. *Numbers*. Grove Press, 1967.

———. *Our Lady of Babylon*. Arcade, 1996.

———. *Rushes*. Grove Press, 1997.

———. *The Sexual Outlaw*. Grove Press, 1977.

———. *This Day's Death*. Grove Press, 1969.

Rivera, Carmen Haydée. "Diasporic Journeys: Memoirs by Puerto Rican Writers in the US." *Camino Real: Estudios de las Hispanidades Norteamericanas*, vol. 1, no. 2, 2010, 103–22.

Rodriguez, Ralph E. *Latinx Literature Unbound: Undoing Ethnic Expectation*. Fordham UP, 2018.

Roon, Kenneth E., Jr. "John Rechy's Borderless *City of Night*." *The Idea of the City: Early-Modern, Modern, and Post-Modern Locations and Communities*, edited by Joan Fitzpatrick, Cambridge Scholars, 2009, 181–92.

Saldaña-Portillo, Josefina. "'Who's the Indian in Aztlán?': Rewriting Mestizaje, Indianism, and Chicanismo from the Lacandon." *The Latin American Subaltern Studies Reader*, edited by Ileana Rodríguez, Duke UP, 2001, 402–23.

Santiago, Esmeralda. *When I Was Puerto Rican*. Vintage, 1993.

Schaeffer, Felicity Amaya. "Spirit Matters: Gloria Anzaldúa's Cosmic Becoming across Human/Nonhuman Borders." *Signs*, vol. 43, no. 4, Summer 2018, 1005–29.

Sedgwick, Eve Kosofksy. *Epistemology of the Closet*. U of California P, 1990.

———. *Tendencies*. Duke UP, 1993.

Segal, Lynne. "Who Do You Think You Are? Feminist Memoir Writing." *New Formations*, issue 67, Summer 2009, 120–33.

Singer, Linda. *Erotic Welfare: Sexual Theory and Politics in the Age of Epidemic*, edited by Judith Butler and Maureen MacGrogan, Routledge, 1993.

Smith, Barbara, editor. *Home Girls: A Black Feminist Anthology*. Kitchen Table, 1983.

Smith, Sidonie. *A Poetics of Self-Representation: Marginality and the Fictions of Self-Representation*. Indiana UP, 1987.

———. *Subjectivity, Identity, and the Body: Women's Autobiographical Practices in the Twentieth Century*. Indiana UP, 1993.

Smith, Sidonie, and Kay Schaffer, editors. *Human Rights and Narrated Lives: The Ethics of Recognition*. Palgrave, 2004.

Smith, Sidonie, and Julia Watson, editors. *De/Colonizing the Subject: The Politics of Gender in Women's Autobiography*. U of Minnesota P, 1992.

———. *Rereading Autobiography: A Guide for Interpreting Life Narratives*, 2nd ed. U of Minnesota P, 2011.

———. *Women, Autobiography, Theory: A Reader*. U of Wisconsin P, 1998.

Soto, Sandra. *Reading Chican@ Like a Queer: The De-Mastery of Desire*. U of Texas P, 2011.

Sundberg, Juanita. "Decolonizing Posthumanist Geographies." *cultural geographies*, vol. 21, no. 1, 2014, 33–47.

Thomas, Piri. *Down These Mean Streets*. 1967. Vintage, 1997.

Thompson, Mary. "Misconceived Metaphors: Irene Vilar's *Impossible Motherhood: Testimony of an Abortion Addict*." *Frontiers*, vol. 35, no. 1, 2014, 132–59.

Todd, Zoe. "An Indigenous Feminist's Take on the Ontological Turn: 'Ontology' Is Just Another Word for Colonialism." *Journal of Historical Sociology*, vol. 29, no. 1, March 2016, 4–22.

Torres, Lourdes. "The Construction of the Self in U.S. Latina Autobiographies." *Third World Women and the Politics of Feminism*, edited by Chandra Talpade Mohanty, Ann Russo, and Lourdes Torres, Indiana UP, 1991, 271–87.

Trinh Minh-ha. "'Speaking Nearby': A Conversation with Trinh T. Minh-ha" [Interview by Nancy Chen]. *Visual Anthropology Review*, vol. 8, no. 1 1992, 82–91.

Trujillo-Pagán, Nicole. "Crossed Out by LatinX: Gender Neutrality and Genderblind Sexism." *Latino Studies*, vol. 16, no. 3, Fall 2018, 396–406.

Tuana, Nancy. "Viscous Porosity: Witnessing Katrina." *Material Feminisms*, edited by Stacy Alaimo and Susan Hekman, Indiana UP, 2007, 188–213.

Tuhkanen, Mikko. "Mestiza Metaphysics." *Queer Times, Queer Becomings*, edited by E. L. McCallum and Mikko Tuhkanen, SUNY P, 2011, 259–94.

———. "Ontology and Involution." *Diacritics*, vol. 35, no. 3, Autumn 2005, 20–45.

Vasconcelos, José. *La raza cósmica*. Mexico City: Colección Austra, 1966.

Vázquez, David. *Triangulations: Narrative Strategies for Navigating Latino Identity*. U of Minnesota P, 2011.

Vidal-Ortiz, Salvador, and Juliana Martinez. "Latinx Thoughts: Latinidad with an X." *Latino Studies*, vol. 16, no. 3, Fall 2018, 384–95.

Vilar, Irene. *Impossible Motherhood: Testimony of an Abortion Addict*. Other Press, 2009.

———. *The Ladies Gallery: A Memoir of Family Secrets*. Translated by Gregory Rabassa, Vintage, 1996.

Wadman, Monika. "Multiculturalism and Nonbelonging: Construction and Collapse of the Multicultural Self in Rosario and Aurora Levins Morales's *Getting Home Alive*." *Literature, Interpretation, Theory*, vol. 11, 2000, 219–37.

Wolfe, Cary. *What Is Posthumanism?* University of Minnesota P, 2010.

Wolfe, Cary, editor. *Zoontologies: The Question of the Animal*. U of Minnesota P, 2003.

Woolf, Virginia. "A Sketch of the Past." *Moments of Being*, edited by Jeanne Schulkind, Harcourt Brace, 1976.

Ybarra, Patricia Solis. *Writing the Goodlife: Mexican American Literature and the Environment*. U of Arizona P, 2016.

Zaytoun, Kelli. "'Now Let Us Shift' the Subject: Tracing the Path and Posthumanist Implications of La Naguala / The Shapeshifter in the Works of Gloria Anzaldúa." *MELUS*, vol. 40, no. 4, Winter 2015, 1–20.

Index

SUZANNE BOST is a professor of English at Loyola University Chicago. She is the author of *Encarnación: Illness and Body Politics in Chicana Feminist Literature* and *Mulattas and Mestizas: Representing Mixed Identities in the Americas, 1850–2000*.

TRANSFORMATIONS: WOMANIST, FEMINIST,
AND INDIGENOUS STUDIES

Teaching with Tenderness: Toward an Embodied Practice
  Becky Thompson
Building Womanist Coalitions: Writing and Teaching in the Spirit of Love
  Edited by Gary L. Lemons
Hungry Translations: Relearning the World through Radical Vulnerability
  *Richa Nagar, in journeys with Sangtin Kisan Mazdoor Sangathan
  and Parakh Theatre*
Shared Selves: Latinx Memoir and Ethical Alternatives to Humanism
  Suzanne Bost

The University of Illinois Press
is a founding member of the
Association of University Presses.

Composed in 10.25/13 Goudy Old Style
with Avenir display
by Jim Proefrock
at the University of Illinois Press
Cover designed by Becca Alexander
Cover illustration: Anatomical illustration
by L. W. Yaggy, Chicago, 1884

University of Illinois Press
1325 South Oak Street
Champaign, IL 61820-6903
www.press.uillinois.edu